John Howard Yoder

John Howard Yoder

MENNONITE PATIENCE,
EVANGELICAL WITNESS,
CATHOLIC CONVICTIONS

Mark Thiessen Nation

WILLIAM B. EERDMANS PUBLISHING COMPANY
GRAND RAPIDS, MICHIGAN / CAMBRIDGE, U.K.

Wm. B. Eerdmans Publishing Co.
255 Jefferson Ave. S.E., Grand Rapids, Michigan 49503 /
P.O. Box 163, Cambridge CB3 9PU U.K.

Printed in the United States of America

10 09 08 07 06   7 6 5 4 3 2 1

Library of Congress Cataloging-in-Publication Data

Nation, Mark.
    John Howard Yoder: Mennonite patience, evangelical witness,
    catholic convictions / Mark Thiessen Nation.
        p.   cm.
    ISBN-10: 0-8028-3940-1 / ISBN-13: 978-0-8028-3940-4 (pbk.: alk. paper)
    1. Yoder, John Howard.   I. Title.

BX8143.Y59N38   2005
230′.97092 — dc22

                                                      2005032811

www.eerdmans.com

For my mother
Shirley (Morris) Nation

Contents

Foreword

John Howard Yoder died in 1997. It will take many years to receive his work. Yoder tried to help Christians change the questions. Those reading Yoder want him to answer the questions they have learned to ask. So it will take some time — but even more demanding, a change in our habits as Christians — to understand the work of John Howard Yoder.

But that work toward understanding has begun. The essays in the *Festschrift* for Yoder, *The Wisdom of the Cross,* certainly began the process. The book edited by Ben Ollenburger and Gayle Gerber Koontz, *A Mind Patient and Untamed,* is also a wonderful collection, mainly by Mennonite authors about the significance of Yoder's work. Craig Carter's *The Politics of the Cross* is also a very helpful overview of Yoder's work. But now we have this essential study of Yoder in Mark Nation's *John Howard Yoder: Mennonite Patience, Evangelical Witness, Catholic Convictions.*

For many years Mark Nation has collected Yoder's work and has read everything he has written — no small feat. Yoder's published work is but the tip of the iceberg. He wrote constantly and in an extraordinary variety of venues. Indeed, much of his work is still not published. I once thought no one could publish more obscurely than I have. But reading through Nation's book and his extensive bibliography of Yoder's work, I know my claim to obscurity to be sheer pretension. Of course, John had an advantage. He was a Mennonite, and Mennonites have a gift for in-group publications.

Not only has Nation read Yoder, but he's also read much of what Yoder read. Again, no small feat. To know what Yoder read is very important because Yoder did not always reveal his sources or his conversation partners. Nation helps us see that Yoder read widely not only in theology and Scripture but also in history and the social sciences. I should say, however, I could never convince John he needed to read as much philosophy as I thought I needed to read. Of course in many ways he did not need to read philosophy the way I need to because John seems to have been born with a clear mind. However, he read more philosophy than he often acknowledged. For example, I recently learned from one of my students that Yoder had read Elizabeth Anscombe's *Intention*. It never occurred to John he should display his erudition.

This book will clearly make Mark Nation the scholar of record about matters Yoder. But Nation does not write in a hagiographical mode about his friend's life or work. He knows that Yoder would not have credited any work that was uncritical. Yoder was a rigorous critic, and he would not have expected anyone reading him not to try to teach him how to think more faithfully. Indeed one of the great contributions Nation makes in his book is to show the polemical Yoder. Yoder could be extraordinarily critical, particularly of his Mennonite sisters and brothers whom he thought too often simply created small versions of Constantinian social establishment without acknowledging what they were doing.

Nation makes wonderfully clear that Yoder had little use for what he called "methodologism." So there is no "center" to Yoder's thought. Not even nonviolence is a systematic principle for him. Jesus is central, of course, but since Jesus is the Son of God, that means he is the center that cannot be summarized, because Jesus makes a difference for how everything is understood. Yoder's work, therefore, is not "systematic"; but Nation helps us see how everything is connected to everything else in Yoder. Particularly interesting is how Nation helps us see the interconnectedness of Yoder's published work and especially his great book, *The Christian Witness to the State*.

Wisely, however, Nation does not try to make the ecumenical focus more than it should be to organize Yoder's thought. One can enter Yoder's thought and its interconnections in a number of ways. No doubt other books will be written on Yoder that stress this or that aspect of his thought in relation to its overall form. But Nation's focus on Yoder's ecumenical commitments proves particularly fruitful for helping us see the connectedness of his life and work. Nation is quite right that not only is Yoder's theology ecumenical in character, but his life was committed to healing the wounds of our divisions. He knew such healing was crucial for peace. That is why it is so important to understand Nation's point that Yoder did not write *The Politics of Jesus* as a Mennonite book.

Particularly important is how Nation helps us see the significance of Yoder's early historical work. That work, which concentrated on disputes between the early Anabaptists and the Reformed, served to convince Yoder that early Anabaptists did not seek to separate themselves from other Christians. Indeed, Yoder is quite insistent that the early Anabaptists did not know they were Anabaptists just to the extent that description might suggest a separatist movement. Yoder's historical work, moreover, complicates the picture of the early Anabaptists, so often drawn as a caricature by those who would want to leave the Anabaptists behind.

Nation also rightly stresses the significance of the congregation for Yoder's understanding of the Mennonite contribution to the ecumenical world. I am sure Nation is right that not only is the disciplined congregation a significant theme in Yoder's work, but also it is an extremely important emphasis for the future of the ecumenical church. As Yoder once observed, the alternative to Constantinianism is not another false universality, but locality. The relationship between locality and catholicity was an ongoing issue for him.

Finally, Yoder was deeply committed to what he called "word care." That he was means his work must be read with equal care. The fundamental themes of his work were established early and changed little. Nor did he ever abandon his unswerving commitment to think through what he thought he had learned from the early Anabaptists for our overall understanding of the church of Jesus Christ. He pursued these tasks with unrelenting intensity and care. It is the great virtue of Nation's book that he has — with the care worthy of Yoder — helped us understand the intensity and passion that shaped this extraordinary man's work.

STANLEY HAUERWAS

Acknowledgments

There are many people I wish to thank as this book goes to the publisher. First, my thanks to Jon Pott, David Bratt, and the other editorial staff at Eerdmans for their diligent work on this project. Second, I want to thank the staff at the London Mennonite Centre for their support as I wrote this there, while director. Third, I give thanks to the three people who read the first draft. In the midst of a fatal health condition, Jim McClendon read this manuscript quickly and carefully, for which I am very grateful. Glen Stassen offered many helpful detailed criticisms. Glen and I first connected almost thirty years ago because of a common passion for peace and justice. His ongoing witness is much appreciated. Stanley Hauerwas, who has been a wonderful friend for sixteen years, has been invaluable in shaping me theologically since I first read *A Community of Character* in 1982. I appreciate his willingness to write a gracious foreword. Fourth, of course, I am grateful for John Yoder, of blessed memory. I often miss him. I continue to be convinced that his witness to the gospel of Jesus Christ — in its fullness — is a timely gift for the church in the twenty-first century. Fifth, I want to thank my wife, Mary, for the many hours she gave to this book — through conversations, editing, and compiling the index. She has not only worked very hard on it directly, but she has also been very supportive of me as I've worked on it. That she has become an inspiring preacher, teacher, and theologian only makes me regret that this has slowed down her progress on her own book(s).

Finally, I dedicate this book to my mother, Shirley (Morris) Nation. She has been a wonderful parent. This book would not have been written without her faithful support. I am so grateful that as of about eight years ago she is also a sister in Christ.

Introduction   Yoder's Broad Reach

"Nineteen seventy-four, I believe, was the year I read John Yoder's *Politics of Jesus*."[1] James McClendon opens his three-volume systematic theology with this sentence, thereby signaling not only that John Yoder had made a substantial contribution to his thinking, but more importantly, that reading Yoder had transformed his whole approach to the enterprise of theology. Similarly, I could begin by saying: Nineteen seventy-six, I believe, was the year I read John Yoder's *The Politics of Jesus*. That book initiated a reorientation in my thinking about theology, social ethics and the church — and the interdependence of these large topics. To understand Yoder's theological project, centered in the politics of Jesus (the subject, not just the book by that title), is to realize the need for a transformation in one's approach to theology. It is to understand why Stanley Hauerwas would write: "When Christians look back on this century of theology in America *The Politics of Jesus* will be seen as a new beginning."[2]

1. James Wm. McClendon, Jr., *Systematic Theology*, Vol. 1: *Ethics* (Nashville: Abingdon Press, 1986), 7. In the revised and expanded edition of this same book McClendon no longer opens with this sentence. However, he still maintained that "John Howard Yoder's writings changed my life" (revised and enlarged edition [Nashville: Abingdon Press, 2002], 7).

2. Stanley Hauerwas, "When the Politics of Jesus Makes a Difference," *The Christian Century*, October 13, 1993, 982.

Not everyone who has read John Yoder's writings, or even has some appreciation of them, would say that they are indebted to Yoder for their basic approach to theology or ethics. In fact, as James McClendon has pointed out, John Yoder has been "the *bête noir* of contemporary moral theology, especially of mainline Protestant ethics."[3] Nonetheless, over a period of almost fifty years of diligent, patient work Yoder convinced more than a few that his views deserved serious consideration. Richard Mouw was more than simply clever when he began his foreword to Yoder's 1994 book, *The Royal Priesthood,* as follows: "The views contained in this book are not detestable," a reference to the language of the Belgic Confession of 1561, a Reformed confession that proclaimed detestation of "Anabaptists and other seditious people."[4] Mouw knows that before Yoder came on the scene, if theologians and ethicists did not assume that Anabaptist views were "detestable," they at least did not think they were worth considering. He notes that "John Howard Yoder has demonstrated the deep folly of this portrayal. He offers us an Anabaptist perspective that, in a decent and orderly manner, forces us to retrace our historical and theological steps as we take an honest look at questions that have long been ignored — yes, even suppressed — by those of us who have found it easy to marginalize the 'free church' tradition."[5] Yoder's influence indeed became significant enough that J. Philip Wogaman, in his recent history of Christian ethics, named Yoder as one of a handful of the "formative Christian moral thinkers" of the twentieth century.[6]

There were at least three responses to Yoder's work. McClendon and Hauerwas represent those who came to see and accept that Yoder's approach required a radical re-thinking and re-orientation of

---

3. McClendon, *Ethics,* 73.

4. Richard J. Mouw, "Foreword," in *The Royal Priesthood,* ed. Michael G. Cartwright (Grand Rapids: Eerdmans, 1994), vii.

5. Mouw, "Foreword," ix.

6. J. Philip Wogaman, *Christian Ethics: A Historical Introduction* (Louisville: Westminster/John Knox Press, 1993), 233-35. Wogaman had given significant attention to the work of Yoder as early as 1976 in his *A Christian Method of Moral Judgment* (Philadelphia: Westminster Press, 1976), 32-35, 123-31, 187-93. Yoder was not happy with some of Wogaman's characterizations of his positions in this 1976 book and wrote a lengthy letter in response (John Howard Yoder to Philip Wogaman, March 27, 1978).

their own approach to theology (and thereby theological ethics). Mouw represents those who grasped something of Yoder's overall theological approach, accepted his critique of their stereotypes of his approach, and even incorporated elements of his approach into their own, while simultaneously not embracing key elements of his radically reforming project. A third category of reader did not fully engage the contours of Yoder's theological approach, but they did engage his views on violence. Some of the latter accepted his corrections of stereotypes regarding pacifism, while others responded to his challenge to take the just war tradition seriously.

Yoder knew that his pacifism created a stumbling block for many. Thus Yoder offered powerful arguments that often either removed or at least softened this offense. As Walter Wink put it, "More than any other person, Yoder has labored to bring the Peace Church witness against violence into the mainstream of theological discussion."[7] In Philip Wogaman's words, "The Christian pacifist tradition gained unusually articulate interpretation in the twentieth century through the work of John Howard Yoder."[8]

These three levels of influence testify to the brilliance of John Howard Yoder. They also testify to the power of what Yoder referred to as his "ecumenical vocation and patience" — what becomes, in my title, Yoder's Mennonite patience, evangelical witness, and catholic convictions.

The Reason for This Book

John Howard Yoder died at the end of 1997, the day after his seventieth birthday. Many tributes were offered during the ensuing months. William Klassen noted that the one thing that was absent from these various tributes was Yoder's contributions to ecumenism: "Yoder opened up the world of the Anabaptists . . . to the ecumenical world.

7. Walter Wink, *The Powers That Be* (New York: Doubleday, 1998), 204. Also see Marlin Van Elderen, "John Howard Yoder: On Studying War . . . ," *One World: A Monthly Magazine of the World Council of Churches* 109 (October 1985): 18-19.

8. Wogaman, *Christian Ethics*, 233.

One of Yoder's abiding convictions, which he wrote about and labored for, was the need for Mennonites to be in dialogue with the larger church."[9] Klassen was right. Insufficient attention has been given to Yoder's ecumenical — or catholic or evangelical — vocation. Commentators are often well aware that Yoder was a Mennonite and that he was a pacifist. For some it is precisely because of their knowledge of these two facts that they are sure Yoder must have been both narrow in his understanding of the Christian faith and limited in his serious engagement with other Christian traditions. Nothing could be further from the truth. Yoder, as a committed Mennonite, was in fact profoundly evangelical in his witness while being broadly catholic in his Christian sensibilities and relationships. This book unfolds how Yoder's whole life and his writing demonstrated his commitment to what he referred to as a "special ecumenical vocation" and, often, an embodiment of "ecumenical patience."

John H. Yoder: Mennonite, Evangelical, Catholic[10]

Mennonite

John Howard Yoder is largely responsible for the fact that Mennonites are now on the theological map. If the name "Yoder" is mentioned in academic theology circles in North America — at the annual meetings of the American Academy of Religion or the Society of Christian Ethics — most would know not only that the speaker was referring to *John Howard* Yoder, but also that this influential theologian was Mennonite and pacifist. In fact, in American academic theology circles, the name of John Yoder is largely synonymous with what it means to be Mennonite.

While Mennonites themselves know that there are other Mennonite theologians than John Howard Yoder, and in fact some Menno-

9. William Klassen, "John Howard Yoder and the Ecumenical Church," *The Conrad Grebel Review* 16 (Spring 1998): 77-81.

10. I have published a brief biographical sketch of Yoder: "John Howard Yoder: Mennonite, Evangelical, Catholic," *The Mennonite Quarterly Review* 78 (July 2003): 1-13. Some paragraphs from that sketch have been used here, with permission.

nite theologians would distance themselves in significant ways from Yoder's theology, what is beyond doubt is that Yoder's theology has deep roots in Mennonite soil. Yoder sometimes emphasized that his theological or ethical approach was not peculiarly Mennonite, but he well knew that he was nothing if not Mennonite. Yoder was nurtured in a Mennonite community and drew deeply from the Anabaptist roots of his own denomination. Through careful study of the Anabaptist tradition — in conjunction with a broad theological education and active and intentional engagement with Christians from a broad array of traditions — he remained convinced throughout his life that there were important insights derived from the Anabaptist tradition that could be of benefit to all Christians.

Evangelical

Some might have been surprised to see John Howard Yoder pictured along with Billy Graham, Carl F. H. Henry, Francis Schaeffer, and George Marsden on the cover of *The Christian Century* in February, 1989, when the cover story read: "The Years of the Evangelicals."[11] More recently, in April 2000, some might have been surprised that *Christianity Today,* the flagship of American evangelicalism, would list *The Politics of Jesus* by John Yoder as one of the ten best books of the twentieth century.[12] Or that evangelical publishers in England and the U.S. would include John Yoder in a *Biographical Dictionary of Evangelicals.*[13]

But these inclusions and descriptions are not really all that surprising. By instinct, John Yoder knew the world of evangelicalism as well as any Christian world outside that of the Mennonite church. He would always have an appreciation for the world of American evangelicalism, a world not entirely dissimilar to that of his childhood in a

---

11. Martin E. Marty, "The Years of the Evangelicals," *The Christian Century,* February 15, 1989, 171-74. (Also see the cover picture.)

12. "Books of the Century," *Christianity Today,* April 24, 2000, 92-93.

13. See "Yoder, John Howard," in *Biographical Dictionary of Evangelicals* (Leicester, England, and Downers Grove, IL: InterVarsity Press, 2003).

Mennonite church. Yoder was critical of the American evangelical world and certainly, after he was an adult, did not identify fully with it. Still, it didn't bother him to be considered a part of it by others; he seemed to have no hesitation about giving the subtitle *Essays Public and Evangelical* to the last book he published.[14] Yoder knew that the word "evangelical" was broader than this one American tradition.[15] He was relatively comfortable that his most famous book was published by an evangelical publisher, that he was referred to by more than a few as an evangelical, and that he was often asked to address evangelical gatherings. He knew that if anyone was really paying attention, they would not confuse him with Billy Graham. On the other hand, Yoder did not want anyone to imagine that he was ashamed of the "evangel," the Gospel of Jesus Christ.

Catholic

Although some might have assumed that he was an evangelical, probably no one ever mistook John Howard Yoder for a Roman Catholic. It is, of course, worth noting that he taught courses at the University of Notre Dame for thirty years. His first invitation to teach there, in the autumn of 1967, was orchestrated by John L. McKenzie, the well-known Roman Catholic Old Testament scholar (and pacifist), a faculty member at Notre Dame at the time. From 1967 until 1977 Yoder taught at Notre Dame part-time; he taught there full-time from 1977 until he died in 1997.

However, by referring to Yoder as catholic I do not primarily mean Roman Catholic. I mean what he meant when he said, in *The Priestly*

14. John Howard Yoder, *For the Nations: Essays Public and Evangelical* (Grand Rapids: Eerdmans, 1997).

15. On some of Yoder's reflections on the word "evangelical" and American evangelicalism see especially John H. Yoder, "The Contemporary Evangelical Revival and the Peace Churches," in *Mission and the Peace Witness,* ed. Robert L. Ramseyer (Scottdale, PA: Herald Press), 68-103; Yoder, "On Not Being Ashamed of the Gospel: Particularity, Pluralism, and Validation," *Faith and Philosophy* 9 (July 1992): 290 ff.; and Yoder, *For the Nations,* 6-8.

Kingdom, that "the vision of discipleship projected in this collection is founded in Scripture and catholic tradition."[16] Throughout his adult life John Yoder sought to be broadly catholic or ecumenical, seeking to understand and to engage various Christian traditions. In fact, from early in his adult life he sensed a call to articulate a catholic vision for the church. He referred to this as a "special ecumenical vocation."

Yoder's "special ecumenical vocation" was twofold. Yoder always called his own Mennonite church to be outwardly focused — missionary, ecumenical, and engaged in current issues, but he wanted that engagement to be defined by their rootedness in the Anabaptist tradition. Yoder admitted the need to learn from others outside the Mennonite world, but such learning, such borrowing, should happen through careful, critical appropriation. In his own ecumenical engagement with non-Mennonites he sought to interpret the radical reformation tradition in a way that was accessible, indeed compelling, to a broad range of Christians. His desire was that others would see how the various components of his position fit together as a whole, but he would rather have them engage certain central elements of his position than see them ignore it altogether. Even if he accomplished nothing else, he sought to influence Christians and others to exercise greater discipline in their use of violence.

Yoder was aware that his tradition was a minority tradition. He also knew that pacifism was offensive to some and simply weird to others. He recognized from the beginning that the task of getting a hearing for his tradition and his convictions presented a considerable challenge. He had no desire to remove the offense, at least not inasmuch as the offense was the offense of the cross. However, he did desire to render intelligible the ways in which his convictions, rooted in a tradition, were derived from the claims of Jesus Christ, not only on Mennonites but upon all who claimed to follow Christ. Throughout the almost fifty years during which Yoder exercised "ecumenical patience" he accomplished this goal to a considerable extent.

16. John Howard Yoder, "Introduction," in *The Priestly Kingdom* (Notre Dame: University of Notre Dame Press, 1984), 8. He emphasizes numerous times throughout this introduction that his convictions, vision, theology, and ethics are catholic.

What I find most remarkable — and what we most need to learn from and live with today — was Yoder's ability to combine his deep commitment to his own tradition with a tenacious dedication to various ecumenical engagements. This combination was embodied in Yoder's "special ecumenical [or catholic] vocation" and made possible by his own "ecumenical [or Mennonite] patience."

I hope through this book to further the catholic conversations that John Yoder so diligently and patiently undertook. I want to challenge stereotypes that at times prevent the fullness of Yoder's voice from being heard. And, finally, I hope to encourage Mennonites and others who are convinced of these radical reformation views that they need not shed the particularities of their traditions in order to be fully engaged in the world. We can learn from Yoder how we can join in discussions across convictional lines from a position of humble confidence coupled with patience.

A Note on Terminology

Although I have begun to clarify what I mean when I introduce Yoder as Mennonite, evangelical, and catholic, a few more comments on the use of the words "catholic" and "ecumenical" may be helpful. Although "catholic" and "ecumenical" can be used interchangeably, inasmuch as the fundamental meaning of both words is identical, the word "ecumenical" appears with greater frequency in these pages. I do this because "ecumenical" was the term Yoder preferred when referring to Christians from all traditions or to the church universal. I am conscious that either term is attractive or unattractive to various people for different reasons. I trust the reader will grow to understand what Yoder intended when he used either of these words.

Chapter 1

John Howard Yoder, a Particular
          Mennonite, a Catholic Vision:
          A Biographical Sketch

Stanley Hauerwas is right: if there was anything that could make John
Yoder "testy" it was to be "pigeonholed" as a "Mennonite thinker."[1]
Yoder knew that such pigeonholing was done to dismiss or, at least, to
marginalize what he had to say. This marginalization had happened
often enough that when he wrote the introduction to *The Priestly
Kingdom* in the early 1980s he sought to make it clear that "these
pages do not describe a Mennonite vision":[2] "Without disavowing my
ethnic and denominational origins, I deny that this view is limited to
people of that same culture or derived in its detail from that experience."[3] Rather, he made the "claim that the vision of discipleship projected in this collection is founded in Scripture and catholic tradition,
and is pertinent today as a call for all Christian believers."[4]

One can certainly argue that the vision of discipleship articulated by
Yoder is a catholic or evangelical or ecumenical vision. He himself made
such arguments throughout most of his adult life. However, like all of us,
Yoder was shaped by a particular time and a particular people. His roots,

---

1. Stanley Hauerwas, "When the Politics of Jesus Makes a Difference," *Christian
Century,* October 13, 1993, 984.

2. John Howard Yoder, *The Priestly Kingdom* (Notre Dame: University of Notre
Dame Press, 1984), 8.

3. Yoder, *The Priestly Kingdom,* 4.

4. Yoder, *The Priestly Kingdom,* 8.

the "mother's milk" that nurtured his soul and shaped his life when he was young, were Amish Mennonite. But we make a serious mistake if we imagine that we can pigeonhole John Howard Yoder simply by knowing he was raised Amish Mennonite. On the other hand, we cannot fully understand him without knowing the Christian tradition in which he was raised as well as the various worlds he entered as he matured.

It was his discovery of the Anabaptist heritage of his own denomination that especially captured his imagination. It was his passion in life to share what he discovered from that tradition with the broader Christian world; one way to describe him is to say that he was a catholic neo-Anabaptist.[5] Using the Anabaptist tradition as a hermeneutic, he sought to provide a compelling voice for a catholic, radically reforming way of understanding the Christian faith that he hoped would, in its main outlines, be embraced by all Christians.[6] Knowing that not everyone would embrace his form of the Christian faith, he sought to call Christians (and others who would listen) to live disciplined lives in relation to violence.

The Yoders, the Goods, and Oak Grove Mennonite Church

"Biography begins with parents and ancestors."[7]

"Without disavowing my ethnic and denominational origins. . . ."[8]

5. Yoder used the term "neo-anabaptist movement" to refer to the recent revival of interest in sixteenth-century Anabaptists in his quickly written summary of an April 1952 meeting of Mennonite graduate students, "Reflections on the Irrelevance of Certain Slogans to the Historical Movements They Represent." See also "The Cooking of the Anabaptist Goose" or "Ye Garnish the Sepulchres of the Righteous," unpublished paper, Mennonite Church Archives, Goshen, Indiana, 1. (Yoder provided these three titles for this brief piece.)

6. See John Howard Yoder, "Anabaptist Vision and Mennonite Reality," in *Consultation on Anabaptist-Mennonite Theology*, ed. A. J. Klassen (Fresno, CA: Council of Mennonite Seminaries, 1970), 5: "what is meant here by the label 'Anabaptist' is not a century but a hermeneutic."

7. John Howard Yoder, "1980 Autobiography," unpublished transcript of an autobiographical tape made by Yoder for James Wm. McClendon, Jr., and Karen Lebacqz in 1980, in possession of author, 1.

8. Yoder, *The Priestly Kingdom*, 4.

John Howard Yoder was reared in Oak Grove Mennonite Church, just outside of Smithville, in northern Ohio. This Mennonite church was founded around 1816.[9] John Howard Yoder's great-great grandfather, his great-grandfather, and his father successively provided leadership at Oak Grove for over one hundred years.

John K. Yoder (1824-1906), John Howard Yoder's great-great grandfather, and his family moved to Wayne County, Ohio, from Mifflin County, Pennsylvania, in the spring of 1855. This was five years after John K.'s ordination to the ministry. He would come to be one of the most powerful, influential, and widely known bishops in the Amish Mennonite church in the later part of the nineteenth century.[10]

---

9. Strictly speaking, until the 1920s, the church was Amish Mennonite. However, to refer to Oak Grove as Amish Mennonite is confusing for those who are unfamiliar with American Mennonite (and Amish) history. Oak Grove was founded by those standing within Anabaptist/Mennonite history who are descended from the followers of Jakob Ammann, who separated from other Mennonites in the late seventeenth century. In the third quarter of the nineteenth century in the U.S. the followers of Ammann found two different ways of appropriating their tradition. One way — the way many Americans now associate simply with the term "Amish" — came to be designated by the term "Old Order Amish" and the other as "Amish Mennonite." John Howard Yoder's great-great grandfather, John K. Yoder, was one of the leaders who helped to lead one segment of the descendants of Ammann in the progressive direction to become Amish Mennonites. (On the beginnings of the Amish branch of the Mennonite tradition see Steven M. Nolt, *A History of the Amish* [Intercourse, PA: Good Books, 1992], 23-41, and John D. Roth, trans. and ed., *Letters of the Amish Division: A Sourcebook* [Goshen, IN: Mennonite Historical Society, 1993]. On the divisions that developed in the second half of the nineteenth-century see Paton Yoder, *Tradition and Transition: Amish Mennonites and Old Order Amish, 1800-1900* [Scottdale, PA: Herald Press, 1991].)

10. A note on the word "bishop" here: "It does not mean a person exercising responsibility over a diocese. [A bishop] was considered a sufficiently mature and responsible leader that he sometimes became a resource to other congregations in matters of reconciliation and ordination of leadership" (James O. Lehman, *Creative Congregationalism: A History of the Oak Grove Mennonite Church in Wayne Country, Ohio* [Smithville, OH: Oak Grove Mennonite Church, 1978], 25). It is also worth noting that ministry was not how John K. earned a living — he was a businessman. However, Theron Schlabach is right that "quite probably he did business mainly to carry on his larger role as religious and moral leader in church and community" (Theron F. Schlabach, *Peace, Faith, Nation: Mennonites and Amish in Nineteenth-Century America*, The Mennonite Experience in America, Vol. 2 [Scottdale, PA: Herald Press, 1988], 53).

It was largely his churchwide leadership, especially in the third quarter of the nineteenth century, that determined the future direction of the Amish Mennonites (as distinct from what would come to be known as the "Old Order Amish").

Early in his ministry John K. was seen to be "forward-looking in his progressiveness, but his deep respect for meaningful patterns and traditions of the past gave him restraint and caution," according to historian James Lehman. He "always insisted upon a strong congregationalism in the government of his church, even if it meant leaving the older ways considerably. . . . He preached and taught powerfully and led his congregation to discipline rigorously. Yet he had a very democratic spirit. And he displayed unusual confidence in the involvement of lay members in church matters."[11] Two guiding principles shaped his policies, according to historian John Umble: "the maintenance of the fundamentals of the Dordrecht Confession as laid down in the Eighteen Articles; and the unity and peace of the brotherhood."[12] This approach to the church influenced John K. Yoder's style as he provided leadership within his own congregation, in offering counsel to other congregations, and in the nationwide meetings.

Christian Z. Yoder ("C.Z.," 1845-1939), the youngest son of John K., did not become a minister until age 58. This delayed ordination was because ministers in the Amish Mennonite church were chosen by lot at that time; he had been through the lot nine times, until it finally fell to him in 1904. By this time C.Z. was already a successful farmer and very actively involved in the Oak Grove church.

Long before C. Z. Yoder was chosen as a minister he organized the Oak Grove Sunday School, serving as its superintendent for 33 years. He also assisted in the organization of the Ohio Sunday School

11. Lehman, *Creative Congregationalism*, 78.

12. John Umble, "The Oak Grove-Pleasant Hill Amish Mennonite Church in Wayne County, Ohio, in the Nineteenth Century (1815-1900)," *Mennonite Quarterly Review* 31 (July 1957): 205. The Dordrecht Confession, from 1632, has been called "the mother among Mennonite confessions": Howard John Loewen, *One Lord, One Church, One Hope, and One God: Mennonite Confessions of Faith* (Elkhart, IN: Institute of Mennonite Studies, 1985), 24. Also see Gerald C. Studer, "The Dordrecht Confession of Faith, 1632-1982," *The Mennonite Quarterly Review* 58 (October 1984): 503-19.

Conference, which began in 1895. For many years he served on the music committee of the Mennonite general conference.[13] C.Z. was on the Board of Directors for the Elkhart Institute as well as its successor, Goshen College, and he served in several capacities with Mennonite mission agencies in their embryonic stages. He became the first vice president and then for nine years served as the president of the Mennonite Board of Missions and Charities and for another eight years as chairman of the Missions Committee of the board. About two months after the U.S. declared war on Germany in 1917, C.Z. co-authored a letter to President Wilson, reminding him that nonresistance "has always been an essential principle in our creed."[14] He also served as an evangelist, a role that took him to Amish and Mennonite communities all over the country, making him a household name throughout the church.[15]

During his stint as an evangelist in Virginia, he worked with another Christian, Christian Good (1842-1916), a Mennonite minister from Harrisonburg. This man would become John Howard Yoder's maternal great-grandfather.[16] Among the facts that were passed down to John Howard about his great-grandfather Good was that he was a conscientious objector during the Civil War. When commanded to shoot, he protested, "But those are people. I don't shoot people." The Confederate army pulled him from battle and put him to work in the kitchen instead.[17]

Christian Good and Anna Heatwole Good (1841-1889) had nine

13. The Mennonite general conference was the general governing body for the ("Old") Mennonite Church. This general governing body came into existence around 1900 (James J. Juhnke, *Vision, Doctrine, War: Mennonite Identity and Organization in America, 1890-1930*, The Mennonite Experience in America, Vol. 3 [Scottdale, PA: Herald Press, 1989], 124-30). This governing body is not to be confused with The General Conference Mennonite Church, a separate Mennonite branch that began in 1860 (see Schlabach, *Peace, Faith, Nation*, 117-40).

14. Lehman, *Creative Congregationalism*, 206-7.

15. Umble, "The Oak Grove-Pleasant Hill Amish Mennonite Church," 196.

16. Lewis Christian Good, *A Good Tree Grew in the Valley: The Family Record of Christian Good, 1842-1916* (Baltimore: Gateway Press, Inc., 1974).

17. John Howard Yoder, memo to the author, November 28, 1995. Also see Good, *A Good Tree Grew in the Valley*, 1-3.

children. Four of their sons moved to Sterling, Illinois, and became a part of the Science Ridge Mennonite Church. One of their sons, Samuel Good (1878-1905), John Howard Yoder's grandfather, became a leader in the church. He died of tuberculosis at the age of 27.[18] A daughter, Ethel (1903-1992), was born to Samuel and his wife, Mary Ellen (Reisner) Good (1881-1973), two and a half years before Samuel died.[19] Family members helped Mary Ellen (Mamie) and Ethel as they could, but it was difficult for the young widow. Mamie was first an apprentice to a dressmaker and then worked as a doctor's assistant. When Ethel was ten years old she and her mother moved to Chicago where Mamie became a volunteer in the Mennonite city mission in Chicago. Mamie married Amos Neff (1887-1951) when Ethel was twelve. Ethel spent the rest of her childhood in Chicago. She moved to Indiana to attend Goshen College in the fall of 1920. There Ethel, the granddaughter of Christian Good, met Howard C. Yoder (1897-1983), the grandson of Christian Z. Yoder. By October 7, 1925, they were married and moved to the Smithville area, worshiping in Oak Grove Mennonite Church, Howard's home church. Howard C. and Ethel were John Howard Yoder's parents.

For our purposes, John S. Yoder, John Howard Yoder's grandfather, is significant for one particular reason: John S. was the only one of C.Z.'s seven sons who remained in the Mennonite church. John S.'s son Howard C. Yoder was John Howard Yoder's father. Howard C. served with the Mennonite Central Committee for two terms — one in the 1920s and one in the 1940s — first in Russia and then in Western Europe.[20] Howard C. was a leader in the Oak Grove congregation for many years. When it was suggested that Howard C. should be the bishop for the Oak Grove congregation, he responded from London,

---

18. On more than one occasion John Yoder mentioned that Samuel's brother, Aaron C., in sixty years following Samuel's death was one of the most visible (Old) Mennonite ministers, a much traveled evangelist. Yoder, memo to the author. Also see index, under Aaron C. Good, in Willard H. Smith, *Mennonites in Illinois* (Scottdale, PA: Herald Press, 1983).

19. The following information is from Ethel G. Yoder, "My Story," an unpublished autobiographical essay.

20. Mennonite Central Committee (MCC), founded in 1920, is the joint relief and service agency of nearly all North American Mennonites.

where he was serving in relief work, "I do not feel in the least that that is where God wants me. I do not see what I could do for the congregation in that office that I can not do as a member."[21] As a layperson he had, at several critical junctures, offered wise counsel, some of it given during his years of service as chair of the church council. In fact his widow, Ethel Yoder, believed that "at one time in the middle 40s it was his gift as a mediator that held the church together."[22] But why would the church needed someone to hold it together?

In 1927 the eastern Amish Mennonite conference of Pennsylvania and Ohio, of which Oak Grove was a member, merged with the Ohio Mennonite Conference of the "Old" Mennonite Church.[23] At that time some Amish congregations were more progressive in matters of education and dress than were the "Old" Mennonite conferences they joined.[24] Oak Grove was one such progressive congregation, a fact that prevented it from joining this newly formed conference for ten years.

By the second decade of the century a number of young people from the Oak Grove congregation were dissatisfied with trends they detected in Mennonite Church leadership. Some of these sentiments were captured in a report of the Clermont Conference held in June 1919 at Clermont-en-Argonne, France. The report included calls for closer cooperation among Mennonites, efforts to address pressing social concerns, an aggressive peace program, including the production of literature and curricula for schools and colleges and a program of witness to the state against military training and imprisonment of conscientious objectors, and the development of a relief and service organization ready to deal effectively with emergencies, such as wars and natural disasters.[25] Another manifestation of the tensions between the

21. Quoted in Lehman, *Creative Congregationalism*, 247.

22. Ethel G. Yoder, "My Story," 11. For the situation in the Oak Grove Church in the 1940s see Lehman, *Creative Congregationalism*, 237-55.

23. The "Old" Mennonite Church (sometimes simply called The Mennonite Church) is the oldest (founded ca. 1683) and largest of the Mennonite bodies in North America. The "Old" Mennonite Church and the General Conference Mennonite Church (the second largest Mennonite body in North America, founded in 1860) merged to form one denomination in 1999.

24. Juhnke, *Vision, Doctrine, War*, 121.

25. Lehman, *Creative Congregationalism*, 211-12.

Oak Grove congregation and many in the larger Mennonite Church was the congregation's support of Goshen College, which many in the leadership in the Mennonite Church thought too liberal, going so far as to close it for a year (1923-24). Oak Grove consistently supported Goshen College; in 1918, for example, it responded to Goshen's plea for help in reducing their indebtedness by giving the college $5,325, a considerable sum for that time.

But at the heart of the disagreement between the newly merged conference and Oak Grove was the fact that the congregation was not ready to bow to conference power and legislation.[26] Oak Grove had gone to some effort to spell out their reaffirmation of distinctive doctrines of the Mennonite Church, such as footwashing, devotional covering, the marriage ordinance, the holy kiss, nonresistance, nonsecrecy, non-swearing of oaths, and non-conformity to the world. Furthermore, they said, "we admire simplicity of attire, and yet we bear in mind that Christ and His Apostles continually emphasized the inner life, purity of heart, etc., more than outward appearance."[27] "We admire simplicity of attire" was precisely the vague commitment that the conference balked at; it stated specifically what dress was appropriately expressive of "simplicity of attire." To deviate from such specified dress (and to deviate from other specified behaviors befitting nonconformity) was to flout the authority of the conference. Oak Grove, coming from the Amish Mennonite heritage and rooted in a different understanding of church polity, had problems with this understanding of authority. For them decisions regarding specific behaviors, appropriate to the convictions they shared with the conference, were to be discerned within the local church.

Working out the differences in understandings of church polity continued to be an issue for the next ten years, until in 1937 Oak Grove did join the conference. Ten years later, however, they were ejected from the conference over a disagreement over whether the congregation could ordain the person of their choice or had to bow to the wishes of the conference. Oak Grove remained independent for the

26. Lehman, *Creative Congregationalism*, 235.
27. Lehman, *Creative Congregationalism*, 235.

next twenty-two years, at which time they affiliated with both the (Old) Mennonite Church and the General Conference Mennonite Church, making this decision to dually affiliate partly under the guidance of John Howard Yoder.[28]

This is the church in which John Howard Yoder grew up. Without question it shaped him to be profoundly Mennonite. It also gave him a sense of freedom:

> I grew up in a relaxed relationship to that culture, never needing, as many do, to prove my independence of it. Never sensing any coercion to stay within it. So that my choice to stay within it, although predisposed obviously by generations of ethnic continuity and by the church faithfulness of my parents, was by no means a matter of bowing to superior pressure but was rather a willing choice made in small stages in young adulthood. That makes it difficult to this day for many Mennonites, especially younger ones, to understand me when they, although chronologically younger than I, are, in a sense, representative of an earlier phase of the denominational quarrel with culture because they still had to fight Mennonitism in its more conservative forms to prove their independence of it. Whereas I had greater freedom and was therefore able progressively to accept that as my story without being coerced to do so.[29]

But, of course, Oak Grove was only one Mennonite church. John Howard Yoder also related to the larger Mennonite world.[30]

---

28. Lehman, *Creative Congregationalism*, 269-70.

29. John Howard Yoder, "1980 Autobiography," 3-4.

30. For a picture of something of the various Mennonite worlds throughout the first forty years of Yoder's life see Paul Toews, *Mennonites in American Society, 1930-1970: Modernity and the Persistence of Religious Community*, The Mennonite Experience in America, Vol. 4 (Scottdale, PA: Herald Press, 1996).

Toward a "Usable Past" and a Peace Theology

"In [Harold S. Bender's] work, for the first time, the renewal concern reached all the way back to the sixteenth-century sources."[31]

"I deny that this view is limited to people of that same culture or derived in its detail from that experience."[32]

For most nineteenth-century North American Mennonites German was the language of worship, religion, and everyday life. The peculiarities of dress, nonresistance, and other ways of living in a nonconforming manner were reinforced by the barrier of language. As with the Amish today, most nineteenth-century Mennonites knew and accepted that they were different from "the English." Put positively, their language connected them with their history. The *Ausbund*[33] from which they derived their hymns, and the *Martyrs Mirror*[34] from which they derived models of discipleship, reminded them that *Gelassenheit* (yieldedness) and *Demuth* (humility) were the way prescribed for them, even if not for "the English." They stemmed from an honored tradition of Anabaptists who spoke the same language they did. "German," however, did not refer only to their language; it was integrated with their pattern of life.

Around the turn of the century the changes that were already well under way began to accelerate.[35] Leonard Gross has dubbed the

---

31. Yoder, "Anabaptist Vision and Mennonite Reality," 25.

32. Yoder, *The Priestly Kingdom*, 4.

33. On the *Ausbund* see Harold S. Bender et al., eds., *The Mennonite Encyclopedia*, Vol. 1 (Scottdale, PA: The Mennonite Publishing House, 1955). On its waning influence after 1800 see Schlabach, *Peace, Faith, Nation*, 91ff.

34. Thieleman J. van Braght, *Martyrs Mirror*, third English edition (Scottdale, PA: Herald Press, 1886 [from 1660 Dutch edition]), still in print. According to Robert S. Kreider and John S. Oyer, "[F]or Mennonites in their 465 years of history, no book except the Bible has been more influential in perpetuating and nurturing their faith than the *Martyrs Mirror*" (John S. Oyer and Robert S. Kreider, *Mirror of the Martyrs* [Intercourse, PA: Good Books, 1990], 7). See also James W. Lowry, *The Martyrs' Mirror Made Plain* (Lagrange, IN: Pathway Publishers, 1997).

35. Leonard Gross, "The Doctrinal Era of the Mennonite Church," *The Menno-*

half-century from 1898 to 1944 "the doctrinal era of the Mennonite Church": "The uniqueness of this era lay in its ahistorical nature, in its doctrinal center and in the fact that it was an extended interlude, the likes of which were not experienced in preceding centuries nor in the decades after 1944."[36]

In 1898 the Mennonite General Conference was formed. That same year Daniel Kauffman, a prominent Mennonite newspaper publisher, published his book, *Manual of Bible Doctrines*.[37] While previously there had been a complementarity of doctrines based on the corporate faith of the church and rooted consciously in the faith of their forebears, according to historian Leonard Gross, Daniel Kauffman's Mennonitism turned virtually ahistorical, "with an imposed unity of doctrine brought to bear upon the Mennonite Church from a newly organized center, the results of which were supposed to unify all believers within the Mennonite Church." But the new doctrinal approach and authoritarianism of church polity resulted in "a definite narrowing of the theological scope and precipitated as well a radical shift in the Mennonite group dynamic."[38]

In 1901 the German Mennonite paper, *Herold der Wahrheit,* came to an end. Seven years later a new Mennonite magazine emerged, the *Gospel Herald,* which Daniel Kauffman edited from 1908 until 1943.[39] Kauffman also edited a 1914 book entitled *Bible Doctrines,* which he revised in 1928 and renamed *Doctrines of the Bible.* As James Juhnke points out, these books were not an official creed, but "they provided an

---

nite Quarterly Review 60 (January 1986): 86. James Lehman says about Oak Grove, "German continued as the basic language of the Sunday school even until the turn of the century" (*Creative Congregationalism,* 98).

36. Gross, "The Doctrinal Era," 83. See also J. Denny Weaver, "The Quickening of Soteriology: Atonement From Christian Burkholder to Daniel Kauffman," *The Mennonite Quarterly Review* 61, no. 1 (January 1987): 5-45, and J. Denny Weaver, *Keeping Salvation Ethical: Mennonite and Amish Atonement Theology in the Late Nineteenth Century* (Scottdale, PA: Herald Press, 1997).

37. Daniel Kauffman, *A Manual of Bible Doctrines* (Elkhart, IN: Mennonite Publishing House, 1898).

38. Gross, "The Doctrinal Era," 92.

39. J. Daniel Hess, "One Magazine, Five Editors, and 90 Years of Journalism," *Gospel Herald* 90 (January 27, 1998): 2.

accepted standard for 'old' Mennonite congregations, Bible conferences, winter Bible schools, and other forums." They also reflected the escalating Modernist-Fundamentalist controversy in American Protestantism. "In his 1898 volume Kauffman had simply assumed the authority of the Bible without worrying much about a theory of inspiration," but the 1914 book included "a conservative theory of biblical revelation."[40]

Kauffman died in 1944. The two decades before his death saw considerable turmoil in the Mennonite Church, much of it related to the debates between Modernists and Fundamentalists. The turmoil led to the aforementioned closing of Goshen College in 1923-24, prompted by the fact that many of its constituents feared for its orthodoxy. In the 1920s, the Mennonite Church district of Indiana-Michigan, where the college was located, lost four congregations, six ministers, and an eighth of its members to the controversy over orthodoxy.[41] When Goshen College began hiring new faculty for the re-opening in the fall of 1924, one of the professors, Harold S. Bender, was hired to teach history and sociology rather than theology because he was considered by some to be theologically unsound.[42]

This was a time of transition, an opportune time to set new directions for the Mennonite Church. In 1927 Harold S. Bender began *The Mennonite Quarterly Review,* a magazine that provided a vehicle for Bender and his many students to search for a "usable past."[43] That same year, Guy Hershberger suggested that focusing on peace theology might be a way to avoid becoming mired down in the debates then raging about doctrine.[44] Ironically, this was also the year in which John Howard Yoder was born. He would both make the most of the "usable past" and, out of that past, spend many fruitful years articulating a peace theology.

40. Juhnke, *Vision, Doctrine, War,* 129.

41. Toews, *Mennonites in American Society,* 71. On the general struggle see pp. 64-83.

42. Albert Keim, "The Anabaptist Vision: The History of a New Paradigm," *Conrad Grebel Review* 12 (Fall 1994): 241.

43. I am borrowing a chapter title, the first part of which is on Bender, from Toews, *Mennonites in American Society,* 84-106.

44. Toews, *Mennonites in American Society,* 64.

A Neo-Anabaptist Vision: Formation and Articulation

"I . . . was . . . able progressively to accept that as my story without being coerced to do so."[45]

"[This] vision of discipleship . . . is founded in Scripture and catholic tradition, and is pertinent today as a call for all Christian believers."[46]

John Howard Yoder was born on December 29, 1927, in Smithville, Ohio. He was not born into some backwater Mennonite world; Oak Grove probably had more college graduates in its membership than any other Mennonite church except those located near Mennonite colleges.[47] Furthermore, in the summer of 1935 John's family moved from Smithville to Wooster because they were dissatisfied with the schools in Smithville. Thus John spent most of his childhood in a community and in a school not populated by ethnic Mennonites. He was the only Mennonite in his classes. As a child John went to Fellowship of Reconciliation meetings with his parents in Wooster.[48] In high school John participated in extemporaneous speech competition and was on a debate team that won the state championship, debating, among other topics, the issue of pacifism. During his last year in high school he took a few classes at The College of Wooster, a Presbyterian college.

When the time came to enter college full-time, John did not want to attend a Mennonite college. He wanted to attend one of the two universities he knew of that offered a "great books" curriculum. He had secured acceptance and scholarships in special programs at the University of Chicago and St. John's College, Annapolis, Maryland,

---

45. Yoder, "1980 Autobiography," 3-4.

46. Yoder, *The Priestly Kingdom*, 8.

47. In fact, Steven Nolt says that more than half of the faculty and staff of Goshen College were from the Oak Grove church. Steven Nolt, "Critic and Community: John Howard Yoder Among the Mennonites," *Christian Living* 45 (April-May 1998): 6.

48. At that time the Fellowship of Reconciliation was an international Christian pacifist organization with local chapters.

both of which would have allowed him to begin study after finishing only two years of high school. However, his parents, especially his mother, wanted him to go to Goshen College, the Mennonite college that both of his parents had attended. Out of respect for his parents he went to Goshen, but he wanted to spend no more than two years there. He made arrangements with the college to complete all of the requirements for a B.A. in Bible within two years, which he did.[49]

John began college at Goshen in the fall of 1945. It was an exciting time to be at Goshen College. Guy F. Hershberger and Harold S. Bender were among John's teachers. A year earlier, Hershberger had published *War, Peace, and Nonresistance,*[50] which "became a benchmark in the legacy of Mennonite peacemaking."[51] According to Paul Toews,

> Hershberger positioned historic Mennonite understandings to make them relevant for the larger ecumenical world and even for the nation at large. He was traditionally Mennonite in his argument that Christian ethics was for Christians only, yet he enlarged the boundaries in which nonresistance had effect. . . . Hershberger offered a radically two-kingdom theology but one in which Christians clearly contributed to the social order.[52]

Still, it was Bender who had the more profound influence on John Yoder. Although Bender's area of expertise was church history, he taught a wide range of courses.[53] Bender's seminal essay, "The Ana-

---

49. He did this in the midst of, at various times throughout the two years, being in the A Cappella Chorus, the French club, the German club, the Mennonite Historical Society, the Devotional Life Committee, the college debate team, and serving as editor of the college newspaper. He also won the peace oratorical contest. During his second year of college he was taking thirty-three hours per term. According to one of his roommates he rose at 4 a.m. and went to bed at about 10 p.m. virtually every day.

50. Guy F. Hershberger, *War, Peace, and Nonresistance* (Scottdale, PA: Herald Press, 1944). This book was revised first in 1953 and a second time in 1969.

51. Leo Driedger and Donald B. Kraybill, *Mennonite Peacemaking: From Quietism to Activism* (Scottdale, PA: Herald Press, 1994), 72.

52. Toews, *Mennonites in American Society,* 127.

53. Albert N. Keim, *Harold S. Bender, 1897-1962* (Scottdale, PA: Herald Press, 1998), 342. Of the courses Bender taught, it is likely that Yoder took Ethics, Mennonite History, and Apostolic History. He may also have taken others with him as well.

baptist Vision," had been published a little more than a year ear-lier.[54] This essay was part of a dramatic shift among historians from ignoring or rejecting Anabaptists to taking them seriously as a sub-ject for Reformation-era research.[55] It encapsulated key elements of a vision he transmitted to his eager students, a vision that would pro-vide impetus for years of research and writing. The basic elements of "The Anabaptist Vision" included *discipleship* as "a concept which meant the transformation of the entire way of life of the individual believer and of society so that it should be fashioned after the teach-ings and example of Christ"; "*a new concept of the church* as cre-ated by the central principle of newness of life and applied Christian-ity"; and "*the ethic of love and nonresistance* as applied to all human relationships."[56] According to Albert N. Keim, Bender's biog-rapher, "It was Bender's luck to articulate a new interpretation of history which influenced how historians understood the Anabaptists. Only after the fact did he come to understand that he had also pro-vided his fellow Mennonites with a new self-definition of who they were and where they came from. He gave Mennonites a 'usable past.'"[57] It was John Yoder's luck to be one of those fellow Menno-nites who studied with Bender in his prime. Yoder was later to be recognized by some as "the most gifted theologian of that gifted gen-eration of Bender's protégés."[58]

In the summer of 1946, between his first and second year at Goshen College, Yoder went on an assignment with the Mennonites and Brethren to help care for a shipload of horses that were being

54. Harold S. Bender, "The Anabaptist Vision," *Church History* 13 (March 1944), 3-24; reprinted, with slight revisions, in *The Mennonite Quarterly Review* 18 (April 1944): 67-88. On the history and context surrounding this influential address see *The Conrad Grebel Review* 12 (Fall 1994), 233-82 and Keim, *H. S. Bender*, 306-31.

55. Keim, *H. S. Bender*, 32.

56. H. S. Bender, "The Anabaptist Vision," in *The Recovery of the Anabaptist Vi-sion*, edited by Guy F. Hershberger (Scottdale, PA: Herald Press, 1957), 42-43, 47, 51, em-phasis mine.

57. Keim, *H. S. Bender*, 327; "Bender's luck" was the expression Keim used in an earlier, e-mailed, version of this chapter, in possession of author. The published version has the expression "Bender's calling."

58. Keim, *H. S. Bender*, 506.

transported to Europe.[59] His ship, the S.S. *Virginian,* docked for a few days in Poland. While there John decided to search for a Mennonite church in Gdansk. He was arrested and brought before the mayor of the town as a spy, and only with the help of a Russian-English dictionary could he convince them he was not a spy and be released.

After graduating from Goshen College in 1947 Yoder returned to Ohio to work as a research assistant in the field of plant nutrition at the Yoder Brothers greenhouse in Barberton. He did this until the summer of 1948, when he traveled from eastern Iowa to western Pennsylvania on a "peace team," speaking about peacemaking in various Mennonite churches and camps. This gave him exposure to a broader range of Mennonites than he had encountered previously.

Meanwhile, John had applied for overseas service with the Mennonite Central Committee. The processing of his request took considerable time. While waiting, John took some religious studies courses at the College of Wooster, studied Hebrew at Goshen College, and researched and wrote his first scholarly essay for publication. This essay was on the legal status of church discipline among the Old Order Amish.[60]

On April 1, 1949, John Yoder arrived in France to begin a Mennonite Central Committee assignment. Harold S. Bender told Yoder, "We are assigning you to France to do youth work and to give a peace testimony."[61] John's work included more than this. In the late 1940s and the early 1950s, according to Keim, French Mennonites split into a conservative majority and a younger group that wanted a deeper, more expressive spiritual experience, and an important part of Yoder's assignment was to help mediate the tensions between the two groups.[62] It was an unusual assignment for someone so young and inexperienced,

---

59. "Brethren" is a term connected to numerous Christian groups. These particular Brethren trace their roots to 1708 in Germany. They have, from their beginnings, had a close tie to Mennonites. See Donald F. Durnbaugh, *Fruit of the Vine: A History of the Brethren, 1708-1995* (Elgin, IL: Brethren Press, 1997).

60. John Howard Yoder, "Caesar and the Meidung," *The Mennonite Quarterly Review* 23 (April 1949): 76-98.

61. Keim, *H. S. Bender,* 458.

62. Keim, *H. S. Bender,* 459.

but according to French Mennonite historian Jean Séguy, Yoder was "one of the most effective instruments of the reorganization of the [French Mennonite] churches after 1945. . . . Few men will have exercised such a profound influence in [the churches'] transformation in this post-war period."[63]

Yoder's daily work consisted of overseeing first one and then two children's homes. For the next five years he oversaw the transformation of the Mennonite relief program in France from primarily feeding people to having children's homes, based "on the notion that stranded children are the people most in need of being fed and the best way to feed them is also to house them."[64] John met and married Anne Marie Guth, a French Mennonite who was working in one of these children's homes. They were married on July 12, 1952. John and Anne had seven children between 1953 and 1969, though one died in infancy.

From the beginning of his time in Europe Yoder was involved in ecumenical conversations about pacifism.[65] "Harold Bender took me along to the International Mennonite Peace Committee," he later recalled, "and the people who represented the Mennonites ecumenically took me along very soon in 1950."[66] Some of these conversations were in the context of formal conferences, among them the ones that came to be called the Puidoux theological conferences. Albert J. Meyer has pointed out that these conferences were "the first extended theological conversations in over four hundred years between the Historic Peace

63. Jean Séguy, *Les Assemblées Anabaptistes-Mennonites De France* (Paris: Mouton & Co. and Ecole des Hautes Etudes en Sciences Sociales, 1977), 637. The first sentence is a slightly altered translation of the one provided in the quotation in Neal Blough, "The Anabaptist Vision and Its Impact Among French Mennonites," *The Mennonite Quarterly Review* 69 (July 1995): 383.

64. John H. Yoder, "1980 Autobiography," 11.

65. According to Albert Meyer, Yoder was, until sometime toward the end of 1954, the Mennonite Central Committee Peace Section representative for Europe. "The three of us part-time MCC Peace Section representatives were to replace John H. Yoder, who had been MCC Peace Section representative before our arrival [in October 1954] and was moving to Basel for [full-time, residential] theological study" (Albert J. Meyer, "The Beginnings of the Puidoux Theological Conference Series, 'Church and Peace,' and Eirene,'" unpublished paper, February 12, 1999, in the Archives of the Mennonite Church, Goshen, Indiana, p. 1).

66. John H. Yoder, "1991 Interview Supplement," 1.

Churches . . . and the official churches of Central Europe."[67] John Yoder played a central role in these events, delivering significant lectures at most of them.[68] During his last three years in Europe Yoder was a member of the ecumenical committee of the German Protestant *Kirchentag* and the Europe Council of the International Fellowship of Reconciliation.

While in Europe Yoder also pursued graduate studies, receiving a Dr. Theol. *(insigne cum laude)* from the University of Basel (1962).[69] He studied with a number of the luminaries there, including Walter Eichrodt and Walter Baumgartner in Old Testament, Oscar Cullmann in New Testament, Karl Jaspers in philosophy, and Karl Barth in dogmatics.[70] Under the supervision of Ernst Staehelin, John wrote his doctoral thesis (and a subsequent volume) on the disputations between the magisterial Reformers and the Anabaptists in early sixteenth-century Switzerland.[71]

67. Albert J. Meyer, "Mennonites," in *On Earth Peace: Discussions on War/ Peace Issues Between Friends, Mennonites, Brethren and European Churches, 1935-1975*, edited by Donald F. Durnbaugh (Elgin, IL: The Brethren Press, 1978), 14.

68. See the appropriate sections of Donald F. Durnbaugh, *On Earth Peace.*

69. Between 1950 and 1957 Yoder took sixty-three structured courses and five colloquiums at the University of Basel. These included eight survey courses on church history/historical theology, seven courses in dogmatics/doctrine, fourteen courses on the Old Testament (specific books/topics/surveys), twelve courses on the New Testament (specific books/topics/surveys), one on a survey of the Bible, four courses in philosophy or philosophy of religion, seven courses in theological ethics, two courses on comparative religion, one course on liturgics, and separate seminars specifically on Kant, Luther and the Enthusiasts, Aquinas, Peter Lombard, Martin Bucer, Augustine, and Calvin and pedobaptism. Among his teachers were Karl Barth (five courses), Oscar Cullmann (nine courses), Walter Eichrodt (eleven courses), Karl Jaspers (one course), Walter Baumgartner (four courses), Hendrik van Oyen (eight courses), Felix Flückiger (three courses), Heinrich Ott (co-taught one course), Fritz Buri (one course), Bo Reicke (one course), Martin Rissi (two courses), Heinrich Barth (one course), and his doctoral advisor, Ernst Staehelin (five courses). In addition he attended five of Barth's colloquiums.

70. Yoder attended a number of Barth seminars offered in both French and English. Among other lectures, Yoder heard Barth present what became Volumes III/iv (dealing with war) and IV/ii (dealing with sanctification, discipleship, and peace) of *Church Dogmatics.* The claim by David Hughes, which is quoted by Philip LeMasters, that "'Yoder never studied directly under Barth,'" is incorrect. See Philip LeMasters, *The Import of Eschatology in John Howard Yoder's Critique of Constantinianism* (San Francisco: Mellen Research University Press, 1992), 11, fn 30.

71. John H. Yoder, *Täufertum und Reformation in der Schweiz, I: Die Gespräche*

Additionally, it was during his time in Europe that John Yoder, as an academic, was articulating what it meant to engage the larger world in relation to peace. He wrote essays about Karl Barth and Reinhold Niebuhr, two of the major theological voices of the day who had addressed themselves to the question of violence.[72] He also made his first efforts at formulating a theological rationale for Christians to be actively involved in the world, something he would continue to write about for the rest of his life.[73] During his last three years in Europe, while a full-time student at the University of Basel (1954-1957), Yoder oversaw the Mennonite Board of Missions and Charities relief program that had begun in Algeria in response to the earthquake there in 1954. He wrote a series of five articles about his experiences in Algeria, reflecting on Islam, the war, and the relief efforts.[74]

Another significant development during Yoder's time in Europe was what came to be called the "Concern" group.[75] This group began, innocently enough, with a "European Study Conference of American Mennonite Students in Europe," April 14-25, 1952. The core "Concern" group consisted of seven Mennonite men who were doing graduate studies. Yoder noted that "Sociologically, the group begins with people who shared in some degree the experiences of CPS [Civilian Public Service, a plan of service for conscientious objectors], MCC [Mennonite

---

zwischen Täufern und Reformatoren 1523-1538 (Karlsruhe: Verlag H. Schneider, 1962) and *Täufertum und Reformatoren im Gespräch: Dogmengeschichtliche Untersuchung der frühen Gespräche swischen Schweizerischen Täufern und Reformatoren* (Zurich: EVZ-Verlag, 1968). These are now published in English translation, in one volume, as *Anabaptism and Reformation in Switzerland: An Historical and Theological Analysis of the Dialogues Between Anabaptists and Reformers*, ed. C. Arnold Snyder, trans. David Carl Stassen and C. Arnold Snyder (Kitchener, ON: Pandora Press, 2004).

72. John Howard Yoder, "Reinhold Niebuhr and Christian Pacifism," *The Mennonite Quarterly Review* 29 (April 1955): 101-17 (original pamphlet, 1954); John Howard Yoder, *Karl Barth and the Problem of War* (Nashville: Abingdon Press, 1970) (greatly expanded from a 1954 essay).

73. Portions of one of these lectures are published as "The Theological Basis of the Christian Witness to the State," in Durnbaugh, ed., *On Earth Peace,* 136-43.

74. See Mark Thiessen Nation, *A Comprehensive Bibliography of the Writings of John Howard Yoder* (Goshen, IN: Mennonite Historical Society, 1997), 16-17.

75. See *Conrad Grebel Review* 8 (Spring 1990). Also see Keim, *Harold S. Bender,* 450-71.

Central Committee], study of history and theology, travel abroad, evangelism and the peace witness. Not all are (Old) Mennonite but most have had contact with the revival of interest in Anabaptist studies and many have been at Goshen."[76] What they had in common was that they had been energized by the rediscovery of the Anabaptist heritage of the Mennonite Church.

As a result of their own studies of the Anabaptist tradition these students came to be critical of those, such as Harold S. Bender, who had led them to these studies in the first place. The group came to the conclusion, as John Yoder put it, "that if we were to make sense of North American Mennonitism, it would have to become more Anabaptist, more radical, more self-critical, less mainstream Evangelical, less institution centered."[77] As Yoder put it in a letter to Bender, "What has happened to me is that in the process of growing up I have put together an interest in Anabaptism, which you gave me, an MCC experience to which you were instrumental in assigning me, and theological study to which you directed me, to come out with what is a more logical fruition of your own convictions than you yourself realize."[78] It would not be a stretch to see such a response as a kind of adolescent disparagement of an elder's point of view.[79] John Yoder is probably right that "creating this group gave us a young Turk image within the Mennonite institutions back home. And young Turks were not yet welcome."[80]

76. John Howard Yoder, "What Are Our Concerns?" *Concern* 4 (June 1957): 20.

77. Yoder, "1980 Autobiography," 18-19.

78. Yoder letter to Bender (1952), quoted in Keim, *H. S. Bender,* 456.

79. John Yoder reflects on adolescence and maturation in the "Addendum to Cooking the Anabaptist Goose," unpublished paper, Mennonite Church Archives, Goshen, Indiana, July 27, 1952, 1-2. However much there may have been some "adolescent" reaction to their elders on the part of the "Concern" group, it should not be imagined that there was loss of respect for these elders. It was apparently John Yoder's idea to compile a Festschrift for Harold S. Bender. (See Letter from Paul Peachey to John Howard Yoder, April 1, 1955 [year unclear], Mennonite Church Archives, Goshen, Indiana.) Paul Peachey and John Yoder were part of the planning committee of what became *The Recovery of the Anabaptist Vision: A Sixtieth Anniversary Tribute to Harold S. Bender,* ed. Guy F. Hershberger (Scottdale, PA: Herald Press, 1957). Many years later, Yoder also dedicated a book to the memory of Harold S. Bender: John H. Yoder, *He Came Preaching Peace* (Scottdale, PA: Herald Press, 1985), 5.

80. Yoder, "1980 Autobiography," 19.

Still, this group was certainly not an adolescent "flash in the pan." The "Concern" group convened a number of meetings over the next six years and edited a pamphlet series from 1954 to 1971.[81] The purpose of the pamphlet series, as announced in the first issue, was "to stimulate informal discussion and common searching within the brotherhood for a strengthening of prophetic Christian faith and conduct." By the third issue the statement of purpose had changed to "an independent pamphlet series published by a group of Mennonites, dealing with questions of Christian renewal."[82]

Yoder finished his European graduate studies in 1957 and returned to the U.S. For the first year he returned to the family greenhouse business in Ohio. During the summer of 1958 he was invited to speak about Mennonite theology and to serve as a resource person for the faculty from the three Mennonite Church colleges. It was in this setting that he addressed himself to the concept of Christ and culture for the first time. During the 1958-59 academic year Yoder filled in for J. C. Wenger at Goshen College Biblical Seminary during his sabbatical, teaching New Testament Greek and Contemporary Theology. He also did theological research and writing regarding Christian attitudes toward the state for the Institute of Mennonite Studies.[83]

From 1959 to 1965 Yoder worked full-time as an administrative assistant for overseas missions at the Mennonite Board of Missions. Already at the beginning of his tenure in this position he initiated contacts with evangelical leaders, the National Association of Evangelicals, and the National Council of Churches. For a period of nine years, beginning in 1960, he worked in several official roles with the National Council of Churches, and, over a period of more than twenty years beginning in 1961, he worked in various capacities with the World Council of Churches (WCC).[84] With the WCC he served as a member of

81. See the "Concern Chronology," *Conrad Grebel Review* 8 (Spring 1990): 201-4.

82. "Editorial note," *Concern* 1 (June 1954): inside front cover. "Concern," *Concern* 3 (1956): inside front cover.

83. This culminated in the publication of *The Christian Witness to the State* (Newton, KS: Faith and Life Press, 1964) and *The Christian and Capital Punishment* (Newton, KS: Faith and Life Press, 1961).

84. See Marlin Van Elderen, "John Howard Yoder: On Studying War . . . ," *One*

both the Study Commission on the Theology of Mission and the Faith and Order Colloquium. He also served the WCC as an adjunct staff member of the Commission on World Missions and Evangelism, and as a consultation speaker for the Commission on Justice, Peace, and the Integrity of Creation.[85]

While on the Mennonite Student Services Committee of the Mission Board, Yoder helped create the university campus ministry program. This program offered a summer educational experience that was organized to provide theological education of college quality for those studying at non-Mennonite colleges. Yoder's papers on H. Richard Niebuhr and biblical realism had their beginnings as presentations at these sessions. Yoder also was instrumental in creating patterns of conference affiliation that permitted a congregation to be affiliated with both the "Old" Mennonite Church and the General Conference Mennonite Church. The Mission Board provided the channels through which Yoder was able to actively continue both his Mennonite and ecumenical contacts in Europe, including, but not limited to, promoting pacifism.

From 1960 to 1965 Yoder was a part-time instructor at the Mennonite Biblical Seminary in Elkhart.[86] During this time he was often called on to be the faculty spokesperson for inter-seminary meetings. Representatives from a variety of seminaries in the region participated

---

World: A Monthly Magazine of the World Council of Churches 109 (October 1985): 18-19.

85. In addition to formal roles within the WCC, Yoder worked in various capacities to bring the Historic Peace Church witness to bear upon the WCC. See John Howard Yoder, "Appendix C: 40 Years of Ecumenical Theological Dialogue Efforts on Justice and Peace Issues by the Fellowship of Reconciliation and The 'Historic Peace Churches,'" in *A Declaration of Peace* by Douglas Gwyn, George Hunsinger, Eugene F. Roop, and John Howard Yoder (Scottdale, PA: Herald Press, 1991), 93-105.

86. Goshen College Biblical Seminary (later Goshen Biblical Seminary) was, at this point, the ("Old") Mennonite Church seminary, located in Goshen, Indiana. The Mennonite Biblical Seminary was the General Conference Mennonite Church seminary, located in Elkhart, about ten miles from Goshen. They merged onto one campus in the fall of 1970 in Elkhart, but continued to have two separately identified staff. Yoder was the first president for Goshen Biblical Seminary after the move. Together the seminaries formed the Associated Mennonite Biblical Seminaries. They currently have one president and one staff.

in these meetings, where Yoder spoke on such topics as baptism, ministry, and the just war theory.

Beginning in 1965 Yoder became a full-time professor at Goshen Biblical Seminary (1965-1977) and became an associate consultant with the Mennonite Mission Board (1965-1970). From 1970 to 1973 he was president of Goshen Biblical Seminary, although he also taught in Argentina in 1970-71. He was also acting dean at the seminary from 1972 to 1973. Among other courses, Yoder taught Systematic Theology; Anabaptist Theology; Issues in Ecclesiology; Christology and Theological Method; Christian Attitudes to War, Peace, and Revolution; History and Theology of Ecumenical Renewal;[87] and Theology of Christian World Mission at the seminary.

Yoder taught an occasional course at the University of Notre Dame as early as 1967 and already served as chair of the program in nonviolence there in 1973. Beginning with the autumn of 1977 he became a full-time professor at Notre Dame, with Goshen Biblical Seminary buying a portion of his time from Notre Dame until the spring of 1984. Beginning in 1986, Yoder was a Fellow of the Joan Kroc Institute for International Peace Studies. As a Fellow of the Peace Institute Yoder gave a number of lectures and wrote numerous occasional papers.[88] While at Notre Dame he regularly taught two courses to undergraduates: Voices in Non-Violence and Christian Attitudes to War, Peace, and Revolution. He team taught The Legality and Morality of War. His graduate-level courses included History of Christian Social Ethics, Method in Christian Social Ethics, Christian Social Ethics, Radical Reformation,[89] Religious Roots of Non-Violence, The Theology of the Churches' Social Ministry, and The Just War Tradition (on ethical method). In addition, he coordinated a multi-departmental

87. This interest was also expressed through his involvement, at various points, as a consultant for several intentional Christian communities, including Reba Place Fellowship, Fellowship of Hope, Sojourners Community, and for the network, Community of Communities.

88. See Nation, *A Comprehensive Bibliography*, especially unpublished listings 1990-1996.

89. Another expression of this interest was his service as co-convener for the committee on continuing conversations for the Believers' Church Conferences from 1967 until his death.

course on the Catholic Bishops' Pastoral letter *The Challenge of Peace* that was offered twice.[90]

Over the years Yoder conducted lecture tours in more than twenty countries, including various Latin American, Asian, and Western European countries, as well as South Africa, Poland, and Australia. He taught for one year each in Argentina and France, and was at the ecumenical study center, Tantur, in Jerusalem for a year (1975-76). His fluency in French, German, and Spanish was of great benefit in many of these situations. Yoder also taught intensive courses at New College, Berkeley, California; Regent College, Vancouver, B.C.; and Asia Theological Seminary, Manila, the Philippines. Of course, this is to say nothing of the many, many speaking engagements Yoder gladly accepted over the years in the U.S. These speaking engagements ranged in their location and venue from the most prestigious schools in the country to the most humble, from conservative evangelical to liberal Protestant, from mainstream Catholic to fringe Catholic, from religious to non-religious, and from pacifist to non-pacifist.

Yoder's other professional involvements were also multiple and varied. He was a member, at various times, of nine professional organizations. He was associate director of the Institute of Mennonite Studies from 1965 to 1973. He was on the board of directors of the Mennonite Historical Society in 1947 and then from 1965 to 1986. He was the president of the Society of Christian Ethics from 1987 to 1988 after serving a term as a member of the board of directors. For the same organization he was the co-chair of the special interest group on war, religion, and society from approximately 1970 to 1992. He was a member of the board of editors of the *Journal of Religious Ethics* from approximately 1978 to 1990, a member of the board of editors of *The Mennonite Quarterly Review* from 1961 to 1992, and he was a contributing editor of *Sojourners* (formerly *Post-American*) from 1973 to 1988.[91]

---

90. National Conference of Catholic Bishops, *The Challenge of Peace: God's Promise and Our Response* (Washington, D.C.: United States Catholic Conference, 1983).

91. Yoder was a contributing editor to *Sojourners* from the January-February 1973 issue (then called *The Post-American*), when they first started having contributing editors, until the December 1988 issue.

No summary of John Yoder's life and work would be complete without mention of his many writings.[92] As Stanley Hauerwas noted, "When Christians look back on this century of theology in America *The Politics of Jesus* will be seen as a new beginning."[93] Without question *The Politics of Jesus* was a watershed in John Yoder's career; it is what he will always be best known for. Its central claims were straightforward. As David Weiss puts it,

> His thesis, simply put but thoroughly and eloquently argued, was that Christian ethics begins not by finding ways to set aside the radicalness of Jesus' ethics, but rather by finding ways in community to take those ethics seriously. In other words, the church is to bear the message of the gospel by *being* that message. If the gospel of God's reconciling love had political implications for the community of followers called into being by Jesus — if it decisively shaped the pattern of their life together — then it will continue to have such implications among those of us who link ourselves to that heritage and that calling.[94]

This message touched a nerve. The first edition sold roughly 75,500 copies. The second edition, published in 1994, had sold 11,000 by April

92. One other thing should be mentioned before bringing this biographical sketch to an end. I have not dealt with the church disciplinary process Yoder lived under from the summer of 1992 until the summer of 1996. It is unnecessary within this book to discuss any of the specifics of the allegations regarding inappropriate sexual activity on Yoder's part. What is most relevant here is to mention that Yoder submitted to a very painful discipline process by his church for four years. His submission indicated his willingness to live consistently with his own views on church discipline as articulated in several essays. The discipline process was successfully concluded in the early summer of 1996, with the church "encouraging Yoder and the church to 'use his gifts of writing and teaching.'" (See "Disciplinary Process with Yoder Concludes," *Gospel Herald*, June 18, 1996, 11.)

93. Stanley Hauerwas, "When the Politics of Jesus Makes a Difference," 982. J. Philip Wogaman, in his *Christian Ethics: A Historical Introduction* (Louisville, KY: Westminster/John Knox Press, 1993), 233-35, in naming only a handful of people who deserved their own section in his chapter on "Formative Christian Moral Thinkers," entitled one of the sections, "John Howard Yoder and the 'Politics of Jesus.'"

94. David Weiss, "In Memory of John Yoder: Scholar, Professor, Friend," *The Observer*, January 27, 1998, 9.

of 1998.[95] It has been translated into ten languages. None of these figures — as impressive as they are — begin to convey adequately the influence of *The Politics of Jesus*. In 1970 Brevard Childs indicated that there was no "outstanding modern work . . . in English that even attempts to deal adequately with the biblical material as it relates to ethics."[96] Two years later, John Yoder, in *The Politics of Jesus*, presented what Bruce Birch and Larry Rasmussen referred to as a "welcome and glowing exception" to this omission.[97] By the early 1980s Edward LeRoy Long, Jr., stated that *The Politics of Jesus* "has become as frequently cited in discussions of social ethics as Paul Ramsey's *Deeds and Rules* in the discussion of norm and context."[98] *The Politics of Jesus* has in various ways helped to re-shape the field of Christian ethics over the last twenty-five years.

Richard Hays observed in 1996:

> Yoder's hermeneutic represents an impressive challenge to the church to remain faithful to its calling of discipleship, modeling its life after the example of the Jesus whom it confesses as Lord. As Christian theologians increasingly are forced to come to grips with the demise of Christendom and to acknowledge their minority status in a pluralistic world, Yoder's vision offers a compelling account of how the New Testament might reshape the life of the church.[99]

But the influence of *The Politics of Jesus* and Yoder has reached far beyond the academy. As Jim Wallis said, "John Yoder inspired a whole generation of Christians to follow the way of Jesus into social action and peacemaking."[100]

---

95. Letter from Anne Salsich, Wm. B. Eerdmans Publishing Co., to Mark Thiessen Nation, London, April 16, 1998.

96. Quoted by Bruce C. Birch and Larry L. Rasmussen, *Bible and Ethics in the Christian Life* (Minneapolis: Augsburg Publishing House, 1976), 16.

97. Birch and Rasmussen, *Bible and Ethics*, 18.

98. Edward LeRoy Long, Jr., *A Survey of Recent Christian Ethics* (New York: Oxford University Press, 1982), 90.

99. Richard B. Hays, *The Moral Vision of the New Testament: A Contemporary Introduction to New Testament Ethics* (San Francisco: HarperSanFrancisco, 1996), 253.

100. Jim Wallis, "Lives of Peacemaking," *Sojourners* 27 (March-April 1998), 8.

In fact, no topic received more of Yoder's time and attention than the subject of peace.[101] The breadth, depth, and variety of his writings on peace are astounding. Walter Wink is undoubtedly right that "more than any other person, Yoder has labored to bring the Peace Church witness against violence into the mainstream of theological discussion."[102] This labor included "the seriousness with which he has carried out his role as a friendly critic of just-war thinking."[103]

Yoder did not seem concerned that many wrote and talked almost as if *The Politics of Jesus* was the only thing he ever wrote. However, it is important to note that Yoder also wrote sixteen other books, hundreds of articles, and hundreds of unpublished essays.[104] He wrote in five languages on a wide range of subjects. For the average person or even the average theologian it is certainly not necessary to master the bulk of John Yoder's writings. However, it is not fair to imagine one has "read" Yoder and adequately assessed his arguments if one has barely begun to read the mass of material he produced over a period of more than fifty years.

Summary: Creative Reworking

How does one describe the continuities and discontinuities between the life of John Howard Yoder and the heritage passed down to him through his family and church? At first glance the discontinuities may be more obvious. The rural world of the Amish Mennonites in nineteenth-century America was significantly different from the world of an internationally known theological ethics teacher at the University of Notre Dame in 1997. There are many differences between the world of a farm or greenhouse and that of a university. But the larger

---

101. See Mark Thiessen Nation, "He Came Preaching Peace: The Ecumenical Peace Witness of John H. Yoder," *Conrad Grebel Review* 16 (Spring 1998): 65-76.

102. Walter Wink, *The Powers That Be* (New York: Doubleday, 1998), 204.

103. Drew Christiansen, S.J., "A Roman Catholic Response," in *When War Is Unjust*, rev. ed., by John Howard Yoder (Maryknoll, NY: Orbis Books, 1996), 102.

104. See Nation, *A Comprehensive Bibliography.* Additional books have been published posthumously.

differences are between the world of the nineteenth century and today, not, as we might be tempted to think, between Amish Mennonites and the rest of the "modern" world. As for all of us, it was "familiar people and familiar things" that shaped John Yoder to be who he was early in his life. His mother and father were committed to the church. Both parents had attended Goshen College, a Mennonite Church college. Howard C., John's father, had served two terms with the Mennonite Central Committee, in Russia and Western Europe. During much of John Yoder's childhood his father had provided wise leadership within their church, especially during the difficult period of the 1940s. Ethel, John Yoder's mother, had been raised in an urban ministry in Chicago, a world apart from the ethnic Mennonite world. Certainly as an adult John Yoder was conscious of having been closely connected to the world beyond that of ethnic Mennonites. Yoder was also freed from the more enclosed world of rural ethnic Mennonites by living most of his childhood in the city of Wooster.

But it was not only the immediate world that shaped Yoder. He was also conscious of a rich heritage to which he was heir. C. Z. Yoder, John Yoder's great-great grandfather, was alive until John was eleven, so John could see the depth of commitment and the active involvement of this Mennonite leader. Later, when John Yoder worked for the Mennonite Board of Missions (MBM), he was frequently reminded of C.Z.'s commitment to mission work. The hoe that C.Z. used to cultivate a special patch of crops, the profits from which he would regularly donate to the Mission Board, was enclosed in a glass case in the MBM building. John Yoder knew of the commitment not only of C.Z., but also of John K., Christian Good, grandma Mamie Neff, and others in his family who had given sacrificially of their time for convictions they held dear — nonresistance, non-conformity, serving the poor, mission, and evangelism.

John Yoder was surrounded by a cloud of Mennonite witnesses who in part shaped who he was. As he reflected on this heritage as an adult, John Howard Yoder knew his heritage was Mennonite, much of it specifically Amish Mennonite. However, he was also aware that his great-great grandfather had led a branch of the Amish Mennonites in a progressive direction, thereby enabling them to avoid being physically separated from the rest of the world as some who came to be called Old Order Amish chose to live. Relatives on both sides of his family engaged in mission work. They related to the larger (non-ethnic Mennonite) world. His own home congregation often — under his father's discerning leadership — interacted in creative, progressive, and (as he would see it) faithful ways with their Mennonite heritage. John Yoder sought to take his Mennonite heritage seriously, being faithful to it, while creatively reworking it in various ways. Later we will see that through a vast array of writing that articulated what might be described as an ecumenical or catholic neo-Anabaptist vision, or a vision for continual radical reform, Yoder continued and carried forward this creative reworking of his heritage.

Chapter 2   Anabaptism, Neo-Anabaptism, and Radical Reform

One could argue that John Howard Yoder's entire academic career was committed to communicating in broadly Christian terms what he learned through his studies of sixteenth-century Anabaptism in the 1950s in Europe. It was through those studies that he came to the central convictions that he would subsequently spend a lifetime articulating. His resulting body of writings called for an ongoing program of radical reform that Yoder believed applied to all who call themselves Christian.

Sixteenth-Century Anabaptist Soundings

As Albert Keim put it, "During the 1950s the earth moved in Anabaptist studies." During that decade at least fifty-nine doctoral theses on Anabaptism were either in progress or completed. About half of these were done by Mennonites, including John Howard Yoder.[1]

It may seem predictable that a student of Harold S. Bender would do graduate studies on Anabaptism. After all, Bender was one of the scholars responsible for the renaissance of Anabaptist studies that began in the 1920s. As we saw in the previous chapter, the "Concern"

1. Keim, *Harold S. Bender*, 495.

group, of which Yoder was a member, consisted of students who were doing graduate studies on Anabaptism. Although Yoder did not originally go to France in April 1949 in order to do graduate studies in theology, he was not in Europe long before he began such studies.[2] His studies included the full range of courses offered in the faculty of theology, and when it came time to choose a topic for his doctoral thesis he chose sixteenth-century Anabaptism.

In 1952 Yoder wrote a letter to Harold S. Bender, stating that it was Bender who inspired his "interest in anabaptism."[3] Yoder's initial interest in Anabaptism did, in fact, show the influence of Bender. Just as Bender had focused chiefly on the beginnings of Swiss Anabaptism, so did Yoder.[4] Yoder focused on the theological colloquies between the Reformed theologians in Switzerland (especially Zwingli) and those who were (or, in the beginning, were becoming) Anabaptist. He wrote what became a two-volume work.[5] William Klassen speculates on why Yoder chose to focus on the colloquies, or disputations, as they are also called:

> The Anabaptist research of Bauman, Bender, Yoder, Wenger, C. J. Dyck, Walter Klaassen, et al., and myself is done in the context of a concern for the church in the twentieth century. Certainly our interest in research and our focusing of the issue were determined by what was going on in the larger world. . . . Yoder, gifted in the art of debate and challenged as he was by the promise of ecumenical dialogue, turned to the disputations that showed most clearly the Anabaptist commitment to dialogue.[6]

2. In the fall of 1950 Yoder began studies part time at the University of Basel. He was a full-time student and resident from the fall of 1954 until June of 1957.

3. Quoted in Keim, *Harold S. Bender,* 456.

4. Bender's doctoral thesis was on Conrad Grebel, leader among the earliest Swiss Anabaptists. Written in 1935, it was published as Harold S. Bender, *Conrad Grebel, c. 1498–1526* (Scottdale, PA: Herald Press, 1950).

5. His manuscript, completed in 1957, offered both a historical description of the colloquies and his theological reflections upon them. However, his doctoral advisor, Ernst Staehelin, wanted only the historical part as the thesis.

6. William Klassen, "History and Theology: Some Reflections on the Present Status of Anabaptist Studies," *The Mennonite Quarterly Review* 53 (July 1979): 198.

The first volume largely described some twenty colloquies between 1525 and 1538.[7] Yoder subsequently translated into English what he apparently saw as two of the most significant pieces of this first volume. He entitled the first article, "The Turning Point in the Zwinglian Reformation."[8] In this essay Yoder, countering earlier research by Fritz Blanke and Harold S. Bender, dates the break between Zwingli and his (future Anabaptist) followers to December rather than October 1523.[9] Bender himself considered Yoder's arguments convincing.[10] But it is not the dates themselves that are important, but rather the reason for the break. Yoder believes Zwingli held back on instituting reforms on which he and his followers had agreed because of the unwillingness of the Zurich Council:

> By thus seeing the basic nature of Zwingli's shift in position we have at the same time found the crux of Grebel's clash with him. To place the unity of Zürich above the faithfulness of the church is not only to abandon the church; it is also the demonization of the state, for persecution becomes a theological necessity. The suppression of dissent is for the Zwinglian Reformation from this point on not an unfortunate expedient but a matter of faith. Grebel did not reject the state as an agent of the church as long as there was some hope that it might carry through the Reformation on a basis of tolerance. Grebel's and Mantz's own proposals to Zwingli also had involved the use of the state. But when at the same time Zwingli accepted that the state should not have to carry through the Reformation immediately, and insisted that it should be intolerant for reasons of principle, Anabaptism had become a necessity even though infant baptism had as yet not become an issue.[11]

7. John Yoder, *Täufertum und Reformation in der Schweiz.*

8. John Howard Yoder, "The Turning Point in the Zwinglian Reformation," *The Mennonite Quarterly Review* 32 (April 1958): 128-40.

9. Bender, *Conrad Grebel,* 97-98; Fritz Blanke, *Brothers in Christ* (Scottdale, PA: Herald Press, 1961), 7ff.; James M. Stayer, *Anabaptists and the Sword,* 2d ed. (Lawrence, KS: Coronado Press, 1976), 97, fn. 6.

10. "Editorial," *The Mennonite Quarterly Review* 32 (April 1958): 82. (This is an unsigned editorial. Since Bender was at this time the editor I am assuming he wrote the editorial.)

11. Yoder, "The Turning Point," 140.

For Yoder this points to what can be seen in retrospect as a crucial difference between these Anabaptists on the one side and the Catholics and magisterial Reformers in the sixteenth century on the other. Yoder argues that the church should not compromise its faithfulness to the gospel because of the wishes of the governing authorities. The inverse of this is also true: the state does not have the prerogative to enforce Christian convictions or persecute those who do not abide by the church's teachings.

In January 1959 Yoder published a second essay, an adaptation of three sections of his doctoral thesis.[12] Again Harold S. Bender commended the essay, saying that "in his thorough and detailed study [Yoder] . . . proves beyond doubt that Hubmaier was not substantially connected with the origins of Anabaptism in Switzerland."[13] Perhaps a part of what Yoder attempts to do in this essay is to distinguish between Hubmaier and others who were a part of the beginnings of Swiss Anabaptism. However, to be more specific, Yoder, utilizing his original research in the sixteenth-century sources, provides a detailed, nuanced discussion of Hubmaier's relationship with the nascent Swiss Anabaptist movement. His conclusion expresses well his central findings:

> Balthasar Hubmaier differed from the Zürich Anabaptists not in the content of his conviction but in its depth. Coming to his antipedobaptist convictions as a theologian, he was the century's best spokesman for that position; but without having founded his commitment either in the experience of becoming a church, which the Zürich circle had come through, or in a general view of the church's relation to the political and economic order, he was not ready as were they for "tyranny, torture, sword, fire, or water." After reaching asylum in Nikolsburg he referred to the Zürich brethren as his "fellows in persecution" and as "righteous people," but he had never really joined their number. Until his death he contin-

12. John Howard Yoder, "Balthasar Hubmaier and the Beginnings of Swiss Anabaptism," *The Mennonite Quarterly Review* 33 (January 1959): 5-17.

13. "Editorial," *The Mennonite Quarterly Review* 33 (January 1959): 4. (Unsigned editorial while Bender was editor.)

ued to follow the Reformers rather than the Brethren in letting the state be master in its own home even if it demanded of Christians that they disobey biblical injunctions (oath, armed defense, interest, defense of the property structure), as well as when it chose to reform the church. That the state which affirms its gracious willingness to reform the church thereby also lays claim to a right to direct, brake, or even halt and reverse the Reformation, is a truth which had become part of the basic spiritual orientation of the Zürich Brethren by 1523, even before baptism became any issue, but which Hubmaier never learned.[14]

In October 1965 Hans Hillerbrand reviewed Yoder's thesis, which had been published in German in 1962. In his review of the book Hillerbrand said that "a word of commendation is in order for the author's industrious gathering of materials. There is no doubt but that we have here as complete a list of colloquies as may be assembled."[15] He went on: "The volume here under review and the author's other contributions to Anabaptist history show him as one of the most promising young Mennonite scholars."[16] However, most of the review was critical. The review, similar to a 1968 article by Robert Walton, dealt with Yoder's arguments about "a turning point" in the Zwinglian Reformation.[17] Both reviewers raised questions about a va-

14. Yoder, "Balthasar Hubmaier," 17. It is interesting to note that thirty years later Yoder reaffirmed his basic interpretation here. He does this in his keynote address at the Conference on the Concept of the Believers' Church, convened at Southwestern Baptist Theological Seminary, Fort Worth, Texas, March 31, 1989. The conference focused on Hubmaier. For his comments on Hubmaier see John H. Yoder, "The Believers' Church Conference in Historical Perspective," *The Mennonite Quarterly Review* 65 (January 1991): 10-17. Even more significantly, also in 1989, the Anabaptist writings of Hubmaier were published in English. Yoder was the co-editor and co-translator of this work. One can see in many of the editorial introductions and footnotes that Yoder is, once again — through direct comments on primary sources — re-establishing the case he made thirty years earlier in this essay and the thesis from which it was taken. See H. Wayne Pipkin and John H. Yoder, eds. and trans., *Balthasar Hubmaier: Theologian of Anabaptism* (Scottdale, PA: Herald Press, 1989), esp. 15-165.

15. Hans Hillerbrand, "The 'Turning Point' of the Zwinglian Reformation: Review and Discussion," *The Mennonite Quarterly Review* 39 (October 1965): 309.

16. Hillerbrand, "The 'Turning Point,'" 309.

17. Robert C. Walton, "Was There a Turning Point of the Zwinglian Reforma-

riety of details related to the depth of Zwingli's shift, the point(s) at which the shift occurred, and whether it was Zwingli or his (nascent Anabaptist) followers who were more right in their views about the city officials, the church, and the progress of reformation.

Yoder responded to Hillerbrand and Walton by publishing another essay from his doctoral work. He responded to Hillerbrand's and Walton's criticisms, reaffirming the accuracy of the basic thrust of his own arguments:[18]

This is the root of Zwingli's inability to understand the Anabaptists. He saw the problem of reformation always from the perspec-

---

tion?" *The Mennonite Quarterly Review* 42 (January 1968): 45-56. See also Robert C. Walton, *Zwingli's Theocracy* (Toronto: The University of Toronto Press, 1967), esp. 185-200. For an article that re-affirms Yoder's basic argument see Paul P. Peachey, "The Radical Reformation, Political Pluralism, and the Corpus Christianum," in *The Origins and Characteristics of Anabaptism,* ed. Marc Lienhard (The Hague: Martinus Nijhoff, 1977), 10-26.

18. John Howard Yoder, "The Evolution of the Zwinglian Reformation," *The Mennonite Quarterly Review* 43 (January 1969): 92-122. It is interesting to note that, fifteen years later, Yoder was given an opportunity to translate primary source material germane to the debates here. Once again he takes the opportunity, through editorial comments and footnotes, to reaffirm the basic arguments of his doctoral work and the essays derived from it. See Leland Harder, ed., *The Sources of Swiss Anabaptism: The Grebel Letters and Related Documents* (Scottdale, PA: Herald Press, 1985), especially pages 234-35, 252-53, 659-64. (Yoder translated these passages. It does not state in the book who wrote which editorial introductions. I am assuming that translators wrote their own editorial introductions to writings they translated, or in some cases the editor. However, it is worth noting that Yoder was on the advisory committee for the whole book.)

It is also interesting to note that a number of the editorial introductions — besides those for Yoder's translations — mention Yoder's essays mostly affirmatively. The most significant comment is that "the overall evidence [of this relevant primary source material, pp. 164-274] tends to confirm Yoder's hypothesis [regarding "a turning point"] against that of Walton" (*The Sources of Swiss Anabaptism,* 267). Reviewing this book, Arnold Snyder criticizes some of these editorial remarks in a book of primary source material. (See C. Arnold Snyder, review of *The Sources of Swiss Anabaptism* in *The Conrad Grebel Review* 4 [Spring 1986]: 172-73.)

Finally, Yoder once again enters briefly into these debates, as an aside, in a 1993 essay: John Howard Yoder, "The Burden and the Discipline of Evangelical Revisionism," in *Nonviolent America: History Through the Eyes of Peace,* ed. Louise Hawkley and James C. Juhnke (North Newton, KS: Bethel College, 1993; reprint, Kitchener, ON: Pandora Press, 2004), 23-27.

tive of the total society which was to be rebuilt in an orderly fashion from the top. The Anabaptist proposals could only become meaningful to him by being transformed in this light. When they asked for a more rapid implementation of the reformation for those whose beliefs calls for it, he understands the coercion of the others as well and therefore answers that it would call forth too much resistance from the Catholics. If they ask of serious Christians the readiness to share with the poor brother, he understands that they want to suspend the institution of private property in the whole civil realm. When they ask of disciples of Jesus Christ the renunciation of violent self-defense, his understanding is that they want to do away with the state. He cannot understand them otherwise than in the way he would think if he were in their place. He therefore remains convinced despite their repeated statements to the contrary that they, like him, really want their convictions to take over the government. Despite their express insistence that that is not their intent, and despite the fact that they did not take advantage of good opportunities to call to their side the support of revolutionary-minded groups, Zwingli remained of this conviction.[19]

Perhaps Yoder's disagreements with Walton and Hillerbrand were finally irresolvable, at least through any straightforward appeal to facts. There are large differences of interpretive frameworks at work here.

Yoder's essay drew from what had become the second volume of his doctoral work, the volume that offered Yoder's theological reflections on his study of the origins of Swiss Anabaptism. These reflections drew a number of contrasts between the Swiss Anabaptists and the Swiss Reformers. Yoder concluded, for example, that these early Swiss Anabaptists saw baptism as the seal of an inner spiritual commitment, whereas the Reformers believed that the sacrament carried weight of itself and was important for institutional order. The Swiss Anabaptists saw the church as a visible, disciplined community of faithful Christians, whereas the Reformers viewed the church as invisible, beyond empirical identification. Furthermore, these Swiss Ana-

---

19. Yoder, "The Evolution of the Zwinglian Reformation," 122.

baptists saw the civil government as a part of the world, whereas the Reformers understood the civil authorities to be bound by a Christian purpose and program. These Anabaptists saw love as Christologically defined, whereas the Reformers saw love as the suppression of the individual will for the sake of civil unity (inseparable from church unity). These early Anabaptists held to a radical Biblicism, whereas Oecolampadius appealed to the universal practice of Christendom as the norm. These Anabaptists believed that the church (as a remnant) was to triumph, if at all in this life, through proclamation, whereas Zwingli, committed as he was to a "Christian" society, thought reform would be achieved through state power. And, finally, these Anabaptists acted upon a Christian mission to "the world," whereas for the Reformers there was no such entity as "the world," except perhaps somewhere outside Christendom.[20]

Yoder's two volumes and the three articles taken from them represent the heart of his original work in sixteenth-century Anabaptism. Beginning in the mid-1950s and continuing throughout the 1960s he drew from that initial research to write encyclopedia articles, extensive reviews, numerous journal articles, and three chapters of a semi-popular history of the Mennonite Church.[21] One of Yoder's last substantive essays on early Swiss Anabaptism argued, contrary to Harold S. Bender, that Michael Sattler, rather than Conrad Grebel, should be considered the founder of the Swiss Brethren. Yoder contended that the "crystallization point" of Anabaptism occurred following attempts at ecumenical dialogue by Sattler in Strasbourg. Only after the failure of such attempts to build connections with the wider reform movement did Sattler formulate the Schleitheim confession that marked the beginning of the Anabaptist movement.[22]

---

20. Yoder, *Täufertum und Reformatoren im Gespräch*.

21. For a listing of other articles see footnotes throughout this section and Mark Thiessen Nation, *A Comprehensive Bibliography of the Writings of John Howard Yoder*.

22. John H. Yoder, "Der Kristallisationspunkt des Täufertums," *Mennonitische Geschichtsblätter* 24 (1972): 35-47. For criticisms of Yoder's argument see Klaus Deppermann, "Die Strassburger Reformatoren und die Krise des Oberdeutschen Täufertums im Jahre 1527," *Mennonitische Geschichtsblätter* 25 (1973): 24-41. For further discussion see

Given the subject of his doctoral thesis, and noting the academic work he published based upon that work, one might have expected that Yoder would spend the rest of his career working in sixteenth-century Anabaptist studies. But of course this was not to be the case. Yoder's primary attention was drawn to other things, but he did not completely leave sixteenth-century Anabaptist studies behind.

The most substantial work Yoder did in this area after his doctoral work and the related writings during the 1960s was in the field of translation. In 1973, while serving as associate director of the Institute of Mennonite Studies, Yoder translated and edited the first volume in "Classics of the Radical Reformation," a series intended to provide English translations of Anabaptist and Free Church primary source material. This first volume made available the writings of Michael Sattler.[23] Twelve years later Yoder was involved directly with the fourth volume, entitled *The Sources of Swiss Anabaptism*,[24] serving on the advisory committee and translating approximately twenty-seven pages.[25] Four years later Yoder served as co-editor and co-translator of the writings of Balthasar Hubmaier for the next volume in the series. Both of the editors assumed responsibility for the final product, but Yoder produced the initial drafts of the introduction, translation, and footnotes for approximately 240 of the 550 pages.[26] What this means is

---

the exchange of letters between Yoder and Depperman: John H. Yoder and Klaus Depperman, "Ein Briefwechsel Über die Bedeutung des Schleitheimer Bekenntnisses," *Mennonitische Geschichtsblätter* 25 (1973): 42-52. For a discussion of the debate between Yoder and Depperman see C. Arnold Snyder, *The Life and Thought of Michael Sattler* (Scottdale, PA: Herald Press, 1984), 89-97. Yoder also offers a brief rejoinder to Depperman and Snyder in John Howard Yoder, "The Burden and the Discipline of Evangelical Revisionism," in Hawkley and Juhnke, eds., *Nonviolent America: History Through the Eyes of Peace*, 25-27.

23. John H. Yoder, trans. and ed., *The Legacy of Michael Sattler* (Scottdale, PA: Herald Press, 1973). It should also be noted that Yoder was on the editorial council for the "Classics of the Radical Reformation" series from the beginning until approximately 1992.

24. Leland Harder, ed., *The Sources of Swiss Anabaptism* (Scottdale, PA: Herald Press, 1985).

25. See Harder, *The Sources of Swiss Anabaptism*, 22.

26. For comments about translation and editing responsibilities see Pipkin and Yoder, *Balthasar Hubmaier*, 14.

that Yoder had a hand in the translation of much of the most significant primary source material related to his own doctoral work in early
sixteenth-century Swiss Anabaptism into the late 1980s.[27]

After the early 1970s, aside from the translations just mentioned,
Yoder wrote much less on sixteenth-century Anabaptism, publishing
only the occasional brief review or essay, based mostly on earlier research. In fact, after the early 1970s, one could say Yoder mostly disengaged from the academic world of sixteenth-century Anabaptist studies. At least two realities converged for Yoder in the early 1970s that
made it easier for him to remove himself from this particular world.

First, the academic world of Anabaptist studies (and Reformation studies more generally) was becoming much more complicated.[28]
There were what might be described as paradigm shifts. One of the
chief paradigms of the past that came to be looked down upon was
what would come to be called the "Bender school," with which
Yoder's name was associated.[29] Though Yoder responded directly to

27. It should perhaps also be mentioned that, because of his knowledge of German and Spanish, Yoder served as editor for a Spanish language collection of Anabaptist sources. See John Howard Yoder, ed., *Textos Escogidos de La Reforma Radical*
(Buenos Aires: Asociasion Editorial Aurora, 1976).

28. For a sense of the complexity in Anabaptist studies see: James M. Stayer,
Werner O. Packull, and Klaus Depperman, "From Monogenesis to Polygenesis: The
Historical Discussion of Anabaptist Origins," *The Mennonite Quarterly Review* 49
(April 1975): 83-121; Hans-Jürgen Goertz, ed., "Problems of Anabaptist History: A Sym-
posium," *The Mennonite Quarterly Review* 53 (July 1979): 175-225; J. S. Oyer, "Histori-
ography, Anabaptist," in *The Mennonite Encyclopedia*, Vol. 5; C. Arnold Snyder, "Be-
yond Polygenesis: Recovering the Unity and Diversity of Anabaptist Theology," in
Essays in Anabaptist Theology, ed. H. Wayne Pipkin (Elkhart, IN: Institute of Mennonite Studies, 1994), 1-33; Werner O. Packull, *Hutterite Beginnings* (Baltimore: Johns
Hopkins University Press, 1995), 1-11; and Thomas Heilke, "Theological and Secular
Meta-Narratives of Politics: Anabaptist Origins Revisited (Again)," *Modern Theology*
13 (April 1997): 227-52.

On the complexity of Reformation studies generally see Thomas A. Brady, Jr., et
al., eds, *Handbook of European History 1400-1600*, Vol. 1: *Structures and Assertions*
(Grand Rapids: Eerdmans, 1994) and Thomas A. Brady, Jr., et al., eds., *Handbook of
European History 1400-1600*, Vol. 2: *Visions, Programs, and Outcomes* (Grand Rapids:
Eerdmans, 1995). Each of the essays in these two large volumes includes a substantial
bibliography.

29. There is no doubt that Yoder, having studied with Bender, and being a Men-

one of the first major contributions to these paradigm shifts, it would be his last substantial contribution to the ongoing discussions.[30] Of course Yoder was quite capable of doing the work that was necessary to engage the new debates emerging in the 1970s in the field of Reformation studies in general and Anabaptist studies in particular. But he was aware that the field was changing substantially. To participate adequately in the debates he would need to give substantial time to a fresh study both of the methodological shifts and the primary sources. Besides, it should be kept in mind that Yoder's central passions were always, even in relation to his original historical work, connected to contemporary Christian faithfulness. He believed that a study of denominational origins could be useful for renewal of contemporary church life. He nonetheless believed this approach had its limitations. As Yoder put it, "Perhaps a Calvinist or a Lutheran needs, for reasons which he can define theologically, to be faithful to his founder. The descendants of churches once led by Menno do not. By the nature of the case the tradition of the sixteenth century is not normative in the free church style. The free church tradition is also a *tradition*, so that guid-

---

nonite of the generation he was, was influenced by Bender. On the other hand, it is a mistake to identify him too closely with Bender. Among other things, it should be noted that Yoder acknowledged, in several places, the diversity of views of various Anabaptists in the sixteenth century. See Yoder, "A Summary of the Anabaptist Vision," in *An Introduction to Mennonite History*, 109-10, and, more fully, John Howard Yoder, "The Recovery of the Anabaptist Vision," *Concern* 18 (July 1971): 5-23, esp. 7-14. He acknowledges both diversity of views and origins of Anabaptist groups in "Anabaptists in the Continental Reformation," *Christian Attitudes to War, Peace, and Revolution: A Companion to Bainton* (Elkhart, IN: Co-op Bookstore, 1983), 163-200.

30. James M. Stayer has been a major player in Anabaptist studies over the last three decades. His doctoral thesis, *Anabaptists and the Sword* (Lawrence, KS: Coronado Press), was first published in 1972. See John Howard Yoder, "Review of *Anabaptists and the Sword* by James M. Stayer," *Church History* 43 (June 1974): 272-73. Yoder wrote another response that should not be seen as a review but rather as a challenge to the interpretive grid of the three authors whose works he reviews; see John Howard Yoder, "'Anabaptists and the Sword' Revisited: Systematic Historiography and Undogmatic Nonresistants," *Zeitschrift für Kirchengeschichte* 85, no. 2 (1974): 126-39.

For a constructive use of Yoder's approach in his "'Anabaptists and the Sword' Revisited'" essay see David S. Fischler, "Undogmatic Anabaptist: Nonresistance and Christian Magistracy in the Thought of Menno Simons," in *Church Divinity 1982*, ed. John H. Morgan (Notre Dame: Church Divinity Monograph Series, 1982), 33-47.

ance is also received from the past. But the *way* that guidance is received is much less firmly structured, and much less concerned for fidelity to any particular father."[31]

Second, at the same time the field of Anabaptist studies was becoming more complicated, Yoder came out with *The Politics of Jesus* in 1972. He had already been extensively involved in ecumenical conversations, but the enthusiastic reception this book received gave him a much higher profile and was to make him much more widely known in the academic world and beyond.

Neo-Anabaptist Possibilities

In 1927, when Harold Bender began *The Mennonite Quarterly Review,* he did so not only because he had a scholarly interest in sixteenth-century history, but also because he had an interest in the renewal of the Mennonite Church. If this was not obvious in 1927, it certainly should have been by 1944 when Bender's well-known essay, "The Anabaptist Vision," was published.[32] Albert Keim notes that with the publication of this essay, Bender "gave Mennonites a 'usable past.' Ultimately, that feature would become the most important effect of his essay."[33] That it pointed to a particular past led some, like Yoder, to study the sixteenth-century Anabaptists. That it was to be a "usable" past meant that what was learned from the sixteenth century was to be used to bring critique and renewal to contemporary Mennonite life.

---

31. John Howard Yoder, "Reformed Versus Anabaptist Social Strategies: An Inadequate Typology," *Theological Students Fellowship Bulletin* (May-June 1985): 5. Or again: "To find your identity in your founders, in your history, in original Anabaptism, is itself already a reformation stance and not a radical free church stance" (John H. Yoder, "Anabaptist Vision and Mennonite Reality," in *Consultation on Anabaptist-Mennonite Theology,* ed. A. J. Klassen [Fresno, CA: Council of Mennonite Seminaries, 1970], 26). See also John H. Yoder, "The Ambivalence of the Appeal to the Fathers," in *Practiced in the Presence: Essays in Honor of T. Canby Jones,* ed. Neil Snarr and Daniel Smith-Christopher (Richmond, IN: Friends United Press, 1994), 245-55.

32. Harold S. Bender, "The Anabaptist Vision," *The Mennonite Quarterly Review* 18 (April 1944): 67-88.

33. Keim, *Harold S. Bender,* 327.

It is no accident that Yoder and a number of the "Concern" group of Mennonites who met in Europe in the early 1950s followed in Bender's footsteps. This group began as a gathering of Mennonites doing graduate studies in Europe who read papers to one another regarding what they were learning about the Anabaptist roots of their Mennonite identity. Their studies of sixteenth-century Anabaptism were used to understand and to offer a critique of contemporary North American Mennonite reality. They became a part of what Yoder dubbed "the neoanabaptist movement."

By 1954 the "Concern" group had decided they would share their findings with a larger audience by publishing a pamphlet series, a periodical they named *Concern*. From 1954 to 1971, the years of the publication of *Concern*, Yoder contributed far more writing to this series than any other author.[34] In an article published about the same time he finished his doctoral thesis, Yoder summarized the theological "concerns" of the "Concern" group:[35]

> There is a definite relation between the group's convictions and reactions and the new understanding of the Anabaptist movement. The Anabaptist fad in American Mennonite circles is already a generation old, but this group has gone beyond studying the Anabaptists and admiring their depth of conviction and reached the conclusion that on many points they were right and should be followed. The claim is not that the Anabaptist movement was infallible but that on a surprising number of points they were led to right answers which retain an exemplary value for our time. Since terms like "Christian," "Biblical," "evangelical" are no longer sufficiently meaningful, and since some label or another is unavoidable, the group accepts the Anabaptist position, by and large, and

---

34. For a discussion and analysis of the writings in *Concern*, see Robert J. Suderman and Bruno Epp, "The Witness of *Concern* Magazine," unpublished paper written for the course, "Theology of Anabaptist Classics," at the Associated Mennonite Biblical Seminaries, 1974, in possession of author.

35. Of course it is difficult to know to what extent this article reflected the thinking of the group. But it is a good summary of Yoder's theological concerns. See John Howard Yoder, "What Are Our Concerns?" *Concern* 4 (June 1957): 20-32.

from it directs its message toward *both Mennonites and non-Mennonites*.[36]

"Toward *both Mennonites and non-Mennonites*": It is not surprising that they intended to address Mennonites. After all, the Anabaptism that had energized them provided the historical roots of the Mennonite churches. And besides, they knew, partly because *Concern* was published by the Mennonite Publishing House, that their readership would mostly be Mennonites. Still, in 1954, when *Concern* was begun, an editorial note stated, "CONCERN is an independent pamphlet series dealing with current Mennonite and general Christian issues."[37] By the third issue, in 1956, the note had changed: "CONCERN is an independent pamphlet series published by a group of Mennonites, dealing with questions of Christian renewal."[38] By issue number 5, in 1958, the cover announced, "A Pamphlet Series For Questions of Christian Renewal."[39] This last stated purpose remained on the cover until the series was discontinued in 1971. Thus from the beginning, this group of Mennonite students wanted to communicate what they were learning from the Anabaptists not only to Mennonites but to other Christians as well. One sign of this ecumenical intent was that in the pages of *Concern* there was surprisingly little reference to sixteenth-century Anabaptism.[40] This in a periodical begun by students, many of whom were studying sixteenth-century Anabaptism and all of whom had caught a vision for the renewal of the church from their own studies and from those, like Harold S. Bender, who had led them to "the Anabaptist vision."

Of course, what these young men were drawing from Anabaptism was not identical to what their teachers had drawn.[41] But, like

36. Yoder, "What Are Our Concerns?" 20-21, emphasis mine.

37. *Concern* 1 (June 1954): inside front cover.

38. *Concern* 3 (1956): inside front cover.

39. This time the intent is stated three places: *Concern* 5 (June 1958): front cover, inside front cover, and p. 1.

40. Robert J. Suderman, "A Brief Commentary and Analysis of the Witness of *Concern*." Unpublished paper prepared for class, "Anabaptist Classics and Discipleship," Associated Mennonite Biblical Seminaries, May 13, 1974, in possession of author, p. 7.

41. On the relationship between Harold Bender and the "Concern" group see Keim, *Harold S. Bender,* 450-71.

their teachers, especially Bender, they did articulate their gleanings from the sixteenth century for the renewal of the contemporary church. In fact, as stated above, in 1957 John Yoder spoke for the "Concern" group when he listed a half dozen issues that the "Concern" group believed needed to be addressed if there was to be Christian renewal. He articulated these issues in the periodical by asking rhetorically: "What Are Our Concerns?" The contents of this 1957 essay highlight the key concerns.

First, *the call to discipleship* belongs within the context of the church. Within the five sub-points under this first point, Yoder attempts to make the call to discipleship solid and accountable, while avoiding what he perceived to be certain Mennonite forms of legalism.[42] The second point, for Yoder, is closely connected to the first: *the local congregation is the primary locus of discernment and authority.* With this twin focus Yoder intends both to keep the authority accountable to those over whom it is exercised and to place within the hands of the local church the process for working out the details of disciplined discipleship. Third, Yoder asserts, *the Bible functions as the authority in the church.* However, as soon as he has made this claim, he intentionally avoids tying it to any particular *theory* of authority: "Our only conclusion for the moment is that there is as yet no satisfying doctrine of Biblical authority. . . . The first question for us . . . is what the Bible says, not a doctrine of authority."[43] Fourth, Yoder states a point at which he believes the Anabaptists were original, namely in their emphasis upon distinguishing *that which was not the church,* that is to say, *"the world."* Fifth, he affirms, without much discussion, that the *church is to be led by the Spirit and to be missionary.*[44] And, finally, he argues

42. It is important to note this twin concern for Yoder as early as 1957, a concern that would continue throughout his life.

43. Yoder, "What Are Our Concerns?" 27.

44. Yoder is brief here: "these two necessities are well enough admitted to need little further development" (Yoder, "What Are Our Concerns?" 28). However, he later makes a further point on the work of the Spirit that is more controversial: "Pentecostalism is in our century the closest parallel to what Anabaptism was in the sixteenth: expanding so vigorously that it bursts the bonds of its own thinking about church order, living from the multiple gifts of the spirit in the total church while holding leaders in

at greatest length for why it is that *the church* (and especially the free church) *should be ecumenical.*

A decade later Yoder wrote an essay wherein he was quite consciously standing on the shoulders of Harold S. Bender. The essay, placed in the context of a book on Mennonite history, is entitled, "A Summary of the Anabaptist Vision."[45] In this essay the focus is on clarifying the distinctiveness of the Anabaptists within the context of the sixteenth-century Reformation. The list is quite similar to that in the previous essay.[46] Seven distinctives are named. (1) Although the common conviction among the Reformers was that the Scriptures were the final authority for faith and practice, the Anabaptists insisted that the scriptural authority superseded the authority of the civil government when the two were in conflict. (2) The magisterial Reformers argued that the theologians or princes were the ones who provided authoritative interpretations of the Scriptures. The Anabaptists believed the Scriptures were to be interpreted within the context of the gathered Christian community under the guidance of the Holy Spirit.[47] (3) The magisterial Reformers and the Roman Catholics appealed to "stations" or "vocations" to provide the standards that guide behavior in daily living.[48] Regarding the use of the sword, they appealed to the Old Testament or an honored Christian emperor. The Anabaptists, however, believed that Christ is to be followed in daily life. Christ's teachings, life, death and

---

great respect, unembarrassed by the language of the layman and the aesthetic tastes of the poor, mobile, zealously single-minded. We can easily note the flaws in Pentecostal theology, organization, or even ethics: — very similar, by the way, to the faults of the early Quakers and Anabaptists, or of the apostolic churches — but meanwhile they are out being the Church." John Howard Yoder, "Marginalia," *Concern* 15 (July 1967): 78.

45. "A Summary of the Anabaptist Vision," in *An Introduction to Mennonite History,* ed. Cornelius J. Dyck (Scottdale, PA: Herald Press, 1967), 103-11. (The names of the authors of the individual chapters are not listed with each essay — only listed in an editorial preface.)

46. One could also compare either list with that provided in John H. Yoder, "The Prophetic Dissent of the Anabaptists," in *The Recovery of the Anabaptist Vision,* ed. Guy F. Hershberger (Scottdale, PA: Herald Press, 1957), 93-104.

47. For more on this see John Howard Yoder, "The Hermeneutics of the Anabaptists," *The Mennonite Quarterly Review* 41 (October 1967): 291-308.

48. For more on this see John Howard Yoder, "The Two Kingdoms," *Christus Victor* 106 (September 1959): 3-7.

resurrection were to guide daily behavior, including the use of money and the sword.[49] (4) Because the magisterial Reformers did not emphasize the teachings of Jesus and their relevance for daily living, they did not emphasize Christ's call for Christians to love their neighbors and enemies. The Anabaptists said that all Christians are called to such love, even if it is costly. (5) It was assumed by the Roman Catholic Church and the magisterial Reformers that everyone was to be a member of the church. This was one factor that made infant baptism intelligible and mandatory. The Anabaptists believed that the church is comprised only of believers. Membership should be voluntary and the church should both be distinguished from the rest of the world and be independent of the state. (6) The civil authorities at the time of the Reformation enforced community membership (and, therefore, church membership) by the sword, by punishment.[50] The Anabaptists believed membership in the church was voluntary. Anabaptists further believed that since membership is voluntary and discipleship is entailed by membership, there should be discipline within the church, the central purpose of this discipline being reconciliation.[51] (7) Concerning "the community of goods," the magisterial Reformers did not teach that Christians were to share their possessions in the way the Anabaptists did. The Reformers worried that the Anabaptists intended the abolition of private property for the whole of society. The Anabaptists taught that believers were to share one another's burdens, that their property was not their own, and that, as stewards, they were to share financially with one another.[52]

---

49. Yoder does not here in this brief, popular treatment deal with various Anabaptist teachings on the use of the sword, but see John Howard Yoder, "Anabaptists in the Continental Reformation," in *Christian Attitudes to War, Peace, and Revolution*, 163-200, and "'Anabaptists and the Sword' Revisited," 126-39.

50. For an interesting recent comparison of Augustinian and Anabaptist forms of discipline see Thomas Heilke, "On Being Ethical Without Moral Sadism: Two Readings of Augustine and the Beginnings of the Anabaptist Revolution," *Political Theory* 24 (August 1996): 493-517.

51. For Yoder's fullest statement on church discipline see John Howard Yoder, "Binding and Loosing," in John Howard Yoder, *The Royal Priesthood: Essays Ecclesiological and Ecumenical*, ed. Michael G. Cartwright (Grand Rapids: Eerdmans, 1994), 323-58.

52. Of course Yoder's whole discussion within this brief essay is intended for a

In both of these essays discussed above Yoder was doing something similar to what Harold S. Bender had done when he provided the list of Anabaptist distinctives in "The Anabaptist Vision." Occasionally Bender was pointed in his critique of the Mennonite Church in relation to "the Anabaptist vision." In June 1953, for example, Bender wrote a much-discussed paper on "Outside Influences on Mennonite Thought." Bender wrote that although there was much to celebrate within the Mennonite Church, some of which stemmed from outside influences on the church, these influences also produced challenges. Bender was concerned about excessive forms of piety, worldliness, and rampant materialism on the one hand, and the need for a revival of nonresistance, nonconformity, and "full discipleship" on the other.[53]

Sixteen years later Yoder offered a similar pointed critique[54] in a lecture entitled "Anabaptist Vision and Mennonite Reality."[55] Yoder presented this lecture at least three times in 1969, to the students and faculty at Mennonite colleges and seminaries. Though the lecture, as the title indicates, is about current Mennonite reality, it is also largely about outside influences on Mennonite thought.[56]

At the outset of the essay, Yoder states that he assumes his audience knows what the "Anabaptist Vision" is. He briefly reformulates

---

general audience, and thus it is not carefully nuanced. On this last topic see especially James M. Stayer, *German Peasants' War and Anabaptist Community of Goods* (Montreal: McGill University Press, 1991).

53. Keim, *Harold S. Bender*, 506-7.

54. Yoder was hardly alone among the "Concern" group in being more harsh in his critique of the Mennonite Church than Harold S. Bender. (On the relationship between Yoder, the "Concern" group and Bender see Keim, *Harold S. Bender*, 450-71.)

55. The lecture was published as John H. Yoder, "Anabaptist Vision and Mennonite Reality," in *Consultation on Anabaptist-Mennonite Theology*, ed. A. J. Klassen (Fresno, CA: Council of Mennonite Seminaries, 1970), 1-46.

56. Five years earlier, Yoder presented less polemical lectures on outside influences. However, they are much less well known, so I do not deal with them here. They should be noted. See John Howard Yoder, "Where Are We Theologically in Terms of 40-75 Years Ago?" and "Streams of Influence — Theological Influences," in *Consultation on Theological Communication* (Scottdale, PA: Mennonite Publishing House, 1964), 8-13, 33-40. Also see Paul Toews, *Mennonites in American Society, 1930-1970*, The Mennonite Experience in America, Vol. 4 (Scottdale, PA: Herald Press, 1996), 277.

the central tenets of this vision, tenets he will use as the norms by which contemporary Mennonite reality is judged. First, the Anabaptist vision calls for a believers' church. On the inside this means that members are not just born into this fellowship, they are there by free adult decision. This also makes such a church a missionary church to all who do not belong. Second, the Anabaptist vision requires the way of the cross. Within the fellowship this will imply a renunciation of the use of power and the refusal to reduce people to objects in decision-making. In relation to those who are outside, this second criterion implies a refusal to engage in war and an insistence on a redemptive sharing in the world's struggles and suffering.[57]

As Yoder proceeds with the discussion of current Mennonite reality, he seems to want to root his critique in recent retrievals of sixteenth-century Anabaptist teachings as well as to create some distance. Thus, at the outset, he writes, "What is meant here by the label 'Anabaptist' is not a century but a hermeneutic. It is [representative of] certain types of discussion by the 16th century movement, but it can be valid apart from that particular period."[58] Halfway through the essay, when speaking of the need for renewal within the Mennonite Church, he notes: "Now the best picture of this renewal according to the model of Jesus is the radical reformation or the Anabaptist vision."[59]

Having set up the Anabaptist vision as the norm by which to measure Mennonite reality, Yoder concludes that the reality of the Mennonite world almost totally fails. Though Yoder acknowledges that the outward marks of Anabaptism remained for centuries, even at great cost (for example, in refusal of military service and infant baptism), he states that "the inner meaning of Mennonite identity [has] changed."[60] There is "no longer a conscious rejection of the use of power and persons within the life of the church, nor is there any sense of missionary reconciliation in the midst of the wars of the

---

57. Yoder, "Anabaptist Vision and Mennonite Reality," 4.

58. Yoder, "Anabaptist Vision and Mennonite Reality," 5. The text says "represented for," which I believe must be a typographical error. Thus I have altered the text as indicated.

59. Yoder, "Anabaptist Vision and Mennonite Reality," 23.

60. Yoder, "Anabaptist Vision and Mennonite Reality," 6.

world."[61] In short, the Mennonite Church "is not an Anabaptist community. . . . It is rather a small Christendom."[62] That is to say, by and large the Mennonite Church is more concerned to defend its ethnic identity and retain its own children than it is to be a "believers church" or to embrace the Anabaptist agenda of mission and social change.[63] Yoder notes that the reason Mennonites are not really Anabaptist is because they have borrowed so much from the non-Mennonite Christian world.[64]

At a 1994 conference commemorating the fiftieth anniversary of Bender's "Anabaptist Vision" essay, John D. Roth, editor of the *Mennonite Quarterly Review,* presented a critique of Yoder's essay, "Anabaptist Vision and Mennonite Reality."[65] As Roth sees it, "In Yoder's reading, virtually the entire history of the Mennonite church — presumably beginning with the second generation of Anabaptists, although Yoder is not very clear on the point — has been a story of acculturation and decline."[66] Roth proceeds to name three specific criticisms of Yoder's critique.[67] First, Yoder writes as if he believes that the embodiment of the Anabaptist vision is a historical possibility, even though almost all the references in his essay point to the failure to meet the standard. As such, the essay is in reality quite ahistorical. Second, culture always seems to be a problem for Yoder. Culture always seems connected to "acculturation." Roth asserts that "Yoder was never clear what 'good' culture — what legitimate appropriations of language, memory and social institutions — might look

61. Yoder, "Anabaptist Vision and Mennonite Reality," 6.

62. Yoder, "Anabaptist Vision and Mennonite Reality," 6.

63. These charges are stated repeatedly throughout the essay, but see especially Yoder, "Anabaptist Vision and Mennonite Reality," 17, 18-27, 27-28, 31, 34, 45-46.

64. Again this is mentioned several places, but see especially, Yoder, "Anabaptist Vision and Mennonite Reality," 7-17, 23-25. Three times (17, 38, 40) Yoder comments that, contrary to the responses he received from audiences, he intended his discussion of the "borrowings" from other traditions to be description, not critique. Given his need to respond to the criticism three times, this was clearly not the way it was heard.

65. Published as John D. Roth, "Living Between the Times: 'The Anabaptist Vision and Mennonite Reality' Revisited," *The Mennonite Quarterly Review* 69 (July 1995): 323-35.

66. Roth, "Living Between the Times," 325.

67. Roth, "Living Between the Times," 328-30.

like."[68] Third, and most grievous, according to Roth, Yoder has not taken seriously enough "the joyful messiness of lived experience": "The 'Anabaptist Vision and Mennonite Reality' model seems to force the Anabaptist Vision and contemporary Mennonites into a pernicious dualism: *either* our institutions, congregations, families, ethics are in perfect alignment with the standard *or* we must accept the fact that we are acculturated, middle class, complacent accommodators to the status quo. There is no middle ground."[69]

While Roth's criticisms of Yoder's essay are helpful, two points should be made. First, Roth may be wrong when he writes, "The address shared the strengths typical of John Howard Yoder's published works: it was incisive, keenly argued and carefully nuanced."[70] Indeed, these are *usually* the strengths of Yoder's writings. However, none of these terms — incisive, keenly argued, or carefully nuanced — fits this particular essay. Roth is more accurate when he goes on to say that "there is also a certain 'slippery' quality to the paper, most evident in Yoder's repeated — and disingenuous — claim that his intent was to be 'purely descriptive'; that he was simply carrying out an assignment to 'describe what is going on while [not] taking sides.'"[71] One might deduce from either Yoder's essay or, even more, from Roth's essay on Yoder, that this is typical Yoder, especially if one accepts Roth's claim that this address "shared the strengths typical" of John Yoder, which is not necessarily true. The second point to bear in mind is that what is missing from this particular essay can be gotten elsewhere in Yoder's writings. Yoder offers other well-articulated responses to the questions raised by Roth. But, more importantly, most of Yoder's numerous other writings that were intended to challenge the Mennonite Church to faithfulness have a different tone and character. They manifest more fully what Roth claims concerning the "Anabaptist Vision and Mennonite Reality" essay, namely, "it clearly was written out of a deep love for the Mennonite church and a passionate commitment to the church's renewal."[72]

---

68. Roth, "Living Between the Times," 329.

69. Roth, "Living Between the Times," 329, emphasis his.

70. Roth, "Living Between the Times," 324.

71. Roth, "Living Between the Times," 324-25.

72. Roth, "Living Between the Times," 324. One question that begs to be asked

An instance of Yoder's careful tone and incisive thinking is found in one of his first published articles in the magazine of the Methodist student movement, *Motive*. Here Yoder commended the Mennonite postwar relief efforts in Europe, using the opportunity to state the theology underlying this work.[73] Yoder's series of nine articles on nonconformity written for the Mennonite periodical *Christian Living* in 1955 and 1956[74] — when Yoder was in his mid-twenties — are models of incisiveness, keenly argued and carefully nuanced. These articles certainly present challenges; they intend to. But the challenges they issue are not unheard of in Mennonite circles. For instance, in the first article on money, Yoder reflects on the live issues (in 1955) of whether or not Mennonites should buy life insurance or save money for the future: "the alternative to commercial endowment and life insurance is not a rule against them, but the kind of Christian giving for which they are a secular substitute. That confidence in commercial insurance has become prevalent is a sign that the church has not responded to her obligation to care for the needy *as one cares for oneself.*"[75] The article is full of such challenges. Yoder also writes that "the Christian life is not a matter of rules, definable once for all and for everyone, but of constantly living under the leading of God. The Bible's prohibitions show us the minimum, not the maximum

---

is: Why did "Anabaptist Vision and Mennonite Reality" lack several of the qualities usually present in Yoder's work? We can only guess. Yoder was passionate about the church being outwardly focused through ecumenism, mission work, and work on behalf of peace and justice. My hunch is that this particular lecture expressed some of his frustrations, in 1969, with the extent to which the Mennonite Church was still too inwardly focused, too filled with "ethnic" Mennonite concerns and preoccupied with its own inner life.

73. John Howard Yoder, "Inasmuch as Unto the Least of These," *Motive* 9 (December 1948): 33-34. One might think the "commendation" is understated. However, one must realize that Yoder would have thought it lacking in humility to write otherwise.

74. For full references for the whole series see Mark Thiessen Nation, *A Comprehensive Bibliography*, 15. One might also compare what he says in these articles with what he said in 1963 and 1964 to students at Goshen College and Bethel College on the subject of nonconformity. (See Nation, *A Comprehensive Bibliography*, 21, 22.)

75. John Howard Yoder, "The Respectable Worldliness," *Christian Living* (January 1955): 15, emphasis his.

level of obedience."[76] Yoder argues that what it means to be fully obedient in relation to economics, "to forsake all and follow Christ," is to be discerned within a local body of believers.[77]

Yoder continued to address specific challenges and current issues among Mennonites in numerous lectures and articles over the years.[78] Even more often, Yoder sought to articulate a theology, rooted in the Anabaptist tradition, that would help the contemporary Mennonite Church to be faithful. At the same time, Yoder was concerned about the renewal of the church as a whole. His burden was to articulate a theology that would respond to the continuing need for radical reform within Christianity.

Radical Reform Contours

As mentioned in the first section of this chapter, Yoder's life and the focus of his research and writing changed after the publication of *The Politics of Jesus* in 1972. Yoder became much better known in a broader range of circles, and more of his writings were written with non-Mennonites in mind. However, we should not overstate the discontinuity with his life before 1972. He was already actively engaged in diverse Christian conversations in the 1950s in Europe. Between 1957, when he returned to the U.S., and the early 1970s Yoder was presenting lectures and writing essays addressed to Christians from a variety of theological traditions. In the mid-1960s he helped establish the "Believers Church Conferences." He was co-convener of these until he died.[79] During this time he gave some of his first lectures and wrote his

76. Yoder, "The Respectable Worldliness," 48.

77. Yoder, "The Respectable Worldliness," 48.

78. See Nation, *A Comprehensive Bibliography,* 15-53, where I list over seventy essays or lectures addressed primarily to Mennonites. This summary does not mention the twenty-six years he taught, full- or part-time, at the Mennonite seminaries in Elkhart, Indiana.

79. See Donald F. Durnbaugh, "Afterword: The Believers Church Conferences," in *The Believers Church: A Voluntary Church*, ed. William H. Brackney (Kitchener, Ontario: Pandora Press, 1998), 217-27.

first articles on just war theory.[80] And he pursued a new audience entirely by learning Spanish and lecturing in Latin America.[81]

Nonetheless, it was early in the decade of the 1970s that Yoder's theological engagement of the ecumenical world moved to a higher plane. Within a period of three years Yoder published four ecumenically oriented books. First, in 1970 he published a book on Karl Barth and war.[82] In 1971 he published two further books, one on a variety of approaches to religious pacifism and a second that was a collection of ecumenical theological essays about pacifism.[83] One year later came *The Politics of Jesus*. The first of these four books gained some academic attention; the middle two were initially read mostly by Mennonites and others in the historic peace churches.[84] This was in part due

---

80. For example, see, John Howard Yoder, "The Christian and War in the Perspective of Historical and Systematic Theology," unpublished seminar paper presented at a conference on The Evangelical Christian and Modern War at Winona Lake, Indiana, August 26-28, 1963, 21 pp., and John Howard Yoder, "Vietnam: a Just War?" *His* (April 1968): 1-3.

81. John Howard Yoder, "Lecture Series in South America," 1966. Typescripts exist in English and Spanish. For the listing of the individual lectures see Nation, *A Comprehensive Bibliography*, 23.

82. John H. Yoder, *Karl Barth and the Problem of War* (Nashville: Abingdon Press, 1970). This has recently been re-released, accompanied by other essays on Barth; see *Karl Barth and the Problem of War and Other Essays on Barth*, ed. Mark Thiessen Nation (Eugene, OR: Cascade Books, 2003).

83. John H. Yoder, *Nevertheless: Varieties of Religious Pacifism* (Scottdale, PA: Herald Press, 1971) and John H. Yoder, *The Original Revolution: Essays on Christian Pacifism* (Scottdale, PA: Herald Press, 1971).

84. One of the scholars who noticed Yoder's work on Barth was James Gustafson. Yoder had originally written a forty-seven-page essay on "Karl Barth and Christian Pacifism" in 1957 while still in Europe. This was mimeographed and circulated by Mennonite Central Committee. In 1968 Gustafson remarked, "For a remarkable critical study of Barth on the point of pacifism, see John Howard Yoder, *Karl Barth and Christian Pacifism*" (James M. Gustafson, *Christ and the Moral Life* [Chicago: The University of Chicago Press, 1968], 208, fn 38). Gustafson was on the editorial board of Abingdon Press's "Studies in Christian Ethics," the series that published Yoder's book in 1970. It is quite likely that Gustafson was responsible for having the bookstore at Yale Divinity School purchase Yoder's mimeographed study. This was where Stanley Hauerwas purchased this paper that introduced him to Yoder. (See Stanley Hauerwas, "When the Politics of Jesus Makes a Difference," *The Christian Century*, October 13, 1993, 984.)

to the fact that they were published by the Mennonite Church press. *The Politics of Jesus,* however — perhaps partly because it was published by a mainstream religious press, but even more because of the way it presented an argument — caught the attention of many in the Christian world, including evangelical Christians, peace activists, and various scholars.

I will discuss *The Politics of Jesus* in some detail later on, but a few comments are in order here. *The Politics of Jesus* became as popular and influential as it did partly by accident.[85] However, that it came to be seen as centrally defining of Yoder's project is quite appropriate. Yoder believed that Jesus is central within the Christian faith, not only for doctrine, which is often believed, but also for the moral character of the Christian community. Yoder seeks to do two things in *The Politics of Jesus.* First, he seeks to suggest the contours of the social ethic that Christians should derive from Jesus, an ethic that he believes should be centrally defining for Christians. And second, Yoder responds directly and indirectly to the ways in which Christian ethicists have sought to set Jesus aside when social ethics are formulated. After *The Politics of Jesus,* Yoder did some further writing on biblical studies, but he knew that the real challenges lay in the area of social ethics.[86]

---

85. John Yoder once said that the central reasons why *The Politics of Jesus* struck such a chord in 1972 are that liberal Protestants, who were already committed to peace and social justice, were looking for a biblical rootedness for their concerns, and Evangelicals, who already were rooted in the Bible, were looking for a commitment to peace and justice based upon the Bible.

86. For his more substantial post-1972 writing on the Bible see John Howard Yoder, "Exodus and Exile: Two Faces of Liberation," *Crosscurrents* (Fall 1973): 297-309; John Howard Yoder, "The Apostle's Apology Revisited," in *The New Way of Jesus,* ed. William Klassen (Newton, KS: Faith and Life Press, 1980), 115-34; John Howard Yoder, "Exodus 20:13 — 'Thou Shalt Not Kill,'" *Interpretation* 34 (October 1980): 394-99; *He Came Preaching Peace* (Scottdale, PA: Herald Press, 1985); "'To Your Tents, O Israel': The Legacy of Israel's Experience With Holy War," *Studies in Religion* 18 (1989): 345-62; and "'See How They Go with Their Face to the Sun,'" "Is Not His Word Like a Fire? The Bible and Civil Turmoil," and "Are You the One Who Is to Come?", all in John Howard Yoder, *For the Nations: Essays Public and Evangelical* (Grand Rapids: Eerdmans, 1997), 51-78, 79-93, 199-218. Scriptural images and idioms permeate Yoder's writings.

Yoder recognized that he needed to make his claims about the normativity of Jesus for social ethics not only intelligible, but compelling. The work in which Yoder did this most powerfully is in his first collection of essays after *The Politics of Jesus,* the collection that came to be called *The Priestly Kingdom.*[87] This book should be viewed as complementary to *The Politics of Jesus.* It presents Anabaptism as a hermeneutic (with minimal reference to Anabaptism) in order to enable non-Mennonites to "see Jesus" as the center not only of their creeds, but also of the social ethics that shape their lives.

To illuminate this understanding of these essays I have taken the liberty to rearrange the order in which they appear in the book. I recognize that any categorization of the essays is artificial. They all serve one another and mutually reinforce the central purpose. I have divided them into three categories. The first group of chapters is intended to help the reader to "see Jesus," which is to say, to see that Jesus should be decisive in shaping our lives as Christians who are situated in the midst of a world of plurality and diversity. The second category, which includes only one essay, serves as a bridge. This essay most fully answers the question: "If you are right, John Yoder, then why have we not seen this before?" The third group includes four essays that, in three different ways, display the social ethical thrust of the way of following Jesus.

I propose that the key essay in *The Priestly Kingdom* is "'But We Do See Jesus': The Particularity of Incarnation and the Universality of Truth."[88] Yoder begins this essay with that for which he has become well-known, making lists. He opens the essay by listing nine ways in which particular claims to truth are called into question by the multifaceted reality of our pluralist/relativist world. He then lists six "adaptive strategies" people use to adjust to the awareness that there are other worlds beyond the world in which they grew up. Some of these worlds claim, or seem, to be wider and/or truer than the world of their earlier experience. By thus having named substantial elements of the

---

87. John Howard Yoder, *The Priestly Kingdom: Social Ethics as Gospel* (Notre Dame: University of Notre Dame Press, 1984). Most of the essays gathered in this collection were published previously, between 1976 and 1983.

88. In *The Priestly Kingdom,* 46-62.

current intellectual framework, elements that tend to call into question the claims about truth from particular events (such as the incarnation of the Word of God in Jesus Christ) Yoder proceeds to challenge this framework in three ways. First, he challenges it by giving an initial succinct critique of some of its assumptions:

> What these six patterns have in common, behind a host of variations in secondary characteristics, is the acceptance of one way of putting the problem in the first place: namely, the priority in truth and value of the meaning system of the world claiming to be wider. That priority is not the product of a careful, debatable demonstration. Its own definition of what constitutes a wider or more public proof is precisely what we should be interested in debating. But that wider world, in any one person's experience of pilgrimage or in any interface between two groups, is still a small place. It still speaks only one language at a time, and that is still insider language. One adolescent's breath of fresh air is another's ghetto. Any given wider world is still just one more place, even if what its slightly wider or slightly more prestigious circle of interpreters talk about is a better access to "universality." Thus the first mistake which tends to be made by the apologetic person emerging from the smaller world is thinking that that wider society is itself the universe, or that its ways of testing validity beyond the provincial have succeeded, by dint of a harder and more thorough hauling away at one's own definitional bootstraps, in transcending particularity.[89]

Yoder ends this initial analysis by asking, "How can particular truths be proclaimed publicly?"[90] He responds to this question by drawing five New Testament samples of ways to make public truth claims based upon the particularities of who the New Testament writers have understood this Jesus to be and what he means for them and the world:

---

89. Yoder, "'But We Do See Jesus,'" 49.
90. Yoder, "'But We Do See Jesus,'" 49.

A handful of messianic Jews, moving beyond the defenses of their somewhat separate society to attack the intellectual bastions of majority culture, refused to contextualize their message by clothing it in the categories the world held ready. Instead, they seized the categories, hammered them into other shapes, and turned the cosmology on its head, with Jesus both at the bottom, crucified as a common criminal, and at the top, preexistent Son and creator, and the church his instrument in today's battle.

It is not the world, culture, civilization, which is the definitional category, which the church comes along to join up with, approve, and embellish with some correctives and complements. The Rule of God is the basic category. The rebellious but already (in principle) defeated cosmos is being brought to its knees by the Lamb. The development of a high Christology is the natural cultural ricochet of a missionary ecclesiology when it collides as it must with whatever cosmology explains and governs the world it invades.[91]

Of course our world is far from the world of the New Testament. We use a different language and have different cultural and intellectual categories. To ask whether we shall speak in the language of pluralism and relativism, for instance, says Yoder, is like asking whether in Greece they should speak Greek. We must use the cultural categories that exist. But the question is: what will we do with the categories? What will we say? According to Yoder the central message remains unchanged. "We shall say, 'Jesus is Messiah and Lord'; but how do you say that in pluralist/relativist language? If that language forbids us to say that, do we respect the prohibition? Or do we find a way to say it anyway?"[92]

Yoder's answer is clearly that we must find a way to say it anyway. But that does not mean that we ignore our current context. Nor are we to imagine that we can communicate the message of the gospel in something other than the languages and categories of our time. In fact we might discover, as Yoder says we should, that "reality always was pluralistic and relativistic, that is, historical. The idea that it could

91. Yoder, "'But We Do Jesus,'" 54.
92. Yoder, "'But We Do See Jesus,'" 56.

be otherwise was itself an illusion laid on us by Greek ontology language, and other borrowings from the Germans, the Moors, and other rulers of Europe."[93] Therefore, we may "be tactical allies of the pluralist/relativist deconstruction of deceptive orthodox claims to logically coercive certainty, without making of relativism itself a new monism."[94] In fact, it may just be that such a world is open to hearing the gospel afresh.

> For our world it will be in his ordinariness as villager, as rabbi, as king on a donkey, and as liberator on a cross that we shall be able to express the claims which the apostolic proclaimers to Hellenism expressed in the language of preexistence and condescension. This is not to lower our sights or to retract our proclamation. It is to renew the description of Christ crucified as the wisdom and the power of God. This is the low road to general validity. It frees us from needing to be apologetic in either the popular or the technical sense. It thereby frees us to use any language, to enter any world in which people eat bread and pursue debtors, hope for power and execute subversives. The ordinariness of the humanness of Jesus is the warrant for the generalizability of his reconciliation. The nonterritorial particularity of his Jewishness defends us against selling out to *any* wider world's claim to be really wider, or to be self-validating.
>
> The particularity of incarnation *is* the universality of the good. There is no road but the low road.
>
> The real issue is not whether Jesus can make sense in a world far from Galilee, but whether — when he meets us in our world, as he does in fact — we want to follow him. We don't have to, as they didn't then. That we don't have to is the profoundest proof of his condescension, and thereby of his glory.[95]

More than anything else, Yoder wanted to make it possible for Christian scholars to see that the canonical Jesus could be normative

---

93. Yoder, "'But We Do See Jesus,'" 59.
94. Yoder, "'But We Do See Jesus,'" 61.
95. Yoder, "'But We Do See Jesus,'" 62, emphasis his.

not only for our doctrines but also for the way we live. This essay sought to make the normativity of Jesus intelligible within our world. In some ways, one can see that, as a whole, *The Priestly Kingdom* offers support for this purpose. I have placed three other essays in this first group because they particularly further and serve this purpose.

The first supporting essay is "The Authority of Tradition," a rather straightforward essay about Scripture and tradition.[96] Its arguments are simple. First, Yoder argues that the Scriptures, simply stated, serve as "witness to the historical baseline of the communities' origins and thereby as link to the historicity of their Lord's past presence."[97] Though always read through an interpretive framework, the Scriptures nonetheless serve as the baseline for distinguishing faithfulness from unfaithfulness.[98] Yoder names a half-dozen ways in which the basic thrust of the gospel was betrayed by later developments. He focuses at greatest length on the betrayal as evidenced in the legitimation of violence. His intent is not to show that there is not or should not be development beyond the Scriptures. Such development is assumed: "The clash is not tradition versus Scripture but faithful tradition versus irresponsible tradition."[99] Yoder argues that we need to be able to distinguish faithful from unfaithful Christian teachings, and to embrace practices based upon those teachings. An essential part of that process includes looking at the baseline of the Christian tradition, Scripture.

A second essay within this first group, "Anabaptism and History," continues the preceding argument. He does so by responding to the claim that the approach that is sometimes referred to as "restitutionism" is ahistorical. The critics of this kind of "restitutionism" argue that to use the New Testament to judge current (or past) unfaithfulness ignores history and denies the necessity of historical development. Critics claim

---

96. For many of Yoder's writings on biblical authority and hermeneutics see John Howard Yoder, *To Hear the Word* (Eugene, OR: Wipf & Stock, 2001).

97. Yoder, "The Authority of Tradition," in *The Priestly Kingdom*, 69.

98. For one way to view Yoder's use of the Bible, see Mark Thiessen Nation, "Theology as Witness: Reflections on Yoder, Fish, and Interpretive Communities," *Faith and Freedom* 5 (June 1996): 42-47.

99. Yoder, "The Authority of Tradition," 69.

that such application of Scripture leaps from the first century to the present. Yoder argues that this need not be so. On the contrary, a "view which criticizes what has come into being in the course of history, on the grounds of criteria which themselves are also drawn from within the course of history, is thereby obliged to be concerned with historical data in a way different from those traditions which claim each in its own way to be the 'mainstream.'"[100] However, that different use of history is still a use of history. For instance, many within the radical reformation tradition have believed that, measured by Jesus and the New Testament, Constantinianism was wrong in the fourth century. However, "it was not wrong because it was later than the New Testament, but because wrong fourth-century options were chosen rather than right fourth-century options."[101] Again, nothing about this judgment is ahistorical. Using the Scriptures as the baseline, it merely discerns the difference between faithfulness and unfaithfulness within real history where various options are available.[102]

The last essay within this first grouping is "Radical Reformation Ethics in Ecumenical Perspective." Here Yoder begins by providing a brief description of the believers' church, or free church, which he refers to as the radical reformation tradition. The heart of the essay claims that "the primary substantial criterion of Christian ethical decisions for the radical reformers is the humanity of Jesus of Nazareth."[103] Christ's humanity provides substantial solidity for moral guidance, while allowing for appropriate flexibility. This moral guidance is solid because "the Christ around whom we gather is confessed the same yesterday and today and forever, and since the ground floor of the canonical witness is a body of relatively clear texts."[104] However, there is also flexibility and contextuality because "the knowledge

---

100. Yoder, "Anabaptism and History," in *The Priestly Kingdom*, 127.

101. Yoder, "Anabaptism and History," 129.

102. For some of Yoder's own criticisms of "restitutionist" approaches see John Howard Yoder, "Primitivism in the Radical Reformation: Strengths and Weaknesses," in *The Primitive Church in the Modern World*, ed. Richard T. Hughes (Urbana: University of Illinois Press, 1995), 74-97.

103. Yoder, "Radical Reformation Ethics," 116.

104. Yoder, "Radical Reformation Ethics," 118.

of the meaning for today of participation in the work of Christ is mediated ecclesiastically."[105] Yoder ties this to a particular "radical reformation" understanding of the church. This church is comprised of voluntary members. Because people choose to be members of this church, a church for which God revealed in Jesus is central, it can be assumed that these members want to be faithful disciples of Jesus. Such a church does not feel bound to do ethics for just anyone. Rather, its members do ethics for those who are committed to following Jesus:

> The substantial guidance, the experiential and social resources of conversion and membership are presupposed for it to be possible to speak of one's behavior as expressive of faith and obedience. Cross-bearing in the hope of resurrection, enemy-love as reflection of God's love, forgiving as one has been forgiven, behavior change describable as expressing regeneration or sanctification, do not make sense in the context of unbelief.[106]

In this same essay, Yoder responds to two stereotypes of this radical reformation approach. First, he argues not only that the morality drawn from this tradition is not peculiarly tied to one approach to ethics (say, deontology) but that in practice, most ethical approaches, including his own, borrow from various types of ethics.[107] Second, Yoder makes a brief argument against the notion that this approach to Christian ethics, especially because of its disavowal of violence, leads to a principled withdrawal from society: "Thus to argue that for believers [standing in this tradition] to derive their ethic from Jesus demands that they withdraw from society is petitionary, an argument which follows neither from empirical experience nor from the

---

105. Yoder, "Radical Reformation Ethics," 117.
106. Yoder, "Radical Reformation Ethics," 110.
107. Yoder, "Radical Reformation Ethics," 113-16. For more substantial arguments see John H. Yoder, "Walk and Word: The Alternatives to Methodologism," in *Theology Without Foundations*, ed. Stanley Hauerwas, Nancey Murphy, and Mark Nation (Nashville: Abingdon Press, 1994), 77-90, 312-17, and John Howard Yoder, "'Patience' as Method in Moral Reasoning: Is an Ethic of Discipleship 'Absolute'?" in *The Wisdom of the Cross*, ed. Stanley Hauerwas, Chris K. Huebner, Harry J. Huebner, and Mark Thiessen Nation (Grand Rapids: Eerdmans, 1999), 24-42.

content of the gospel message, but from the hermeneutic aprioris of the majority traditions."[108] Christians, from the radical reformation perspective, can participate in many ways in society.[109] Furthermore, there is "a sense in which the Christian community can and must 'do ethics for the world,' that is, cooperate in ethical discourse beyond the borders of faith, or in language not dependent on faith." Commenting on this ethical discourse with the world, Yoder notes, "that is a different kind of discourse from the ethical deliberation of the believing community."[110]

As I move into the second category, the bridge essay, it is worth noting that *The Priestly Kingdom* is not intended as a Mennonite book; its arguments are intended for a broadly catholic or ecumenical audience.[111] Though Yoder sometimes names his Anabaptist heritage in the book, he more frequently focuses on what he refers to as the radical reformation tradition. Yoder typically begins the narration of the radical reformation tradition by looking at the Waldensians in the twelfth century.[112] He believed that this radical reformation tradition retrieved vital emphases from the early church as it functioned prior to the fourth century, emphases within the canonical witness that are often lost in other traditions.

The question that begs to be asked here is, why is it that the radical reformation tradition retrieves these dimensions of the canonical

108. Yoder, "Radical Reformation Ethics," 115-16. I address this issue at length in Chapter Five.

109. This point will be discussed much more fully in Chapters Four and Five.

110. Yoder, "Radical Reformation Ethics," 110.

111. In the introduction Yoder writes, "These pages do not describe a Mennonite vision. They describe a biblically rooted call to faith, addressed to Mennonites or Zwinglians, to Lutherans or Catholics, to unbelievers or other-believers. . . . Their appeal is to classical catholic Christian convictions properly understood." Yoder, "Introduction," in *The Priestly Kingdom*, 8-9.

112. When I took Yoder's course on the Radical Reformation at the University of Notre Dame in 1980, he structured the course around Donald F. Durnbaugh, *The Believers' Church: The History and Character of Radical Protestantism* (New York: The Macmillan Co., 1968). This book begins its narration with the Waldensians. My memory is that Yoder commented on other traditions with similar characteristics much earlier. But sources for groups before the Waldensians are mostly writings by enemies of the traditions, and thus are hardly reliable as sole sources.

witness and the other traditions do not? Or, put differently, why were these dimensions lost within mainstream Christianity? Yoder answers these questions in "The Constantinian Sources of Western Social Ethics."[113] For Yoder (and others who are convinced by his arguments) it is a very helpful, explanatory piece. In fact, the implications are profound. It serves to make the previous four essays more intelligible and provides a bridge to the four essays in the next group. I should add, however, that I believe the other essays in the book can be quite valuable even if one is left unconvinced by this bridge essay.[114]

Yoder opens the essay with a central premise: Christians were by and large pacifist in the first three centuries.[115] These early Christians believed this ethic was derived from the life, teachings, death, and resurrection of Jesus. However, "the post-Constantinian Christians considered imperial violence to be not only morally tolerable but a positive good and a Christian duty."[116] Yoder argues that this dramatic shift was undoubtedly related to the reign of Emperor Constantine and to a series of events following from that reign.[117] But more important

113. In Yoder, *The Priestly Kingdom*, 135-47.

114. In 1982 I wrote a letter to Yoder asking if he thought the basic thrust of this essay would be supported by historians of that period of history. Yoder responded, "With regard to your other question, about the place of Constantine in the reading of history, I doubt that you would find any major historian of western culture fundamentally rejecting what I have been arguing on this matter." John Howard Yoder, Elkhart, Indiana, to Mark Nation, Urbana, Illinois, July 27, 1982, transcript in possession of author.

115. For Yoder on this question see John Howard Yoder, "The Pacifism of Pre-Constantinian Christianity," in *Christian Attitudes to War, Peace, and Revolution*, 21-35, and John Howard Yoder, "War as a Moral Problem in the Early Church," in *The Pacifist Impulse in Historical Perspective*, ed. Harvey L. Dyck (Toronto: University of Toronto Press, 1996), 90-110. The issue of pacifism and the early church has become a complicated one over the last few decades, but for a guide see David G. Hunter, "A Decade of Research on Early Christians and Military Service," *Religious Studies Review* 18 (1992): 87-94.

116. Yoder, "The Constantinian Sources," 135.

117. Yoder is careful to say that the shift began earlier than Constantine and took some time after Constantine to be complete. Thus, Constantine is a symbol of the shift as much as the cause of the shift. Nonetheless, historians are generally agreed that Constantine's reign was a significant component of the major shift that occurred. (My subsequent uses of the name "Constantine" are intended to reflect this same ambiguity

than naming the historical causes of the shift, Yoder examines some of the subsequent shifts within Christian understanding that made violence "not only morally tolerable but a positive good and a Christian duty." Yoder names six of these shifts.

First, a new understanding of the church arises. Previously the church was assumed to consist only of those who believed in the God revealed in Jesus Christ. This faith often cost Christians dearly, sometimes even their lives. As a result, only those who were serious about faithfulness to Christ claimed membership in the church. After Constantine there is social pressure to be a part of the church. On occasion people are actively coerced to become members; dissenters and heretics are persecuted. In fact, after the reign of Constantine it is difficult not to be a member of the church. Consequently, the church is redefined. It is no longer clear which members within the church "believe" (referring to the New Testament meaning of belief/faith/trust). It becomes possible that many of those who are members of the church (which is effectively everyone in the empire) are not "true" Christians. The concept of the invisibility of the true church emerges. The other shifts follow from this fundamental shift in the understanding of church.

Second, a new understanding of eschatology develops. The early church, the apostolic church, confessed the Lordship of Christ. The firstfruits of Christ's reign were evident within the church, albeit imperfectly. In relation to the world, the church also confessed that Christ was Lord. This confession was made in faith that the future would hold the fullness of this reign, even though persecution and suffering were evidence that Christ's reign was not yet fully manifest in the world. After Constantine this understanding was reversed. Since in the present one can only deduce that the mass church is not really the true church, it is hoped that the true church, rather than being present, will one day be revealed. Conversely, it appears to be a fact that Christ is reigning in the world, because Constantine is a member of the

---

and complexity.) It should be said that though violence is the moral question to which Yoder gave most attention, he would also suggest that the attitude toward money and the loss of rootage in Judaism are likewise connected to the shift.

church, and the "Christian" empire is being expanded — never mind that it is expanded either through the slaughter of pagans or through coercing them to join the empire's religion.

Third, a new central "servant of the Lord" appears. Although the Scriptures record that on occasion the Lord uses pagan rulers or governments to serve God's purposes, such activities are clearly subsidiary to the central "servant of the Lord" in God's purposes. Even a cursory reading of the Scriptures makes it clear that Israel in the Old Testament and the church in the New Testament are the main bearers of God's historical involvement in the world. After Constantine this is reversed. The civil government becomes the main bearer of God's significant involvement in the world. Consequently, the central test of the validity of Christian ethics is changed. The question is no longer whether Christian behavior is consistent with what it means to follow Jesus. Instead, the question becomes whether one can rule an empire effectively while living in the way of Jesus. In other words, can the church ask "that" kind of behavior of the emperor because he is now one of us?

Fourth, Christian moral agency is redefined. Previously it could be assumed that everyone in the church was committed to following Jesus and that they had "numerous resources not generally available to all people: personal commitment, regeneration, the guidance of the Holy Spirit, the consolation and encouragement of the brotherhood, training in a discipleship life-style."[118] Believers knew that without these resources their lives of discipleship were impossible. However, after Constantine, such resources can no longer be assumed. As a result, a call to serious discipleship — servanthood and love of enemies, for instance — makes no sense. Instead there are two new tests for morality: "Can you ask such behavior of everyone?"[119] and "What would happen if everyone did it?"[120] If you cannot ask it of "everyone" then it is heroic behavior that can only be asked of a select few. Whether or not "love of enemies" is a valid Christian ethic is no longer primarily dependent on whether or not Jesus said it should be done. Instead eth-

---

118. Yoder, "The Constantinian Sources," 139.
119. Yoder, "The Constantinian Sources," 139.
120. Yoder, "The Constantinian Sources," 139.

ics are determined by considering what would happen to the empire if everyone (that is, everyone in this Christian empire) were to live this ethic — the empire could not exist in the midst of hostile pagans. Consequently, such ethics are deemed not valid.

Fifth, for the first time, effectiveness becomes inherently valuable in Christian ethical deliberation. For "once the evident course of history is held to be empirically discernable, and the prosperity of our regime is the measure of good, all morality boils down to efficacy. Right action is what works; what does not promise results can hardly be right."[121]

And, finally, a new dualistic metaphysic enters into Christian vocabulary. Somehow those providing Christian moral teachings and biblical studies have to account for the growing distance between Jesus and the teachings of the church regarding matters like violence and wealth. One way to do that is to create dualisms between internal and external, and between individual and corporate. So, love of enemies and the love of money are interpreted as only relevant for inward attitudes or personal behavior. Outward behavior, especially as it relates to ways of structuring society, is guided by other norms than the life, teachings, death, and resurrection of Jesus.

These are the significant shifts affecting social ethics that Yoder believes are a result of "Constantine." They dominated the mainstream church throughout the medieval period, and have continued to influence much Christian thinking about social ethics ever since.[122]

What does Yoder offer as an alternative? First he seeks to make it possible for Christians and Christian ethicists once again to see the possibility that Jesus should be normative. That is what both *The Politics of Jesus* and the first group of four essays I discussed above seek to do. In the four essays I discuss below, Yoder begins an alternative construal of a truly Christian social ethic derived from Jesus.

In the essay "Radical Reformation Ethics in Ecumenical Perspective," which I discussed above, Yoder observed that the "bridge

---

121. Yoder, "The Constantinian Sources," 140.

122. For Yoder's discussion of various historical manifestations of Constantinianism see Yoder, "The Constantinian Sources," 141-44, and John Howard Yoder, "Christ, the Hope of the World," in *The Royal Priesthood*, 195-97.

between the words of Jesus or of the apostolic writings and obedience in the present is not a strictly conceptual operation, which could be carried out by a single scholar at his desk, needing only an adequate dictionary and an adequate description of the available action options."[123] Instead, argues Yoder, the "knowledge of the meaning for today of participation in the work of Christ is mediated ecclesiastically."[124] Yoder develops the preceding points in "The Hermeneutics of Peoplehood,"[125] the first essay in this next group. Yoder's principal claim is that moral discernment, including discernment about what are usually described as social ethics, should centrally take place within the church. This means therefore that moral discernment is not simply left up to specialists, whether ethicists or clergy. Rather all of the people of God who are covenanted together to be faithful to and to worship the God revealed in Jesus Christ together discern what it means to be moral.

This church-based discernment avoids the problems of an autonomous and individualistic approach because the discernment is communal. It also avoids an unhealthy authoritarian approach because the covenanting is voluntary and the leaders are accountable to those they lead. Though everyone contributes to the process of discernment, not everyone has the same gift. Yoder names several distinctive and important roles that are expressed through various gifts. This list is not exhaustive. The roles include what he describes as agents of direction, agents of memory, agents of linguistic self-consciousness, and agents of order and due process. These "agents" are Christians, members of this body, this church that seeks — through liturgy, praise, song, words of instruction, and faithful living — to worship the living God. "Worship," among other things, "is the communal cultivation of an alternative construction of society and of history."[126] This worship reminds those who worship of the centrality of Jesus Christ for their lives. In turn, faithful living reinforces the liturgy, the hymns, and the

123. Yoder, "Radical Reformation Ethics," 117.

124. Yoder, "Radical Reformation Ethics," 117.

125. Yoder, "The Hermeneutics of Peoplehood: A Protestant Perspective," in *The Priestly Kingdom*, 15-45.

126. Yoder, "The Hermeneutics of Peoplehood," 43.

centrality of Jesus. As James McClendon has said, "Christianity turns upon the character of Christ. But that character must continually find fresh exemplars if it is not to be consigned to the realm of mere antiquarian lore."[127]

What the previous paragraphs underscore is that Christian social ethics is rooted in the narrative of the life of the church, a narrative that shapes Christian virtues. One can see that this approach, consistent with some recent trends in Christian ethics, can appreciate a focus on virtues and narrative:

> As contrasted with the punctual understanding of choice, virtue is narrative: it has length. The present is embedded in a past which has made me who I am and reaches toward a hope which is already present to faith. Virtue as well has breadth: it is communal. My decision has neighbors, persons who count on me, persons far and near, and groups, with whom I am bound by reciprocal promises and role expectations. Virtue also has depth: it implies and celebrates understandings about the nature of person, the nature of God, the goodness and fallenness of creation, the inwardness and the transparency of self, the miracles of redemptive transformation.[128]

Along with an appreciation of the relatively recent focus on virtue and narrative, Yoder is also cautious:

> One will welcome the creative imagination of structuralists who protect narration from reduction to 'truths' and 'concepts'; yet an equal vigilance is needed to defend the particularity of Abraham and Samuel, Jeremiah and Jesus from reduction to mere specimens of a new kind of universals, namely, narrative forms, lying deeper than the ordinary events and sufficient to explain them.[129]

---

127. James Wm. McClendon, Jr., *Biography as Theology*, 2d ed. (Philadelphia: Trinity Press International, 1990), 23.

128. John Howard Yoder, *Nevertheless: Varieties of Religious Pacifism*, revised and expanded ed. (Scottdale, PA: Herald Press, 1992), 130.

129. Yoder, "The Hermeneutics of Peoplehood," 36.

Yoder was not primarily interested in some theory about narratives or virtues. He was interested in using language that retained the centrality of the actual worshiping community that itself makes Jesus central in the shaping of the moral lives of Christians as they live in various social worlds.[130]

For Yoder's project it is important that the reader realize that Yoder is already on the subject of Christian social ethics, both because he is discussing how Christians discern, socially, what it means to be moral and because he is discussing the social entity called the church. In the next essay in this group of four, "The Kingdom as Social Ethic," Yoder focuses more directly on the ways in which the church is a social ethic. He begins by repeating things he has said in other essays already discussed, but he develops further insights along the way.[131]

One such further insight is that "the believing community as an empirical social entity is a power for change. To band together in common dissidence provides a kind of social leverage which is not provided by any other social form."[132] As a result, those who are a part of the minority community are socially supported in a variety of ways. Additionally, an alternative perspective is shaped and nurtured by the convictions and lives of those within the community. However, it is not only that those within the community are recipients of the newness wrought in Christ; "The alternative community discharges a modeling mission. The church is called to be now what the world is called to be ultimately."[133] From these assertions flow several implications.

First, the church can undertake experiments, pilot projects.

---

130. Yoder expands upon this in John H. Yoder, "Walk and Word: The Alternatives to Methodologism," 77-90, 312-17.

131. Yoder, "The Kingdom as Social Ethic," in *The Priestly Kingdom,* 80-101.

132. Yoder, "The Kingdom as Social Ethic," 91. On some of the similarities between Yoder's point here and a feminist interpretation see Mark Thiessen Nation, "Feminism, Political Philosophy, and the Narrative Ethics of Jean Bethke Elshtain," in *Virtues and Practices in the Christian Tradition: Christian Ethics after MacIntyre,* ed. Nancey Murphy, Brad J. Kallenberg, and Mark Thiessen Nation (Valley Forge, PA: Trinity Press International, 1997), 289-305. (My original title for the essay was "Fools for Christ, Redeeming Everyday Life: Jean Bethke Elshtain and the Moral Revolution of the Church.")

133. Yoder, "The Kingdom as Social Ethic," 92.

Sometimes when these projects are perceived to be useful they will be adopted more broadly. For instance, "popular education, institutionalized medicine, and the very concept of dialogical democracy in the Anglo-Saxon world generalize patterns which were first of all experimented with and made sense of in free-church Christianity."[134]

Second, "the church represents a pedestal or subculture in which some truths are more evidently meaningful and some lines of logic can be more clearly spelled out than in society as a whole."[135] That is to say, an alternative vision is given greater intelligibility and credibility by being embodied within the social life of a people.

Third, the church may exemplify what might be termed "sacramentality." This may sometimes involve the connecting of what are normally thought of as sacraments (eucharist or baptism, for instance) with relationships within the church or between church and world (sharing food and egalitarianism, as derived from eucharist and baptism).[136] This notion is intended to signal that worship is integrally related to ethics, redemption to relationships.

And fourth, Yoder suggests that "the church can be a foretaste of the peace for which the world was made. . . . Transcendence is kept alive not on the grounds of logical proof to the effect that there is a cosmos with a hereafter, but by the vitality of communities in which a different way of being keeps breaking in here and now."[137] Thus the quality of the witness of the Christian community, the peaceable community, is a sign of the coming Kingdom, a way of keeping hope alive.

In all of these ways, says Yoder, "the church cultivates an alternative consciousness."[138] This alternative consciousness is centered in Jesus. It is also in the context of a community that is centered in Jesus that members learn to view reality from the viewpoint of a minority, a

134. Yoder, "The Kingdom as Social Ethic," 92.

135. Yoder, "The Kingdom as Social Ethic," 93. For his fuller development see John Howard Yoder, "Firstfruits: The Paradigmatic Public Role of God's People," and "The New Humanity as Pulpit and Paradigm," in *For the Nations*, 15-36, 37-50.

136. This is expressed more fully in John Howard Yoder, "Sacrament as Social Process: Christ the Transformer of Culture," in *The Royal Priesthood*, 359-73, and John Howard Yoder, *Body Politics* (Nashville: Discipleship Resources, 1992).

137. Yoder, "The Kingdom as Social Ethic," 94.

138. Yoder, "The Kingdom as Social Ethic," 94.

minority whose imagination is freed from the constraints of "realism" and for whom hope is not tied to short-term success. Space is created for entertaining new possibilities and taking risks appropriate to the following of Jesus. This does not mean that ineffectiveness and irresponsibility are considered virtues. However, it does mean that definitions of effectiveness and responsibility derived from mainstream perspectives are not determinative for Christians. Christians are aware of and learn from others, but in the context of that awareness they seek to live in such a way that their lives give tangible witness to the Lordship of Christ in their communities and, ultimately, over the world.[139] This world includes civil governing structures.

The final two essays in this group address the relationship of the church to the civil governing structures.[140] First, "The Christian Case for Democracy" offers two main sets of points. The first covers what Yoder refers to as "Gospel realism." To explain this realism Yoder draws lessons from a passage in the Gospel of Luke (Luke 22:25-26) "not as a proof text nor as prescription, but as a provocative paradigm."[141] Three statements illustrate the paradigm. First, "the rulers of the nations lord it over them." According to Yoder this statement provides the realism we need. He notes that often rulers engage in the sort of behaviors that can, in a word, be described as "lording it over" others. We need to be honest, conscious, and realistic about this. A second statement follows: "those who exercise authority let themselves be called benefactors." This helps us to see that we do not have to reach far to find a language for holding the rulers accountable. Often they provide the language by allowing themselves to be called benefactors or, especially in the day of media public relations, they generate the language that makes them look like benefactors. When they do not live up to the claims, the language of critique has been provided. Finally, the third statement: "but it shall not be so among you

---

139. Though Yoder deals with the issues raised in this paragraph in various places, see especially Yoder, "Christ, the Hope of the World," in *The Royal Priesthood*, 192-218.

140. Yoder, "The Christian Case for Democracy," and "Civil Religion in America," in *The Priestly Kingdom*, 151-71, 212-14 and 172-95, 214-15.

141. Yoder, "The Christian Case for Democracy," 155.

[my followers]; you shall be servants because I am a servant." Here the followers of Jesus are reminded that their behavior, whatever their roles in life, is to be defined by the Lord, not by the various roles of "lording it over" that are on offer.

These three statements from Jesus as reported in Luke (and similar ones in Matthew and Mark), are reminders of who Christians are to be in relation to the "Lords" of the world and how we can offer critiques of the leaders of the world. However, this language can only function in this manner if we keep the three statements separate:

> Since Constantine we have fused those three levels: the facticity of dominion, the language of legitimation, and the differentness of the disciples. Thereby we have confused rather than clarified the proper diversity of language. This mixes the descriptive and the prescriptive, interweaving the language which justifies coercion with that which guides voluntary discipleship. Since Constantine, when talking about government, we have assumed (as Jesus could not have) that we are talking about government of Christians and by Christians. We have thus lost the distance which Jesus maintained between his realism about power and his messianic liberty in servanthood and that other discourse which talks with the rulers about their claim to be benefactors.[142]

The other main set of points in this essay regards the use of analogy. Yoder discusses the use of analogies in two ways. First, for the purpose of communication with "the children of Troeltsch and Niebuhr," he simply accepts the dominance of the language of the "marketplace." To borrow from his first example (echoing what we just discussed above), in the "world" or the marketplace the rulers let themselves be called "benefactors." In the church, on the other hand, servanthood, the way of the cross, is to define appropriate behavior, including how leadership is exercised. Those in the church do not use their own in-house language to offer a critique of the behavior of the ruler. Rather, Christians, with full knowledge of their convictions, use a mediating language. In this case they would use the ruler's own ac-

---

142. Yoder, "The Christian Case for Democracy," 157.

cepted accolades, the claims of beneficence, to offer a critique that nonetheless calls for the ruler's behavior to move more in the direction of behavior known by Christians to be righteous. A second use of analogy, one that Yoder does not develop in detail here, is from Barth. Within this analogy, the church refuses to allow the marketplace to dictate the terms of conversation. That is to say, "it is the usage of governmental language within the people of God which is the norm. The governmental language used within the wider culture is then only a pale reflection, analogy, dilution, perversion of 'true politics'."[143] Yoder indicates that this is what he had in mind by calling one of his books *The Politics of Jesus.*

The previous essay, "The Christian Case for Democracy," plus the final essay, "Civil Religion in America," clearly indicate that Yoder was quite capable of relating his approach to thinking about governments and politics narrowly defined.[144] Yoder had already demonstrated this at least as early as 1964 when *The Christian Witness to the State* was published. However, rather than arguing here that this was the case, I will address how Yoder's approach relates to governments and politics in Chapter Five, where I focus on what Yoder taught about peacemaking and responsibility.

Summary: Dynamic Consistency

As William Klassen has suggested, it was probably no accident that Yoder chose the debates between the Swiss Anabaptists and the Reformers as the focus of his research in sixteenth-century Anabaptism. Yoder was interested from the beginning of his academic career in ecumenical relations. The biographical sketch in Chapter One demonstrated how Yoder engaged non-Mennonites in ecumenical dialogues

143. Yoder, "The Christian Case for Democracy," 163. This is developed further in John Howard Yoder, "Why Ecclesiology Is Social Ethics: Gospel Ethics Versus the Wider Wisdom," in *The Royal Priesthood,* 102-26. Also see John Howard Yoder, "Firstfruits: The Paradigmatic Public Role of God's People," in *For the Nations,* 15-36.

144. I will not discuss "Civil Religion in America." It is the least original essay in the book and adds little to our discussion.

in Europe. The present chapter has shown how, from the beginning, Yoder interpreted what he learned from Anabaptism, while in Europe, into terms that should matter for all Christians, including Mennonites. Simultaneously, he sought to show Mennonites that their convictions should not be restricted to people who shared their ethnicity. In fact, their convictions should compel them to engage other Christians in mutually challenging dialogue and to engage the world in compassion, precisely because of their convictions.

Yoder's writings and concerns display an amazing consistency from the 1950s to the 1990s.[145] After the publication of *The Politics of Jesus* in 1972, a higher percentage of his writings were consciously directed to non-Mennonites. It was *The Politics of Jesus* that made Yoder a more widely known and public pacifist. But both before and after the publication of his most famous book, he articulated the theology undergirding his pacifism, provided defenses of pacifism, and gave various arguments for why all Christians should be serious about peacemaking and about "the politics of Jesus."

---

145. I am not sure that James Reimer is quite right when he says about Yoder: "here was a man who seemed never to have changed his mind." James Reimer, "Mennonites, Christ, and Culture: The Yoder Legacy," *The Conrad Grebel Review* 16 (Spring 1998): 6.

Chapter 3   Faithful Ecumenism:
A Call to Unity in
Disciplined Discipleship

John Howard Yoder arrived in France in April 1949 to begin a term of service with the Mennonite Central Committee. It is unlikely that as a twenty-one year old he realized how significant the next nine years would be. He could not have known how deeply his thought and the whole course of his life would be shaped by serious ecumenical engagement during these years in Europe.

Prior to this time in Europe, Yoder's life had been largely defined by North American Mennonite forms of Christianity. That was to change after his arrival in Europe. Not only was he to become seriously connected to the French Mennonite Church but he was to become one of the most active ecumenists and also one of the most vocal proponents of ecumenism within the Mennonite Church. In fact, throughout his life and his prolific writing career, the only issue that occupied more of his time was peacemaking. Even the way he dealt with peacemaking, however, was often quite consciously affected by his commitment to ecumenism.

In this chapter we will examine Yoder's central writings on ecumenism.[1] As is true for his views on many issues, the heart of his views

1. I note at the outset of this chapter that I will draw less from secondary sources here than in the rest of the book. That is partly because I want to lay out Yoder's own views without getting distracted by the reflections of others. But it also has to do with the paucity of writings by others on Yoder's views on ecumenism. One article that offers

regarding ecumenism was established in the 1950s while he was still in Europe. He subsequently addressed issues of ecumenism in essays written directly on the theory of ecumenism, on the practicalities of inter-church relations for his own denomination, and, on specific issues as they arose in ecumenical conversations. He also utilized principles he learned in ecumenical relations to formulate some ideas on interfaith dialogue and interfaith relations.

The Ecumenical Movement and the Faithful Church

John Yoder's views on ecumenism were published in 1957. In the first two months of 1957, *The Gospel Herald*, the organ of the Mennonite Church, published a series of articles by Yoder on ecumenism. These articles were gathered together a year later into a single, forty-three-page essay entitled *The Ecumenical Movement and the Faithful Church*.[2] The essay was published as a pamphlet by the publishing house of the same Mennonite denomination. The pamphlet presents the heart of Yoder's views on ecumenism, views that remained substantially unaltered for the next four decades.[3]

a personal testimony to Yoder's commitment to ecumenism is William Klassen, "John Howard Yoder and the Ecumenical Church," *The Conrad Grebel Review* 16 (Spring 1998): 77-81. Michael Cartwright's fine introductory essay to Yoder's essays on ecclesiology and ecumenism is consistent both with the thrust of this chapter and the whole book. See Michael G. Cartwright, "Radical Reform, Radical Catholicity: John Howard Yoder's Vision of the Faithful Church," in John Howard Yoder, *The Royal Priesthood: Essays Ecclesiological and Ecumenical*, ed. Michael G. Cartwright (Grand Rapids: Eerdmans, 1994), 1-49. Gayle Gerber Koontz's treatment of Yoder's views on ecumenism is largely consistent with what is offered here; see Gayle Gerber Koontz, "Confessional Theology in a Pluralistic Context: A Study of the Theological Ethics of H. Richard Niebuhr and John H. Yoder" (Ph.D. dissertation, Boston University, 1985), 148-85. And, finally, see Fernando Enns, "Der kritische 'ökumenische Imperative' in der Theologie John Howard Yoders," in *Jesus folgen in einer pluralistischen Welt: Impulse aus der Arbeit John Howard Yoders*, ed. Hanspeter Jecker (Bienenberg, Switzerland: WB-Druck GmbH, 2001), 139-51.

    2. (Scottdale, PA: Mennonite Publishing House, 1958). Subsequent references will be to this pamphlet rather than the series of articles. Unless otherwise designated, in this chapter these references will be noted in parentheses in the text.

    3. Most of Yoder's important essays on ecumenism were gathered together for the

At the time of the writing of this essay, the 1950s, Yoder recognized he had to convince many Mennonites of the importance of serious ecumenical engagement, especially when that engagement was of a formal, structured variety.[4] He also knew what sort of argument he needed to make in order to convince people of the importance of ecumenical engagement — although, it should be noted, the sort of argument he *needed* to make was not unrelated to his own convictions. These were not artificial arguments for him.

Yoder begins the essay by naming the context: "It is a highly significant fact, worthy of being noted at the very outset, that evangelical Christians see any problem at all [in encouraging ecumenical relations with other Christians]" (p. 1). He will need to explain this claim. Although Yoder acknowledges that there might be some good reasons for caution in ecumenical relations, he asserts that the imperative for Christian unity outweighs such caution.

Yoder begins by noting that the New Testament origin of the word "ecumenical" is the Greek noun *ecumene*. It refers to "that which is inhabited" or, as it is translated in Luke 2, "the whole world" (p. 2). He notes that the adjective "ecumenical" was first used in reference to a series of gatherings that culminated in the formulation of the orthodox doctrine of the Trinity. Yoder then devotes several paragraphs to providing a thumbnail sketch of the ways in which ecumenism has been used to refer to a variety of interchurch and inter-Christian relationships. He ends this brief discussion by mentioning

1994 book *The Royal Priesthood*. I was a party to the essay selection process. I do not remember now why we (or John Yoder and Michael Cartwright) decided not to include this essay. It may be that Yoder thought this essay was too "in-house," too Mennonite. It was also a long essay, and the book was already too long. Whatever the reasons, I now believe the essay should have been included.

4. It may be instructive to note that the second volume of *The Mennonite Encyclopedia* ("D-H"), published in 1956, does not include an entry on ecumenism. Not much has been written on Mennonites and ecumenism. But see J. A. Oosterbaan, "The Mennonites and the Eumenical Movement," *The Mennonite Quarterly Review* 41 (July 1967): 187-99; *The Mennonite Encyclopedia*, Vol. 5, ed. Cornelius J. Dyck and Dennis D. Martin (Scottdale, PA: Herald Press, 1990), s.v. "ecumenism"; and Ivan J. Kauffman, "Mennonite-Catholic Conversations in North America: History, Convergences, Opportunities," *The Mennonite Quarterly Review* 73 (January 1999): 35-60. One should also note the numerous writings of Tom Finger on ecumenism.

the modern variant wherein the major concern is that of crossing the barriers that exist between denominations.

In the next section Yoder looks at the roots of the twentieth-century ecumenical movement, naming three in particular. The first root is found in the revival work of D. L. Moody. In this regard, Yoder mentions how mission efforts deriving from revivals often confronted denominational divisions on the mission fields, divisions missionaries felt a need to confront in that context. The second root of the modern ecumenical movement, according to Yoder, was the peace movement. He specifically names the International Fellowship of Reconciliation as an instance of ecumenical concerns linked to a commitment not to kill other Christians across national borders. The third root Yoder identifies as distinctly American: "[in] the American ecumenical movement the effort has been to minimize differences, if necessary by minimizing the importance of doctrinal fidelity" (p. 8). However, he also makes it clear that the negation of doctrinal fidelity is not a necessary component of ecumenism. He does this by distinguishing American from European forms of ecumenism and by saying that the National Council of Churches is more prone to this negation than was its predecessor, the Federal Council of Churches. Yoder attributes this to the theological atmosphere that changed after 1920. Yoder wrote this material for North American Mennonites. By claiming that the roots of modern ecumenism are in revivalism and the peace movement, and by creating distance from the lack of concern for doctrinal fidelity, Yoder makes several brilliant moves to bring 1950s Mennonites along with him.

In the next section Yoder discusses the growth and various manifestations of the ecumenical movement in the twentieth century. Throughout this discussion Yoder is honest about the liberal elements of some segments of the ecumenical movement. He recognizes that many of his Mennonite readers will have problems with these elements. However, Yoder also continually reminds his readers that there are theologically orthodox concerns expressed by significant groups within the ecumenical movement. In fact, in the concluding paragraph, he states that this diversity is inevitable, "for the movement's reason for being lies in the fact that Christians disagree. The only way to avoid contact with Christians with whom one disagrees would be to have no conversation with them" (p. 15).

The next section is entitled "Stating Our Problem." Here Yoder names some of the central problems any constructive proposal for ecumenism needs to address. He begins by offering an interesting paragraph on the various ways to think about what "joining" an organization might mean, since the problem of "joining" the ecumenical movement, or some expression of it, often stems from the way the question is posed. Yoder seeks to show that this preoccupation with whether or not to join a movement can be distracting. Joining is not the primary issue. The central question is much simpler: "Do we believe seriously that there are other Christians in the world than ourselves?" (p. 16). Yoder says he believes that Mennonites, if asked, would agree that there are other Christians. However, for centuries it was possible for Mennonites to ignore the implications of this question. But if the question is faced honestly, Mennonites must also face that "it is clear that the unity of all believers is a Scriptural command, just as clear as the other commandments which we Mennonites tend to emphasize, and often even more important in the eyes of the apostolic writers" (pp. 16-17). Yoder argues that the central challenge within ecumenism is the call to be faithful to unity as Christians. This is a commandment that cannot be ignored. The hows and wherefores of implementing this call are a secondary matter. They require wisdom and discernment regarding the various opportunities to express unity.

Yoder's next few comments again show his understanding of his 1950s Mennonite readership, and they illuminate his own approach to ecumenical relations. "The 'ecumenical problem,'" writes Yoder, "does not only have to do with other Christians; it has to do with other Christians with whom we seriously disagree" (p. 17). Therefore, "we do well to remind ourselves that we are discussing the Ecumenical Movement and the Faithful Church. This is the only way to approach our question in all its seriousness; for we want earnestly to be faithful — personally, congregationally, and in the broader brotherhood" (p. 17). However, lest he be misunderstood, Yoder immediately adds that "we are not a faithful church" (p. 17).

Though faithfulness is an important issue and there are truth questions involved that Mennonites should care about, Mennonites (or other Christians) should not approach ecumenical relations imagining that their church is the "faithful" one and other churches the unfaithful ones. "It will be a good Anabaptist way of thinking, and a good check on whether the answer we find to the ecumenical question is evangelical, if we ask: 'Where would we be if God took that attitude toward us?'" (p. 18).

Yoder proceeds to set aside two approaches to the ecumenical problem. The first is the approach that has automatically excluded other Christians or groups of Christians from fellowship, as if they had been excommunicated. Yoder asserts that this is against New Testament teaching on excommunication: "Excommunication is, in the faithful church, the result not of disagreement but of persistent and unrepentant disobedience" (p. 18). Discerning whether or not there is in fact unrepentant disobedience involves a lengthy process and an attempt at reconciliation. It will not do to approach the ecumenical problem as if this careful process had already been concluded.

The opposite approach, which Yoder also wants to challenge, is to treat disagreement as normal, with each party regretfully going its own way. Yoder wonders why, if the disagreements are so insignificant, the groups remain separate. Or, if we believe that the principles to which we hold are true only for us, then why are they worth the trouble? But if we believe, rather, that the principles to which we hold are true before God, then they are also true for other Christians, and it is our responsibility to inform them of these principles. On the other hand, Yoder asks, might it not be that our unwillingness to lay these claims before other Christians is based instead on fear? Are we not sure enough of our convictions to believe that they will withstand the scrutiny of other Christians?

After setting aside these faulty approaches, Yoder turns to "The Witness of the New Testament." Yoder begins by establishing that there are divisions within the churches portrayed in the New Testament. In fact, if we look at the root meaning of "denomination," which is a "naming," we can see both that there is a process of forming denominations within the New Testament and that the New Testament is opposed to such divisions. In this regard, Yoder discusses the refusal to name various factions after the various leaders and, more substantially, the conflicts between the "Judaizers" and the Hellenists. Paul becomes a model. According to Yoder, Paul "made no attempt to appear impartial" (p. 20). It was not as if Paul thought it didn't matter what people believed, as if one belief were as good as another. And yet he gave no encouragement to the "Paul people," a faction who saw him as central, to "take over the church." This was not Paul's strategy for unity. Rather "the unity of the church at Corinth was not to be created by the central authority of one group of leaders, even if those leaders were in the right; *Christian unity is not to be created, but to be obeyed*" (p. 21, emphasis his). It would have been far easier for Paul to accept divisions that were created by others, but he refused to do so. Instead, he pursued the more difficult task of seeking the unity mandated by the gospel: "For the Apostle Paul, the unity of all believers, including the attempt to maintain unity with those who seek division, whose doctrine is wrong and whose view of the church is distorted, was the will of God" (p. 23).

> The essence of the Lord's Supper is lost by division (I Corinthians 11); the essence of the Gospel is the destruction of the barrier between Jews and Gentiles (Ephesians 2:3); the essence of discipleship is to follow Christ in the humility which enables unity (Philippians 2); the purpose of the various ministries in the church is unity (Ephesians 4; I Corinthians 12). Even when the work of the church was done for the wrong reasons, Paul could rejoice (Philippians 1:18). This deep concern for unity was not a new idea with Paul; Jesus had said that the unity of the believers was necessary if the world were to accept Him (John 17:23). (pp. 23-24)

Paul's commitment to unity, derived from the essence of the gospel, was profound. Yet, this emphasis on unity for Paul did not entail the sacrifice of faithful living and of correct doctrine. Church discipline was always a possibility, but if any discipline was needed it was applied locally and individually: "Even where Paul was clearly in the right, he did not impose his views on the churches, but left the supervision of doctrine and morals in the hands of local elders" (p. 24).

Next Yoder turns to a discussion of "Christian Unity in Christian History." He argues that while some Roman Catholic readings of early church history suggest that the Church was basically united before the schism between East and West, in fact "there was no time when serious differences in matters of life and doctrine did not divide the church" (p. 26). However, imperially convened councils and the growth in the hierarchy of the church did enforce a semblance of unity, albeit in ways that can seen as inconsistent with what Yoder has just described as the New Testament understanding of unity. Yoder was critical of this medieval arrangement. But he was not only critical: "Whatever were its faults, and however much it failed to unite all Christians in a spiritual way, medieval Catholicism at least had two positive achievements. It was truly international, and there was room within it for a degree of freedom in certain doctrinal matters" (p. 28). These two achievements were lost in the magisterial Reformation.

The remainder of this section of Yoder's essay is devoted to a discussion of what some would see as an unlikely source of inspiration for contemporary ecumenism: the beginnings of Anabaptism in early sixteenth-century Switzerland. Yoder was aware that some perceived the Anabaptist tradition as more sectarian than ecumenical, as breaking with other churches in order to remain faithful.[5] However, near the conclusion of his doctoral thesis regarding the debates between the early Swiss Anabaptists and the Swiss Reformers, Yoder argues otherwise:[6] "Far from using the 'break-to-be-faithful' principle, the Anabaptists refused, for over a year, to accept a break that was already there [between Zwingli and themselves]" (p. 31). "Even when the breach of fellowship was definite and extended all over Eu-

---

5. Yoder would have agreed that this has too often been the approach within Mennonite history.

6. John Howard Yoder, *Täufertum und Reformation in der Schweiz, I: Die Gespräche zwischen Täufern und Reformatoren 1523-1538* (Karlsruhe: Verlag H. Schneider, 1962). Yoder completed writing his doctoral thesis during the first half of 1957, at approximately the same time as the writing of the original series of articles on ecumenism that became the 1958 booklet.

rope, the Anabaptists did not accept it as final. . . . In the small space of Reformed Switzerland and southern Germany, and the short time from the birth of Anabaptism until 1540, more than a score of debates were held, almost always at the initiative of the Anabaptists" (p. 32).

When Yoder summarizes the practices of the Anabaptists he notes remarkable similarities between them and what he has discovered from the New Testament.[7] Referring to the Anabaptists, Yoder writes, "The faithful church will discipline; she will expel, if necessary, one at a time, disobedient individuals. She will not, in so far as the choice is hers, withdraw from the body of believers" (p. 33). He goes on to say that "there are good grounds for saying that the Anabaptists were the first ecumenical movement":[8]

> Alone of all the churches of the Reformation, they were truly international. . . . With their rejection of the state church and of war they broke down the greatest barriers to Christian fellowship which have operated in modern times. Alone of all the churches of the Reformation, they insisted that the church is essentially missionary. . . . Alone among the churches of the Reformation, the Anabaptists refused to define their faith exclusively in terms of hierarchy or a confession. . . . To be a Christian according to 'Anabaptist orthodoxy' you need neither to sign nor join anything; you just practice Biblical baptism, communion, and discipline in your local congregation, and accept Scripture as the criterion for all future discussion. Alone among the churches of the Reformation, the

---

7. The similarities are remarkable. Two things are clearly true for Yoder: he knew the Bible well and, after the mid-1950s, knew Anabaptism well. For Yoder, there was a dialectical relationship between the two throughout his life. Yoder formally held to a strong belief in the authority of the Scriptures and specifically did not believe the Anabaptist tradition was, finally, normative. See John Howard Yoder, "The Hermeneutics of the Anabaptists," *The Mennonite Quarterly Review* 41 (October 1967): 291-308; and "Anabaptism and History," in *The Priestly Kingdom: Social Ethics as Gospel* (Notre Dame: University of Notre Dame Press, 1984), 123-34, 205-9. For some reflections on Yoder's use of Scriptures see Mark Thiessen Nation, "Theology as Witness: Reflections on Yoder, Fish, and Interpretive Communities," *Faith and Freedom* 5 (June 1996): 42-47.

8. Yoder, *The Ecumenical Movement and the Faithful Church*, 33.

Anabaptists refused to accept division as final and came back again and again to discuss.[9]

In the last section of *The Ecumenical Movement and the Faithful Church,* Yoder both summarizes the previous discussions and makes some specific proposals for the Mennonite Church. He wants to make it clear that his proposals can only be tentative and should be discussed before they are acted upon. However, "they are submitted in the conviction that Christian unity is just as clearly a Biblical imperative as are evangelization, nonresistance, and nonconformity, and that, however delicate the question may be, it demands open discussion and action" (p. 35).

Yoder proceeds by naming several specific lessons from the previous discussion. First, he states that the New Testament and the Anabaptists agree that it is the "duty" of evangelical Christians to maintain familial relationships with all others who confess Christ. Second, these relationships require more, not less, than is sometimes supposed in ecumenical discussions, for it is "unity in disciplined discipleship" (p. 36). Therefore, unity "does not mean that we approve of the present belief and behavior of another Christian; it means that we lay upon [that person] the claims which Christ lays upon those who confess His name; we ask of him [or her] Christian obedience, Biblical baptism, separation from the world, and the rest of what the Gospel implies" (p. 36). Third, Yoder argues that fellowship with other Christians should be maintained, if at all possible. If there is a break in fellowship, it should be at their initiative, not ours. Fourth, lest he be misunderstood, Yoder makes it clear that the other Christians with whom we converse may be right and we wrong. He encourages all Christians to realize the need to simultaneously call one another to faithfulness and to acknowledge that where there are differences, either party may be wrong. Fifth, Yoder acknowledges that there are different degrees of unity needed for various forms of ecumenical cooperation. Just because we may not deem it appropriate to

---

9. Yoder, *The Ecumenical Movement and the Faithful Church,* 33-34. Also see John Howard Yoder, "Reformation and Missions: A Literature Survey," in *Anabaptism and Mission,* ed. Wilbert R. Shenk (Scottdale, PA: Herald Press, 1984), 40-50.

work in unity on one thing does not mean we cannot cooperate on something else.[10]

Finally, in the last section of the booklet, Yoder makes three specific proposals. First he encourages continued Mennonite participation in meetings of the "Historic Peace Churches." He suggests that Mennonite involvement may contribute the biblical rooting of a valid peace witness. However, he does not want Mennonites to forget that they too may have something to learn, such as a concern for social justice. Second, he encourages the continued involvement of Mennonites in the National Association of Evangelicals, though he warns Mennonites to continue to wrestle with the "superchurch" tendencies of this organization. And, finally, he encourages Mennonite contact with the World Council of Churches (WCC). He probably uses a rather noncommittal word like "contact" rather than involvement or participation because of the greater resistance on the part of Mennonites in the 1950s to any full-blown "involvement" in the WCC, but what he says about the organization in encouraging Mennonite contact is positive.

The last few sentences of this long essay convey the spirit of the whole. Yoder has expressed what he believes is the New Testament mandate for the unity of the church numerous times throughout the essay. With this mandate in mind, he acknowledges that there will be differences, and it is precisely our differences that provide the justification for both witness and humility:

---

10. For two pages after this (39-40) Yoder digresses to discuss the inadequacies of the typical fundamentalist approach to ecumenical cooperation. Typically, says Yoder, this involves the development of a checklist of four or five doctrinal beliefs that must be accepted by others who would be deemed worthy of consideration as Christian conversation partners. Yoder names three problems with such an approach. First, this is overly simple, for it "forgets that there are a great number of different possible levels of agreement and possible collaboration" (p. 39). Second, the checklist is unsatisfactory because it represents doctrinal criteria derived from debates of one particular era. Even assuming one wants to use such a list of criteria, this particular list may not be the most important in other contexts or in other eras. Third, such a list is always comprised of doctrinal formulae and, therefore, presumes that the most important tests of faith are doctrinal (as opposed to faithful discipleship).

The question raised by Mennonite contacts with the World Council of Churches is not whether we will fellowship with unbelievers. The question is whether, following the example of the New Testament and the Anabaptists, we will give to misinformed and seeking believers the help they are looking for and which only the heirs of the Anabaptist tradition can give; and whether we will seek, as this tradition itself demands, whatever correction, admonition, and instruction may be received from the encounter with fellow confessors of the Lord's name under the norm of Scripture and the guidance of His Spirit. (p. 43)

The Nature of the Unity We Seek

Although his views did not change much over the years, Yoder had more to say regarding ecumenism as early as September 1957, when he participated in a symposium at Oberlin College on "the nature of the unity we seek." He offered "a historic free church view" on this topic.[11] In his contribution he names three dimensions of the unity he believes should be sought with other believers, and he ends with a few comments on a false sort of unity that should be avoided.

Yoder recommends that the first element of the unity we seek is conversation. "True conversation," he says, "exists only where there is movement toward agreement, motivated by appeal to an authority recognized by both parties."[12] Yoder suggests that if there is not such

11. Apparently Yoder's contribution was written sometime before the conference because it was originally published as John Howard Yoder, "The Nature of the Unity We Seek: A Historic Free Church View," *Religion in Life* 26 (Spring 1957): 215-22. Later it was published with the conference proceedings as John Howard Yoder, "A Historic Free Church View," in *Christian Unity in North America: A Symposium*, ed. J. Robert Nelson (St. Louis: The Bethany Press, 1958), 89-97. It was reprinted in *The Royal Priesthood: Essays Ecclesiological and Ecumenical*, ed. Michael G. Cartwright (Grand Rapids: Eerdmans, 1994), 221-30. It should also be noted that a significant portion of a programmatic essay Yoder published in 1957 was on ecumenism. See John Howard Yoder, "What Are Our Concerns?" *Concern* 4 (June 1957): 29-32.

12. John Howard Yoder, "The Nature of the Unity We Seek: A Historic Free Church View," in *The Royal Priesthood*, 223. I refer to this version of the essay in subsequent references.

movement conversation will be destructive rather than constructive, serving to harden differences. Productive conversations must include two components. First, both parties must agree on a recognized authority to which appeal can be made, with the possibility of moving toward agreement. Second, there must be openness to changing positions when compelling evidence is brought forward in relation to this common authority. Furthermore, Yoder claims that churches outside of the free church tradition inherently have barriers to this element of unity because they have authorities (such as a pope or a creed) that others outside of their tradition do not accept as authoritative. Yoder argues that the free church tradition sees "as the only legitimate judge [and authority] *Christ himself* as he is made known through Scripture to the congregation of those who seek to know him and his will."[13] Yoder observes that in spite of this the free church viewpoint has usually not been given much of a hearing within structured ecumenical movements.

The second claim in Yoder's essay is that "the unity we seek is supranational." Here Yoder makes an assertion that animates much of the rest of his long tenure in the ecumenical involvement:

> It would be hard to find a more flagrant implicit denial of the givenness of Christian unity than the churches' unhesitating consent to nationalism in its demonic military form. No doctrine of Christian unity has yet explained why it should be more serious for Christians to disagree about the relative merits of episcopal, synodical, or congregational polity than for them to accept, under formal protest but with no real intention to object effectively, to prepare for, and to carry out if necessary, mass killing of other

13. Yoder, "The Nature of the Unity We Seek," 225. So as not to have his point confused with a fundamentalist, ahistorical, position, Yoder adds, "This would not necessarily mean that all evolution would *ipso facto* be condemned, nor would it commit us to an infantile literalism in the use of Scripture; but there would have to be the mutual abandon of any attempt to have recourse to any particular evolution as a canon of interpretation" (p. 225). It is worthwhile to note that these comments are present in the original 1957 essay, not added to the 1994 reprint. For further, more recent elaboration see also John Howard Yoder, "The Authority of Tradition," and "Anabaptism and History," in *The Priestly Kingdom*, 63-79, 199-201 and 123-34, 205-9.

Christians at the call of their respective governments. (This is not to imply that the mass killing of heathen would be more desirable; but it is a disobedience in the field of missions rather than in the field of ecumenics.)[14]

Because he was speaking to an ecumenical audience, not to Mennonites, he acknowledged the difficulty for most Christians to embrace pacifism, even if they would grant the legitimacy of Yoder's point. Nonetheless, he argued that a realization of the importance of the mandate for Christian unity should revolutionize the typical Christian approach to war.[15]

Yoder's third point is that "the unity we seek is a discipline." In formal ecumenical discussions, Christian behavior is usually subordinated to Christian doctrine and worship. "*That* it is important to be politically responsible is strongly emphasized; *how* it is important to execute that responsibility is much less clear."[16] There seems to be a comfortableness with major differences in matters of moral practice (resulting in less of a need to move toward greater unity on these matters) in a way that is not true for differences regarding doctrine and worship. Yoder argues that this is contrary to New Testament teaching.

> The thought world of the New Testament was entirely different. Unity in ethical commitment was for the apostolic church no less central than unity in faith and worship. Christian behavior was not the lowest common denominator of a fully baptized society but a kind of life strikingly, offensively different from the rest of the world; it dared to claim that Christ himself was its norm and to believe in the active enabling presence of the Holy Spirit.
>
> With Christ as the criterion of obedience and the Spirit as the Guarantor of the possibility of discipleship, the Church cannot but be a disciplined fellowship of those who confess that, if there be

14. Yoder, "The Nature of the Unity We Seek," 226-27.

15. For an expansion of this point see John Howard Yoder, "Let the Church Be the Church," in *The Royal Priesthood*, 168-80. This essay was originally published in 1965.

16. Yoder, "The Nature of the Unity We Seek," 228, emphasis his.

one faith, one body, one hope, there must also be one obedience; that God's will may be known in the church and commitment to its application expected of the church's members.[17]

Yoder ends by arguing against a lowest common denominator approach to Christian unity. It is tempting, he says, for middle-of-the-road Protestants (at least the middle as they see it) to imagine that they have done the full ecumenical task when they have joined hands with each other, even creating new ecumenical structures that express such union. What is much more difficult — and the true, hard work of ecumenism — is working toward unity among much more disparate bodies within Christianity. Yoder emphasizes that working at unity among the Orthodox, Roman Catholics, Pentecostals, evangelicals, the historic peace churches, *and* liberal Protestants is the true and difficult work of Christian unity.

The Free Church Ecumenical Style

The next essay on ecumenism, "The Free Church Ecumenical Style," written in 1968, can be seen as a series of footnotes in which Yoder expands on points already made in *The Ecumenical Movement and the Faithful Church*. Since the essay was originally published in a Quaker journal,[18] Yoder feels free to assume a commitment to a free church understanding. He also refers to the Quakers more often here than in most of his work.

In this essay, Yoder notes that the common approach to ecumenism is rooted in a "magisterial" conception of the church. By this he means that concentration is placed on the church as a structure for governing doctrine and administration. He cites several shortcomings of this approach. But, as in the previous essay, Yoder points out that the central problem is that this approach avoids dealing with the "real

17. Yoder, "The Nature of the Unity We Seek," 228.
18. Yoder, "The Free Church Ecumenical Style," *Quaker Religious Thought* 10 (August 1968): 29-38; it was reprinted in *The Royal Priesthood*, 231-41. References will be to the reprinted version.

divisions" that separate Christians. In this essay, however, his chief emphasis is on differences within denominations: "The real divisions in the churches are between rich and poor, between liberal and conservative, between races, between east and west. These divisions go down through the middle of existing denominations."[19] These are the divisions that matter most and that are the most intractable. Precisely because of this, they are the divisions that should be high on the agenda for those Christians who are committed to ecumenism.

Yoder commends the Quakers for acknowledging through their terminology the commonality of the "meeting" that happens weekly with the ones that happen monthly, quarterly, or yearly: all of these are indeed religious "meetings." This is to say that there should be an "openness, truthfulness, and bindingness" that befits the significance of such meetings. It does not mean there are no differences among the various gatherings. It is simply to acknowledge that the various gatherings of Christians are, in their own ways, forms of church. "Thus instead of the doctrinaire statement that the geographically localized congregation is the *exclusive* reality, there is here a sober affirmation of the *priority* of the group that meets with frequency and continuity of membership and discipline."[20]

The next section of the essay deals with the meaning of membership. Though put in different terms, this section is basically addressing the same set of issues Yoder dealt with in the previous document when he addressed the inappropriateness of making doctrine and church polity more important than ethics. Here he frames the issue as being one of membership. Why is it, he asks, that when the issue of baptism is dealt with in ecumenical conversations the point of debate revolves around its validity as a sacrament rather than the way in which the faith of those baptized relates to baptism? In this regard Yoder suggests that there should be a more substantial ecumenical discussion of the meaning of membership in relation to the mission of the church.

Additionally, he calls for a study of the meaning of apostasy. He acknowledges that the term has been overused in the past. He wonders

---

19. Yoder, "The Free Church Ecumenical Style," 234.
20. Yoder, "The Free Church Ecumenical Style," 236, emphasis his.

whether there has been an adequate ecumenical discussion of the term to discern whether or not the term is dispensable. Might it be that something significant is lost if the possibility of apostasy is ignored?[21]

In the next two brief sections Yoder repeats what he has said elsewhere about historical precedents for free church involvement in the ecumenical movement, particularly as this relates to the free church commitment to biblical authority "over the heads of all particular traditions." More interestingly, Yoder sounds a note here that he sounds in numerous other places, though not often in his essays on ecumenism. He notes that within current debates there are attempts to discuss the relation between church and society through various uses of "two realms" language. He suggests that the free churches offer an alternative view, with a strong emphasis on "the distinction between the believing community and other communities, between covenanting community as a secular social reality and the other secular social realities in the midst of which it lives."[22]

Finally, Yoder concludes by suggesting that the free church or believers' church tradition approaches the question of Christian unity with "another spirit," rooted in "the priority of the congregation."[23] He names three dimensions to this different spirit. First, "the believers' churches are committed to the discovery of a unity that is *personal*. One does not so much encounter another tradition as encounter a brother or sister."[24] Second, "decision making and thereby unity in the believers'

---

21. Yoder does not elaborate on what he means here. (Elsewhere he would mention heresy along with apostasy.) However, I can imagine at least three related examples that might have been in his mind. Yoder was conscious of the past dire situation in Nazi Germany. Some believed that making pronouncements of heresy in this situation of *status confessionis* was crucial for the future of the church. Using this situation as the model, some of the German leaders of the confessing church movement believed that nuclear armaments in the late 1950s called for similar action. (On this latter see John H. Yoder, "Appendix: The Continuing Church Struggle," in *Karl Barth and the Problem of War* [Nashville: Abingdon Press, 1970], 133-37.) Having visited South Africa on several occasions, Yoder might also have been thinking of the apartheid situation there. (See John W. DeGruchy and Charles Villa-Vicencio, eds., *Apartheid Is a Heresy* [Grand Rapids: Eerdmans, 1983].)

22. Yoder, "The Free Church Ecumenical Style," 239.

23. Yoder, "The Free Church Ecumenical Style," 240.

24. Yoder, "The Free Church Ecumenical Style," 240, emphasis his.

church must *begin at the point of offense.*"[25] True unity should not avoid dealing with difficult issues. Rather, in a spirit of openness and with a willingness to repent, there must be a commitment to the hard work of discipline and reconciliation. And, third, repeating what he had said earlier in the essay, *"every meeting of the church is a meeting for worship."*[26] Yoder's insightful deductions concerning the inherent ecumenical contributions of the free church traditions enabled him to further meaningful ecumenical conversations and relationships.

The Imperative of Christian Unity from Below

While Yoder's last three essays on ecumenism do not add significant new arguments to his previous essays, they highlight some of his long-standing emphases and introduce a few new ones as well. In 1983 Yoder presented a guest lecture in a class at the Mennonite seminaries in Elkhart, Indiana, entitled "The Imperative of Christian Unity."[27] In the first section of this lecture Yoder covers much the same biblical ground he had covered in *The Ecumenical Movement and the Faithful Church.*[28] Here he speaks as clearly as anywhere: "The unity of Christians is a *theological* imperative first of all in the sense that its reasons arise out of the basic truth commitments of the gospel and the church's intrinsic mission. Speaking even more precisely, as we turn to the most clearly stated text of the New Testament, it is a Christological imperative: it has to do with who Jesus is."[29] For Yoder there would be no stronger claim.

25. Yoder, "The Free Church Ecumenical Style," 240, emphasis his.

26. Yoder, "The Free Church Ecumenical Style," 240, emphasis his.

27. Published as John Howard Yoder, "The Imperative of Christian Unity," in *The Royal Priesthood,* 289-99.

28. The heart of what Yoder says is true and important, as were his insights in his 1957 essay. However, one has to wonder, in 1983, why Yoder shows no signs of having done any research on the scholarship regarding unity and diversity in the New Testament. The most obvious source in 1983 would have been James D. G. Dunn, *Unity and Diversity in the New Testament* (Philadelphia: The Westminster Press, 1977). (See also the extensive bibliography within Dunn's book.) I think interaction with some of this literature would have enriched, broadened, and strengthened Yoder's views.

29. Yoder, "The Imperative of Christian Unity," 291, emphasis his.

Yoder contrasts appropriate diversity with the "lazy solution" of pluralism: "That diversity is accredited by its being within the fundamental unity with purpose and complementarity of function. Pluralism, on the other hand, is diversity without unity, variation without asking the truth question, work at cross purposes without accountable discipline."[30] Unity with diversity is more difficult, but it is the true gospel call that leads us to work at questions of truth and reconciliation even with difficult issues. Finally, Yoder emphasizes that the priority for unity is on the local level, a theme to which he will give more attention in the last two lectures.

In 1990 Yoder presented the valedictory lecture on the occasion of the departure of James Wm. McClendon, Jr., from the Church Divinity School of the Pacific. Yoder used this occasion to address himself to the Episcopal claims to catholicity. The lecture, "Catholicity in Search of Location," begins by offering some reflections on his chosen title. As in other essays already discussed, he then criticizes some of the standard "magisterial" assumptions that are often presupposed in ecumenical discussions. He cautions against imagining that we can locate the unity we seek before there is a dialogical process; it is precisely the process of dialogue that helps us to see what unity means.[31] However, Yoder argues, a movement toward unity does involve an ecumenical acknowledgment that the Scriptures, as the testimony to common Christian origins, have pride of place in their searching dialogue. The Scriptures have priority over any particular traditions.[32]

In the last portion of this lecture Yoder offers several steps toward locating catholicity.[33] The first step is to renounce any tools of privilege or power to accredit or enforce our understanding of the Word we believe to be catholic. Such renunciation of power will testify to the authenticity of the Word and will display our trust that the truth is, in fact, accredited by the Holy Spirit. The second step is to acknowledge the fallibility of our witness and ministry by stating that reformation is not something needed only at one point in time but is, rather, a

---

30. Yoder, "The Imperative of Christian Unity," 293.

31. Yoder, "Catholicity in Search of Location," in *The Royal Priesthood*, 311.

32. Yoder, "Catholicity in Search of Location," 311-13.

33. For the following see Yoder, "Catholicity in Search of Location," 314-20.

constant need. Third, catholicity that is true to itself must be embraced freely in each locale. This means that ecclesiology must be formulated in such a way that it is capable of being expressed everywhere. Furthermore, there must be rules for dialogue within these local embodiments of the catholic faith. There needs to be an acknowledgment that every member within the unity of the local body is a bearer of a gift of the Spirit; everyone has the authority both to speak and to listen; and everyone is potentially subject to "reconciling admonition."

Yoder concludes with the following summary: Catholicity is not "looking for a home" in the sense of a vagabond who "once lodged will no longer roam." It is a lived reality that will have its place or "location" wherever all comers participate — in the power of the Triune God — in proclaiming to all nations (beginning where they are) all that Jesus taught. Only if the avowed agenda is that broad and that open can we claim the promises of the Lord who pledged that he would accompany us to the end of the age.[34]

The last essay to discuss is, as far as I know, the last lecture John Yoder ever wrote, which also happened to be on ecumenism. It was scheduled to be delivered in January 1998. He died in late December 1997. The lecture was delivered by a former student of a friend of John Yoder. It was entitled "Christian Unity: The Way from Below." It suffers from the same lack of focus as the previous lecture, but it is useful to note some themes that reappear.[35]

Yoder's lecture notes first that one of the most basic tasks of

34. Yoder, "Catholicity in Search of Location," 320. This paragraph is mostly a paraphrase of Matthew 28:18-20, the points of which he had listed much earlier in the essay (p. 309). I think the essay would probably have been significantly strengthened if he had used the passage from Matthew more centrally in organizing the second half of the essay, because the essay suffers throughout for a lack of coherence and clarity.

35. In this eighteen-page lecture, Yoder consciously provides almost eight pages of preamble. (I say "consciously" because on page eight he states: "NOW FOR THE LECTURE PROPER.") Having read many essays and lectures by Yoder, I think it is often a sign that Yoder is lacking focus, perhaps not quite knowing what to say, when his preambles are overly long. Whether that was generally true, it is true for this lecture. The lecture was the Paul Watson Lecture, the Gray Friars, read posthumously by Mike Broadway, January 1998, San Francisco, California. It was published as John Howard Yoder, "Christian Unity — The Way from Below," *Pro Ecclesia* 9 (Spring 2000): 165-83.

working at unity is to define its limits. Heresy and apostasy should be words with meaning, however much they may have been abused in the past.

The second point is somewhat unclear but seems to be that there would be fewer quarrels about ecclesiology if those traditions with episcopal structures would limit the size of each diocese. There could still be a bishop for every church, but the parishes would be more truly congregational.

Third, Yoder raises the specific issue of infant baptism. He points out two facts. One is that some major theologians from pedobaptist traditions have made substantial theological arguments for believers' baptism. The other is that neither these arguments nor the rationales of the anti-pedobaptist traditions themselves have been given serious attention within most formal ecumenical circles.

Yoder connects the fourth point to insights from liberation theology, namely, the epistemological privilege of the "underdog." Although for those who often engage in ecumenical dialogue at the top this is not new, Yoder wants to make it clear that his challenge to epistemological advantage is rooted in the humiliation of God becoming flesh in Jesus and then embracing the cross.

Fifth, Yoder again emphasizes that Christian unity is part of the mission of the church. This unity is to be distinguished from a "lazy solution of pluralism." It should be a disciplined unity, a unity that acknowledges the potential need for reconciling admonition.

Sixth, Yoder insists that we need to avoid the temptation to imagine that polite etiquette equals true unity. We must deal with the root of the most difficult differences squarely.

Seventh, Yoder suggests that the structures of the church must somehow appreciate the need to deal with dividedness on the local level. It is there that differences and conflicts are often most real and most in need of healing.

Eighth, Yoder suggests that Christians on the local level need to practice ways of living in unity. They must do so even if the ecclesial structures and hierarchy do not provide support for such actions.

Ninth, Yoder states that every Christian is a minister; every Christian has a gift of the Spirit. The work of the church, including work for unity, is to be done by all of the people. This does not exclude a role for episcopacy, but it re-defines the work for unity, including the role of those often considered "clergy."

Finally, Yoder asserts that if we are to move forward in embodying unity in a truly Christian manner, we must reconnect with the Jewishness of apostolic Christianity. We must disavow the "Christendom" methods of enforcing unity and subject our standard triumphal visions to the re-definitions of the crucified One whom we proclaim as Lord.

These last three essays, written in 1983, 1990, and 1999, restate the reasons for Yoder's commitment to ecumenism. Time and again he challenges his audience, the church, to strive for unity in Christ.

First to the House of Menno

In addition to Yoder's major essays on ecumenism, he made some further contributions to the Mennonite Church on the subject. Although a number of Yoder's essays or lectures were presented to ecumenical audiences that were significantly different from the Mennonite Church, most of his writings on ecumenism were directed toward his own denomination. In addition to the essays, lectures, and symposia I have already discussed in this chapter, Yoder wrote numerous articles for Mennonite publications. He also wrote many unpublished lectures and memos for his own denomination.[36]

36. In addition to the writings previously dealt with in this chapter, some of the others include: John Howard Yoder, "Mennonites and Contemporary Ecumenical Movements," unpublished lecture presented at the Centennial Study Conference, General Conference Mennonite Church, Christian Unity in Faith and Witness, Donnellson, Iowa, June 1960; "Mennonites and Interdenominational Agencies," *The Mennonite* (March 20, 1962): 81-82; "The Unity We Have," *The Mennonite* (March 13, 1962): 165-66; "The Unity We Seek," *The Mennonite* (March 27, 1962): 213-14; "Christian Unity Within a Divided North American Protestantism," Memorandum on Mennonite Board of Missions and Charities stationery, March 1, 1967; "Memo on World Council of Churches Fourth Assembly, Uppsala," August 6, 1968; "The Case for More Reporting on Interchurch Matters in Mennonite Periodicals," April 15, 1969; "Draft of Possible Communication to Church Reorganization Commission in the Form of a Possible Letter to J. Howard Kauffman," August 7, 1969; "Ecumenical and Counter-Ecumenical De-

In order to help effect changes, he was also a member of the "Interchurch Relations Committee" of the Mennonite Church from 1965 to 1971.[37] As a member of this committee he wrote the initial drafts of at least three committee papers.[38] These papers both provided a rationale and suggested specific steps for active ecumenical engagement on the part of the Mennonite Church and its members.

Ecumenical Engagement: *Baptism, Eucharist and Ministry*

Although this whole book deals with the ways in which Yoder's life and thought were largely shaped by his ecumenical commitments and engagements, it is worthwhile to examine one specific instance where Yoder addressed the ecumenical community directly around an issue both he and they cared about: baptism. A few comments about eucharist and ministry also flow from the discussion of baptism. This is merely an example of how Yoder's ecumenical views related to specific issues; it should not be divorced from his overall project as articulated throughout this book.

Throughout most of the history of the church, Christians have been separated partly by holding to various views on matters of church order. As a result, many in the ecumenical movement considered it important that after several decades of working at these issues, the Faith and Order Commission issued, in 1982, a statement on "Bap-

---

velopments Overseas," October 4, 1969; and "A Plea for a Broader Conception of Evangelical Unity," unpublished paper, 1967. (I have listed these to illustrate the diversity and practical nature of Yoder's input.)

37. For a summary of the work of the Mennonite General Conference Ad Hoc Committee on Interchurch Relations, from 1965 to 1971, of which John Yoder was a member, see James M. Lapp, ed., *Principles and Guidelines for Interchurch Relations* (Scottdale, PA: Mennonite General Conference, 1971).

38. For the papers, see "The Challenge of the Divided State of American Protestantism," and "Christian Unity in a Divided Mennonitism," in *Proceedings of the Thirty-Seventh Mennonite General Conference* (Scottdale, PA: Mennonite Publishing House, 1967), 63-66, 66-71, and "Text on the Organizational Expression of Christian Unity," in *Proceedings of the Thirty-Eighth Mennonite General Conference* (Scottdale, PA: Mennonite General Conference, 1969), 54-63.

tism, Eucharist, and Ministry" (BEM). This text "represents the significant theological convergence which Faith and Order has discerned and formulated."[39]

Within two years of the publication of this statement the ecumenical journal *Midstream* invited John Yoder to write a response to the document.[40] Yoder's essay provides an example of his approach to issues in an ecumenical context. He begins by quoting, approvingly, from two people at the 1952 WCC assembly, who stated that the Faith and Order Commission was biased toward the "mainline" or "high church" perspective over against those of the "free churches." It needs to be recognized, claims Yoder, that the BEM document also represents a similar tilt. That said, Yoder does acknowledge something very positive about the process behind the document. The process was in some ways a truly open dialogical process wherein the various confessional commitments were relativized. This was an important step toward the possibility of fruitful dialogue.

Having begun with this affirmation, Yoder goes on to name various elements within the document that he thinks are wrong. He wonders, for instance, whether the possibility of "unfaithfulness" is given serious consideration. He asks whether there might not have been past acts of unfaithfulness, acts related to baptism, that should be named in order for this document to be truthful and adequately ecumenical. That such unfaithfulness has not been named, argues Yoder, is "of a piece with the wider strategic tendency of inclusive agency leaders to

---

39. Faith and Order Commission, World Council of Churches, *Baptism, Eucharist and Ministry: Faith and Order Paper No. 111* (St. Louis: Association of Evangelical Lutheran Churches, 1982), 4. This text was intentionally published in many different editions through the World Council of Churches and its member churches. The formal text itself is divided into numbered paragraphs for standardized reference. However, the quoted phrase is from the introduction, peculiar to this edition.

40. It should also be noted that shortly after the document was published in 1982, John Yoder, as co-convener, suggested that the Believers Church conferences organize a conference around the BEM document. See Donald F. Durnbaugh, "Origin and Development of the Believers' Church Conferences," in *Servants of the Word: Ministry in the Believers Churches*, ed. David B. Eller (Elgin, IL: Brethren Press, 1990), xviii-xix. Papers from the conference suggested by Yoder were published as Merle D. Strege, *Baptism and Church: A Believers' Church Vision* (Grand Rapids: Sagamore Books, 1986).

believe that ecumenical unity can be achieved by going forward together without repentance."[41] Repentance for what? Anyone who
knows Yoder's writings well knows precisely what he has in mind:
"The early Anabaptists did not die, and the 'Christian' civil authorities
did not kill them, for a quibble about proper ritual form. Although the
words of the debate on baptism were on the level of ritual, the entire
constantinian concubinage was at stake."[42] Yoder not only wants acknowledgment of these past horrendous wrongs; more importantly, he
wants an acknowledgment that there were (and are) significant theological issues at stake regarding the matter of believers' baptism. Serious and needed debates are in fact subverted when the differences between infant baptism and believers' baptism — differences over which
Christians were put to death — are treated as trivial.

Yoder also reflects on "rebaptism" and confirmation in his essay.
The BEM document says that "any practice which might be interpreted as 'rebaptism' must be avoided."[43] But no church would affirm
the practice of rebaptism, argues Yoder. Again, difficult issues are carefully avoided by stating it in this way. Interpreted by whom, of course,
is the begged question. All traditions, Yoder reminds us, have criteria
for determining the validity of the practice of baptism. And, yet, this
statement skirts the issues involved. When Anabaptists in the sixteenth
century were put to death for "rebaptizing," these dissidents did not
believe that was what they were doing. In fact, one way to interpret
their actions is to say that they were protesting against "indiscriminate
baptism," an act also criticized in the BEM document.[44] If, in fact, infant baptism were always understood within the context of a nurturing family and church, and if it was followed by a serious confirmation
process, then, at least by some theological accounts, the differences between believers' baptism and infant baptism would be greatly mini-

41. Yoder, "A 'Free Church' Perspective on Baptism, Eucharist and Ministry," in
The Royal Priesthood, 281-82.

42. John Howard Yoder, "Adjusting to the Changing Shape of the Debate on Infant Baptism," In *Oecumennisme: Opstellen aangeboden an Henk Kossen*, ed. Arie
Lambo (Amsterdam: Algemene Doopsgezinde Societeit, 1989), 206.

43. *Baptism, Eucharist and Ministry*, "Baptism," paragraph 13.

44. *Baptism, Eucharist and Ministry*, "Baptism," paragraph 16.

mized.[45] However, the fact that "indiscriminate baptism" is still practiced by more than a few churches still begs the question: "re-baptism" as interpreted by whom?

Although Yoder focuses mostly on baptism in his essay on the BEM document,[46] he does make a few comments on eucharist and ministry as well. He acknowledges that the issues are different in regard to these latter two issues. With the exception of a few communions, issues regarding the eucharist mostly have to do with understandings of what the eucharist means. Yoder believes that in this regard, again, the tilt is toward a high church understanding.[47] Concerning ministry, Yoder acknowledges that believers' churches disagree greatly among themselves on this topic.[48] However, he is disappointed that the minority tradition that opposes professional ministry seems not to have received a hearing within the document.

Because of Yoder's genuine commitment to unity in Christ, and because of his careful application of the principles he has articulated throughout his writings, he was able to sustain relationships and offer a sustained voice on behalf of the free churches. But how did he apply what he learned through these ecumenical engagements and through his studies to other faiths?

And Those of Other Faiths?

While Yoder was involved extensively in ecumenical conversations, formally and informally, in many different contexts and throughout most of his life, his involvements in and writings about interfaith rela-

45. Yoder, "Adjusting to the Changing Shape of the Debate on Infant Baptism," 206-8. Something like what is stated in this sentence seems to be suggested by BEM, though as Yoder says, it is certainly not spelled out carefully enough to provide any solid guidance. Yoder himself would have been, I believe, reasonably content with this sort of re-interpretation.

46. For some of Yoder's other views on baptism, presented in a less polemical style, see John Howard Yoder, *Body Politics* (Nashville: Discipleship Resources, 1992), 28-46.

47. For some of Yoder's thoughts on the eucharist see Yoder, *Body Politics*, 14-27.

48. For one example of this, with contributions from John Yoder, see David B. Eller, ed., *Servants of the Word: Ministry in the Believers Churches.*

tions and dialogue are more meager.[49] Yoder did publish one substantial essay on interfaith dialogue entitled "The Disavowal of Constantine: An Alternative Perspective on Interfaith Dialogue."[50]

The title, "The Disavowal of Constantine," indicates much of the agenda for this key essay on interfaith dialogue and relations. Yoder opens the essay by commenting on the fact that it is presumed that the interlocutors engaged in dialogue will be the theologically elite from mainstream forms of each of the religions. He wants to make the reader conscious of this presumption because it puts a certain questionable slant on the discussions. As Yoder indicates in several pages, this is quite understandable given that he is speaking for a tradition that believes some fundamental structural mistakes have been made by

49. There would be two ways in which this statement should be modified. First, Yoder engaged the Jewish tradition substantially. He both engaged in extensive dialogues with some contemporary Jewish scholars and wrote at some length on certain dimensions of Judaism and their relationship to Christianity. He clearly saw Judaism as in a special relationship to Christianity, referring to it as a "non-non Christian religion." See John Howard Yoder, *The Jewish-Christian Schism Revisited,* ed. Michael G. Cartwright and Peter Ochs (Grand Rapids: Eerdmans, 2003); John Howard Yoder, "The Nonviolence of Rabbinic Judaism," in *Christian Attitudes to War, Peace, and Revolution: A Companion to Bainton* (Elkhart, IN: Co-op Bookstore, 1983); John Howard Yoder, *Nevertheless: Varieties of Religious Pacifism,* rev. ed. (Scottdale, PA: Herald Press, 1992), 122-25. See also James Wm. McClendon, Jr., *Systematic Theology,* Vol. 2: *Doctrine* (Nashville: Abingdon Press, 1994), 350-54. Second, some of Yoder's writings on religious approaches to, or the effectiveness of, nonviolence are deliberately written to be of use to people of any or no religious persuasion. See, for example, portions of Yoder, *Nevertheless;* Yoder, "The Power of Nonviolence," A Publication of the Joan B. Kroc Institute for International Peace Studies, University of Notre Dame, 1994.

50. This essay was originally presented in Jerusalem in February 1976 at the Ecumenical Institute for Advanced Theological Studies. It was originally published as John Howard Yoder, "The Disavowal of Constantine: An Alternative Perspective on Interfaith Dialogue," in *Aspects of Interfaith Dialogue: Tantur Yearbook 1975-76,* ed. W. Wegner and W. Harrelson (Jerusalem: Tantur Ecumenical Institute for Advanced Theological Studies), 47-68. The version I will refer to is the one reprinted in *The Royal Priesthood,* pp. 242-61. The other substantial essay Yoder wrote was a lecture for a course in 1983. It is drawn from three sources: a brief published essay from 1966, a college chapel talk of 1973, and the 1976 lecture just mentioned. This 1983 lecture, "The Finality of Jesus Christ and Other Faiths," is long (thirty-three pages) but lacks the focus and care of the other published essay and, itself, remains unpublished. Therefore, I will only discuss the published essay.

much of what is usually considered "mainstream" Christianity. Thus, the way in which the critical, radical reformation stream of Christianity approaches many issues, including relationships with other religions, will be different from that of mainstream Christians.

Toward the end of the introductory section Yoder proceeds to list five constitutive components of the position he seeks to represent:

- its concern for the particular, historical, and therefore Jewish quality and substance of New Testament faith in Jesus;
- its holistic inclusion of communal and cultural dimensions of 'way of life' within the faith (decision-making patterns, e.g., or economics) as religious issues, rather than making them peripheral behind the priority of spirituality or dogma;
- its insistence on the voluntariness of membership in the visible church, usually expressed in the baptism of persons old enough to confess responsibly their own faith;
- its rejection of the support, defense, and control of the church by the civil rulers;
- its relativizing of the hierarchical dimensions of the church in favor of maximum freedom and wholeness in the local congregational fellowship.[51]

With this agenda in mind, Yoder proceeds to name some of the ways in which this set of alternative perspectives relates to interfaith relationships. One of the distinctives Yoder has named from this tradition is that it includes an enculturated "way of life." Therefore discussing relations with people from other religions is about much more than just discussing differing dogmas or alternative spiritualities. In fact it is a distortion to discuss only convictions, as if these convictions can be separated from the way of life with which they are integrated. Having said this, Yoder must confront the offense of how the Christian gospel has too often been destructively "enculturated," because a part of the problem is that the Christian faith has too often come in the cultural clothing of the Roman or British or American *empires*.

Yoder criticizes two dimensions of the way in which Western

---

51. Yoder, "The Disavowal of Constantine," 247.

Christian missions have often been expressed. First, there is the uncritical adoption of anti-biblical and pagan convictions and practices that are both different from and counter to Christian understandings of God, human community, morality, or nature. Second, there is the sanctioning of this pagan synthesis by the power of the sword and money. It is the combination of these two as a means of enforcing a certain enculturation that have too often been prominent in the history of Christianity and have made the "witness" of the Christian religion offensive.

Consequently, according to Yoder, a full acknowledgment of the need for repentance is required, both in relation to this past and as a mode of Christian existence today. It is not adequate to say that these mistakes of the past are ones we have outgrown, that we know better now. Nor is it adequate to be embarrassed about the past and therefore in a mode of humility say that we may be wrong and others may be right. Nor need we be hesitant in making repentance a component of the message we now share with those from other religions. The outsiders already know of the past sins of the church. We should renounce them, repent of them, and acknowledge that "at least for Christians, the continuing pertinence of the historical memory of Jesus, via the New Testament, as a lever for continuing critique, is part of the message itself. The capacity for, or in fact the demand for self-critique is part of what must be shared with people of other faiths and ideologies."[52]

It is important to reiterate at this point that interfaith relations are not primarily related to a discussion among elites about religious or metaphysical abstractions. This is why, in fact, we cannot simply discuss interfaith "dialogue," as if an exchange of ideas is all we are discussing. Rather, from Yoder's perspective, such relations are about the concreteness of local communities of Christians who in their particular confession of Christ relate to others who do not share this confession or this way of life shaped around the confession. Some of these "others" will likewise be engaged in their own particular, but different, communities of faith and some of them will, in their own self-understanding, be irreligious. As Christians we (should) have reasons inherent in our confession as to why we respect all "others" who do

52. Yoder, "The Disavowal of Constantine," 251.

not share our confession of faith. Jesus calls us to "love our neighbors as ourselves," even to "love our enemies." Thus we relate to all others, including those of other religions, in ways that are consistent with our confession that Jesus is Lord. However, just as we believe that Christian faith should be voluntary and, therefore, it should not be assumed that any Briton or German or American will necessarily be Christian, so we do not assume, say, that any Iranian will necessarily be Muslim or Burmese be Buddhist.

It may be that the word "mission" has been tarnished by centuries of colonial empire-building practices on the part of Christians. Nonetheless, with an appropriate sense of humility, repentance, and respect, we witness to our faith in the God revealed in Jesus Christ, seeking to testify not only with our words but also with lives lived in accordance with our claims:

> One corrective today, one approach to dialogue, approves of Christendom's vision of an all-englobing unchallenged truth system and apologizes for the narrowness of its continuing confession of Jesus. The other would renew the critical impact of the confession of Jesus but must then apologize — yet repent is the better word — for triumphalism, as well as for Mediterranean and Germanic tribalism, and abandon the assumption that a criterion of the true faith will be that it can sweep everyone in. One corrective relativizes Jesus, seeking dialogue by stripping off distinctiveness. The other radicalizes the particular relevance of Jesus, enabling dialogue through the content of the message:
> - the love of the adversary,
> - the dignity of the lowly,
> - repentance,
> - servanthood,
> - the renunciation of coercion.
>
> One corrects for the error of provincialism by embracing variety: the other corrects for the sin of pride by repenting. Only experience can tell when and where either one of these stances will enable a genuine interfaith meeting.[53]

53. Yoder, "The Disavowal of Constantine," 258. For an article that quite effec-

Summary: Sustained Engagement

John Yoder did not consider working for the unity of the church to be optional; it was an imperative rooted in Jesus Christ and the life of the church. Furthermore, the very form of ecumenical engagement — as well as engagement with those outside the church — should be decisively shaped by the person of Jesus the Christ. That there are substantial disagreements among Christians renders dialogue and attempts to arrive at unity necessary. Disagreements should not be treated as normal. If disagreements are trivial they should not separate Christians from each other; if they are significant enough to separate Christians from each other, they should be confronted. Disagreements should also not be avoided, either by ignoring issues that are difficult to deal with or by excluding certain Christian bodies that make the ecumenical tasks more complicated.

But it must be remembered that when Yoder called for involvement in ecumenism he always had in mind both the ecumenical movement *and* the faithful church. True Christian unity should be expressed through disciplined discipleship. The established ecumenical movement had often focused on differences of doctrine and church order; Yoder wanted Christians to confront differences of ethics. All of us who call ourselves Christian are bound together, accountable to one another. The levels of accountability vary, quite appropriately, depending upon the level of relationship. But appropriate to the level of relationship, we are to call one another to faithfulness as brothers and sisters in Christ. That we differ on what faithfulness means is precisely the value of relationships across communions. These differences are sometimes the source of the challenges that prove difficult. As we seek unity in faithfulness with all who name the name of Christ, we acknowledge, in humility, that it may be others who hold to the truth

---

tively draws from Yoder's broader writings to develop a response to the reality of religious plurality see Gayle Gerber Koontz, "Evangelical Peace Theology and Religious Pluralism: Particularity in Perspective," *The Conrad Grebel Review* 14 (Winter 1996): 57-85. See also A. James Reimer, "Response to Gayle Gerber Koontz," *The Conrad Grebel Review* 14 (Winter 1996): 86-89. In addition see Gayle Gerber Koontz, "Confessional Theology in a Pluralistic Context," 195-205.

that we have yet to learn, the morality that we have yet to embody. Simply put, we may be wrong. We also, inasmuch as it is up to us, refuse to break communion because of our perception of unfaithfulness on the part of others. We simply continue, in ecumenical patience, to press upon others (as upon ourselves) the call to be faithful to our Lord whom we all as Christians seek to serve.

In brief this was John Yoder's understanding of the ecumenical challenge. He believed he had a particular vocation to do his work ecumenically. Knowing full well that many of his central views were minority views within the Christian tradition, he knew that this vocation required ecumenical patience, a patience he sought to embody through a long-term commitment to translating his own Anabaptist tradition for the broad Christian world.

Chapter 4

The Politics of Jesus,
the Politics of John Howard Yoder:
An Evangelical and Catholic
Peace Theology

Over twenty-five years ago Stanley Hauerwas observed:

> An attempt to treat pacifism in a serious and disciplined way is
> particularly important today when many people are emotionally
> predisposed to make vague commitments to the cause of peace. If
> emotional decisions are not refined by intellectual expression, they
> can be too easily transferred to the next good cause, which may en-
> tail violence for its success. Further, if this kind of pacifism is to be
> saved from the perversities of innocence that too often invite ag-
> gression or acquiescence to evil, it will need to be based on a more
> substantive ground than it now possesses. There is no better school
> to go to for such training than the pacifism of John Yoder.[1]

More recently, in 1998, Walter Wink said, "More than any other person, Yoder has labored to bring the Peace Church witness against violence into the mainstream of theological discussion."[2] More than any

---

1. Stanley Hauerwas, "Messianic Pacifism," *Worldview* 16 (June 1973): 29. Also
see Stanley Hauerwas, "The Nonresistant Church: The Theological Ethics of John
Howard Yoder," in *Vision and Virtue* (Notre Dame: Fides Press, 1974), 197-221. Each of
these essays provides a very nice overview of Yoder's theological project as it relates to
his pacifism. Also see Craig A. Carter, *The Politics of the Cross: The Theology and Social Ethics of John Howard Yoder* (Grand Rapids: Brazos Press, 2001).

2. Walter Wink, *The Powers That Be* (New York: Doubleday, 1998), 204.

other theologian, Yoder provided substantive theological grounding for Christian pacifism from within the resources of catholic Christianity. Over a period of more than forty-five years, he truly brought "the Peace Church witness against violence into the mainstream of theological discussion."

Much of Yoder's influence occurred through one book, *The Politics of Jesus*, which was first published in 1972.[3] In 1976 Stephen Charles Mott called it "the most widely read political book in young evangelical circles in the United States."[4] By 1982, Edward LeRoy Long, Jr. claimed that *The Politics of Jesus* was one of the most discussed books in the field of Christian social ethics.[5] By 1994 the first edition of the book had sold approximately 75,500 copies in English alone. From the time the second edition came out, in 1994, through April of 1998 it had sold another 11,000 copies in English.[6] To date the book has been translated into ten languages.

Although Yoder authored many other works besides *The Politics of Jesus*, it is largely this book that sparked Yoder's extensive influence. *The Politics of Jesus* was popular with non-academics, as evidenced by the number of copies sold, but the book also received serious academic attention. In fact, it has helped to reshape the field of Christian social ethics in the last several years.

The Politics of Jesus

The Politics of Jesus was deliberately intended to be an ecumenical book. It was written to provide "a 'peace witness' which Mennonites could recognize as their own, yet which would be aimed at non-

3. John Howard Yoder, *The Politics of Jesus* (Grand Rapids: Eerdmans, 1972). All subsequent references, however, will be to the second edition: John Howard Yoder, *The Politics of Jesus,* 2d ed. (Grand Rapids: Eerdmans, 1994).

4. Stephen Charles Mott, " 'The Politics of Jesus' and Our Responsibilities," *The Reformed Journal* 26 (February 1976): 7.

5. Edward LeRoy Long, Jr., *A Survey of Recent Christian Ethics* (New York: Oxford University Press, 1982), 90.

6. Anne Salsich, of Wm. B. Eerdmans Publishing Co., to author, April 16, 1998.

Mennonite readers."[7] It was quite successful in achieving this aim. The original 1972 edition carried endorsing blurbs from Markus Barth, a respected Reformed New Testament scholar, and from John L. McKenzie, a respected Roman Catholic Old Testament scholar.

Yoder states his central purpose very clearly:

> I propose to read the Gospel narrative with the constantly present question, "Is there here a social ethic?" I shall, in other words, be testing the hypothesis that runs counter to the prevalent assumptions: the hypothesis that the ministry and the claims of Jesus are best understood as presenting to hearers and readers not the avoidance of political options, but one particular social-political-ethical option.[8]

Throughout the book Yoder seeks to present soundings from various strands of the New Testament that display the social-political-ethical option embodied and taught through the life and ministry of Jesus and the communities that took his name. He argues that these teachings are normative for contemporary Christian ethics.[9] I begin here with an examination of the biblical studies sections of the book, leaving aside for the moment chapters one and six, as they do not directly deal with biblical studies.

Three things should be kept in mind when reflecting on these matters from the vantage point of the early twenty-first century. First, Yoder begins with the Gospel of Luke as his focus, in part because in the world of early 1970s biblical scholarship, among the Gospels, Luke presented the greatest challenge to Yoder's thesis. This challenge stemmed from the

---

7. John Howard Yoder, "*The Politics of Jesus* Revisited," unpublished lecture presented as the "Culbert Rutenber Lecture," Eastern Baptist Theological Seminary, Philadelphia, November 4, 1997, in possession of author, p. 1.

8. Yoder, *The Politics of Jesus*, 11.

9. It should be kept in mind that Yoder commented in 1993: "[*The Politics of Jesus*] has quite rightly been found wanting by people who asked for a full contemporary social ethic; that was not intended" (John Howard Yoder, "The Burden and the Discipline of Evangelical Revisionism," in *Nonviolent America: History Through the Eyes of Peace*, ed. Louise Hawkley and James C. Juhnke [North Newton, KS: Bethel College, 1993], 34, fn. 43).

wide influence of the writings of Hans Conzelmann. According to Richard Cassidy, Conzelmann argued that Luke's portrayal of Jesus suggests that "Jesus himself was not in conflict with the existing political order during his ministry, [and therefore] his followers should follow a similar course and seek to act in harmony with the Roman order." Moreover, "in Conzelmann's view . . . Luke entered upon a full-blown political apologetic as an extension of his eschatology, and both elements are important components of his overall theology."[10] Thus, the Jesus portrayed by Luke was typically perceived to be either apolitical or politically innocuous. Yoder believed his case for a political Jesus could be made from any Gospel. But, reasoned Yoder, if he was to use but one Gospel, why not use the one that was deemed the least political. If the case could be made there, people would be more open to seeing it in the other Gospels as well.

Second, in 1972 few were writing about the social dimensions of the New Testament. They were certainly not drawing together the various strands of the New Testament as Yoder did. And, third, virtually no one at this time was connecting the disciplines of biblical studies and Christian ethics in a constructive work. As Bruce Birch and Larry Rasmussen said in 1976, *The Politics of Jesus* was "an outstanding modern work . . . [that was] a welcome and glowing exception to the omission and failure [of communication between those working in biblical studies and those in ethics]."[11]

Two chapters of *The Politics of Jesus* draw on the Gospel of Luke. In chapter two, "The Kingdom Coming," Yoder moves through many of the significant events and teachings of Luke, from the annunciation at the beginning to the crucifixion at the end of the Gospel. Having alerted the reader to a social-political-ethical message, Yoder is convinced the texts will mostly speak for themselves. Thus, with minimal commentary, he seeks to show that the burden of proof is on the shoulders of those who would want to claim there is no political message here rather than the other way around. Toward the end of his overview of Luke, Yoder provides a brief summary of portions of the

10. Richard J. Cassidy, *Jesus, Politics, and Society: A Study of Luke's Gospel* (Maryknoll, NY: Orbis Books, 1978), 8.

11. Bruce C. Birch and Larry L. Rasmussen, *Bible and Ethics in the Christian Life* (Minneapolis: Augsburg Publishing Co., 1976), 18.

Gospel he has not addressed directly earlier in the chapter. One gets a sense of his overall discussion when he concludes,

> Jesus was not just a moralist whose teachings had some political implications; he was not primarily a teacher of spirituality whose public ministry unfortunately was seen in a political light; he was not just a sacrificial lamb preparing for his immolation, or a God-Man whose divine status calls us to disregard his humanity. Jesus was, in his divinely mandated (i.e., promised, anointed, messianic) prophethood, priesthood, and kingship, the bearer of a new possibility of human, social, and therefore political relationships. His baptism is the inauguration and his cross is the culmination of that new regime in which his disciples are called to share.[12]

The third chapter of *The Politics of Jesus* explicates the functioning of the jubilee traditions of ancient Israel within the teachings and community of Jesus as portrayed in the Gospels. This chapter is an adaptation of a portion of a book by André Trocmé.[13] In the 1994 "epilogue" to this chapter Yoder seeks both to show that he never intended the "oversimple relevance" that some of his readers saw in the chapter and he seeks to show that subsequent research has affirmed the basic thrust of the chapter.[14] Yoder might have been better served had he done his own, original work, for many have found this chapter less than convincing.[15] However, the intention of the chapter is reflected in the work of others.[16] In fact, N. T. Wright, in his recent book, *Jesus and the Victory of God*, captures Yoder's intent in this chapter well:

---

12. Yoder, *The Politics of Jesus*, 52.

13. Yoder, *The Politics of Jesus*, 60, fn. 1.

14. Yoder, *The Politics of Jesus*, 71-75.

15. See, e.g., Richard B. Hays, *The Moral Vision of the New Testament* (San Francisco: HarperSanFrancisco, 1996), 246; Sharon H. Ringe, *Jesus, Liberation, and the Biblical Jubilee* (Philadelphia: Fortress Press, 1985), 103, endnote 1; and N. T. Wright, *Jesus and the Victory of God*, Christian Origins and the Question of God, Vol. 2 (Minneapolis: Fortress Press, 1996), 294.

16. See the recent thesis utilizing Yoder and Trocmé, Mark Hrecz Rich, "Jesus' Jubilee Movement as the Chief Exemplar of the Kingdom of God: A Paradigm for Christian Ethics" (Ph.D. dissertation, Garrett-Evangelical Theological Seminary and Northwestern University, 1997).

[A]lthough Jesus did not envisage that he would persuade Israel as a whole to keep the Jubilee year, *he expected his followers to live by the Jubilee principle among themselves*. He expected, and taught, that they should forgive one another not only "sins" but also debts. This may help to explain the remarkable practice within the early church whereby resources were pooled, in a fashion not unlike the Essene community of goods.[17]

The next two chapters, chapters four and five, provide a context both for the preceding discussions of Luke and, really, the whole New Testament. Chapter four offers one way to think about Old Testament conceptions of God and violence. The chapter provides a possible backdrop for thinking about the nonviolence that Yoder argues is implicitly or explicitly taught throughout the New Testament. This is only one of many Yoder writings in which he displays the Jewish roots of New Testament thought (sometimes as it relates to violence) and where he seeks to challenge any Marcionite reading of the New Testament.[18]

Chapter five provides a very brief discussion of some acts of nonviolent resistance on the part of Jews within the first century. This brief discussion is provided to inform the reader that "effective nonviolent resistance was not at all unknown in recent Jewish experience."[19]

17. N. T. Wright, *Jesus and the Victory of God,* 295, emphasis his.

18. For Yoder generally on the relationship between Judaism and Christianity see *The Jewish-Christian Schism Revisited*. Two of his other essays on the Old Testament and violence are "If Abraham Is Our Father," in *The Original Revolution,* 85-104, and "'To Your Tents, O Israel': The Legacy of Israel's Experience with Holy War," *Studies in Religion* 18 (Summer 1989): 345-62.

In 1998 John W. Miller attempted to connect Yoder's theology with Marcion; see John W. Miller, "In the Footsteps of Marcion: Notes Toward an Understanding of John Yoder's Theology," *The Conrad Grebel Review* 16 (Spring 1998): 82-91. Many of Yoder's writings would indirectly refute Miller's claim. Yoder's most direct critical comments on Marcion are John Howard Yoder, "Introduction," in Millard C. Lind, *Yahweh Is a Warrior: The Theology of Warfare in Ancient Israel* (Scottdale, PA: Herald Press, 1980), 17-19.

19. Yoder, *The Politics of Jesus,* 89. In 1988 Ched Myers offered several criticisms of Yoder's *The Politics of Jesus,* including the comment that "[Yoder's] historical example of nonviolent resistance comes not from Jesus but from Josephus" (Ched Myers,

Chapter seven, "The Disciple of Christ and the Way of Jesus," differs from most of the other chapters. The chapter does not draw from one particular book or one author, but rather draws from most of the literature of the New Testament. Yoder does this specifically to make a point: the concept of the imitation of Christ — or discipleship or participation or correspondence or whatever term one wants to use — is pervasive in the New Testament. As his numerous quotations in this chapter seek to demonstrate, there are a variety of ways in which imitation of Christ is expressed. Nonetheless, this *imitation* follows a pattern:

> There is thus but one realm in which the concept of imitation holds — but there it holds in every strand of the New Testament literature and all the more strikingly by virtue of the absence of parallels in other realms. This is at the point of the concrete social meaning of the cross in its relation to enmity and power. Servanthood replaces dominion, forgiveness absorbs hostility. Thus — and only thus — are we bound by New Testament thought to "be like Jesus."[20]

The next four chapters deal with Pauline literature.[21] In chapter eight, "Christ and Power," Yoder discusses the Pauline language regarding "the principalities and powers." Yoder is aware that "Paul's" language is foreign to our modern world. But, argues Yoder, if we can get inside the language, observing how it functions for "Paul" and his

---

Binding the Strong Man: A Political Reading of Mark's Story of Jesus [Maryknoll, NY: Orbis Books, 1988], 462). It should be said that Yoder did, in a footnote, in a 1993 essay, point positively to Walter Wink's book, *Jesus' Third Way* (Philadelphia: New Society Publishers, 1987), which does provide more of a "nonviolent resistance" portrait of Jesus than given in Yoder's book. (See John Howard Yoder, "The Burden and Discipline of Evangelical Revisionism," in *Nonviolent America*, ed. Louise Hawkley and James C. Juhnke [North Newton, KS: Bethel College, 1993], 33, fn. 40.)

20. Yoder, *The Politics of Jesus*, 131.

21. It is not important for the purposes of this book to make judgments about which epistles are genuine writings by Paul and which not. By "Pauline" I simply mean either Paul or those other New Testament witnesses standing within the tradition of Paul. But since the use of "Pauline" can be cumbersome, I will, like Yoder, usually use "Paul" to mean the same thing as "Pauline."

readers, we can see that, in fact, this biblical language connects with our own way of speaking about structures, institutions, and ideologies. Therefore "Paul's" language is very much at home in what we think of as the field of social ethics.[22] As Yoder says in his 1994 epilogue to this chapter:

> If it could be our task here to enter modern conversations about social ethics, the point to make would be that this Pauline vision is far more nuanced and helpful than much contemporary discussion about "the problem of power" in Christian social ethics. . . . The Pauline perspective is far more clear about the intrinsic complexities of institutional and psycho-dynamic structures, such that basically good creaturely structures can nonetheless be oppressive, and basically selfish decisions can sometimes nonetheless have less evil outcomes. Neither guilt about losing personal purity, nor pragmatism about doing lesser evils to achieve greater goods, is then at the heart of "the problem of power" for "Paul," as they are for our contemporaries. The challenge to which the proclamation of Christ's rule over the rebellious world speaks a word of grace is not a problem within the self but a split within the cosmos.[23]

The church by its very existence proclaims Christ's rule. Through the church's redeemed social relations it testifies to the Lordship of Christ over this split cosmos. It manifests the firstfruits of true liberation from the dominion of the powers. "The church does not attack the powers; this Christ has done. The church concentrates upon not being

22. There are many places throughout the book where Yoder carefully nuances his point through the use of footnotes. Here he makes it clear that he is not being reductionistic in the way he uses Paul's language: "The positive emphasis of this present discussion on the relevance of the apostle's powers language to the institutions and ideologies of our times need not imply the rejection of all the more literal meanings which the language of the demonic and of bondage can also have. . . . That these two areas or two kinds of definitions of 'the demonic' are quite distinct from one another would probably have been much less evident to Paul than it seems to be to some moderns" (Yoder, *The Politics of Jesus*, 139-140, fn. 4). For a substantial footnote to these points see John Howard Yoder, Elkhart, Indiana, to John R. W. Stott, London, December 7, 1978.

23. Yoder, *The Politics of Jesus*, 161.

seduced by them. By existing the church demonstrates that their rebellion has been vanquished."[24]

Yoder's next chapter is entitled "Revolutionary Subordination." Here Yoder seeks to explicate what are often referred to as "the household codes" or *Haustafeln* in the New Testament (esp. Col. 3–4 and Eph. 5–6). As Yoder knows, this is a very complicated subject, fraught with interpretive land mines. With this realization, Yoder seeks to interpret the teachings on subordination within these passages both as being more radical than often perceived and as consistent with earlier portraits he has given of the life and teachings of Jesus. He does this by briefly naming the contexts, especially that of the Stoic teachings, within which these New Testament household codes are given. By displaying the contexts Yoder hopes to prevent an anachronistic reading of these texts. He argues that we cannot begin to understand the message of these texts unless we first realize the distance between their world and ours.

Yoder names a number of ways in which these New Testament teachings differ from somewhat similar Stoic teachings. They differ enough, in fact, that Yoder refers to the differences in the New Testament teachings as revolutionary innovations. The first revolutionary innovation Yoder names is that the "*subordinate* person in the social order is *addressed as a moral agent*."[25] That is to say, they are given "responsibility for viewing their status in society not as a simple meaningless decree of fate but as their own meaningful witness and ministry, as an issue about which they can make a moral choice."[26] The second innovation is that the subordinate Christians to whom some of these writings are addressed heard the gospel as one that offered them liberty, making them fully a part of the people of God, thereby challenging their subordinate status. "Only if something in the life or the preaching of the church had given them the idea that their subordinate status had been challenged or changed would there be any temptation to the kind of unruliness to which these texts are addressed."[27] The

24. Yoder, *The Politics of Jesus*, 150.
25. Yoder, *The Politics of Jesus*, 171, emphasis his.
26. Yoder, *The Politics of Jesus*, 172.
27. Yoder, *The Politics of Jesus*, 173.

third revolutionary innovation to which Yoder points is that these New Testament household codes call for a reciprocal subordination on the part of the superordinate persons in these relationships:

> For a first-century husband to love *(agapan)* his wife or for a first-century father to avoid angering his child, or for a first-century master to deal with his servant in the awareness that they are both slaves to a higher master, is to make a more concrete and more sweeping difference in the way that husband or father or master behaves than the other imperative of subordination would have made practically in the behavior of the wife or child or servant.[28]

It is not important whether all of the details of Yoder's argument are convincing. It is important, however, to note Yoder's central purpose: "I was especially concerned to test — and as it turns out, to negate — the widespread view that the ethic of the apostles betrays that of Jesus."[29] "I am not," writes Yoder, "affirming a specific biblical ethical content for modern questions; I am rather observing that where the New Testament did offer specific guidance for its own time, that guidance confirmed and applied the messianic ethic of Jesus."[30]

Some have judged Yoder as less than successful in his attempts to show the continuity between Jesus and the teaching of "revolutionary subordination." According to Richard Hays, who is mostly positive about Yoder's work, "[Yoder's] proposal that the *Haustafeln* should be read as a call for 'revolutionary subordination' leans toward apologetic wishful thinking."[31] Yoder himself, in his 1994 "Epilogue," admits that "no other single chapter provoked as much angry objection as this one when *The Politics of Jesus* first appeared."[32] However, to be fair to Yoder, there are respected Scripture scholars who continue to make arguments similar to Yoder's.[33] And Jean Bethke Elshtain's expo-

---

28. Yoder, *The Politics of Jesus*, 178.

29. Yoder, *The Politics of Jesus*, 187.

30. Yoder, *The Politics of Jesus*, 187.

31. Hays, *The Moral Vision of the New Testament*, 246.

32. Yoder, *The Politics of Jesus*, 188.

33. Ben Witherington, a prolific New Testament scholar, takes an approach that is very similar to Yoder's. See Ben Witherington III, *Women and the Genesis of Christian-*

sition of the "moral revolution" initiated by the early church, would, in its general outlines, be consistent with what Yoder offers in this chapter.[34]

Chapter ten focuses on Romans 13 and the authority of the state, another topic about which there is considerable controversy, though perhaps not as much as the previous one. However, in this case, Yoder's interpretation has stood up well over the period of more than twenty-five years.[35] Richard Hays states that "[Yoder's] exegetical treatment of the passage . . . is detailed, subtle, and persuasive."[36] Furthermore, Hays comments that Yoder appropriately insists that Romans 12 and 13 be read together, which is illustrative of Yoder's "careful attention to the context and shape of the texts he treats."[37] Ben Witherington summarizes Yoder's challenge to the dominant view well:

> [T]his text says absolutely nothing about Christians' participating in government activities such as war or police actions. Christians were not themselves rulers during this period, and the Roman government was not a participatory democracy. Even soldiers were not enlisted through a lottery of citizens. In short, this text is about pagan rulers and their right to govern and bear the sword for some purposes. The text says nothing about a Christian's right, much less duty, to bear arms.[38]

---

ity (Cambridge: Cambridge University Press, 1990), 147-62, and Witherington, *The Paul Quest* (Downers Grove, IL: InterVarsity Press, 1998), 184-203.

34. For a portrayal of Elshtain's thought consistent with what is said here see Mark Thiessen Nation, "Feminism, Political Philosophy, and the Narrative Ethics of Jean Bethke Elshtain," in *Virtues and Practices in the Christian Tradition: Christian Ethics After MacIntyre*, ed. Nancey Murphy, Brad J. Kallenberg, and Mark Thiessen Nation (Harrisburg, PA: Trinity Press International, 1997), 289-305. In Elshtain's work see Jean Bethke Elshtain, *Public Man, Private Woman*, 2d ed. (Princeton, NJ: Princeton University Press, 1993), 55-64.

35. Mark D. Nanos, for example, in his well-received book on Romans, employs Yoder extensively in his chapter on Romans 13: Mark D. Nanos, *The Mystery of Romans* (Minneapolis: Fortress Press, 1996), 289-336. Also Ben Witherington, in his recent survey of Paul studies, recommends Yoder's chapter as a general discussion of Romans 13: Witherington, *The Paul Quest*, 178, fn. 6.

36. Richard B. Hays, *The Moral Vision of the New Testament*, 246.

37. Hays, *The Moral Vision of the New Testament*, 245.

38. Witherington, *The Paul Quest*, 178.

This is Yoder's case put negatively or defensively against the traditional view. But Yoder's central intention is to make his more difficult positive case:

> Romans 12–13 and Matthew 5–7 are not in contradiction or in tension. They *both* instruct Christians to be nonresistant in all their relationships, including the social. They *both* call on the disciples of Jesus to renounce participation in the interplay of egoisms which this world calls "vengeance" or "justice." They *both* call Christians to respect and be subject to the historical process in which the sword continues to be wielded and to bring about a kind of order under fire, but not to perceive in the wielding of the sword their own reconciling ministry.[39]

Though chapter ten of *The Politics of Jesus* can still stand up as solid interpretive work, it is perhaps chapter eleven as much as any that Richard Hays has in mind when he says that "at numerous points, [Yoder's] readings reflect an astute — indeed, almost prescient — grasp of important developments in the field of New Testament studies."[40] This chapter is entitled "Justification by Grace Through Faith." Within the context of late 1960s and early 1970s scholarship as well as popular Christian views, Yoder was again swimming against the stream. Drawing on various scholars, Yoder argued against the notion that the lynchpin of Paul's thought is that as individuals each of us cannot earn the salvation of God but rather is accepted by God by grace through faith. Yoder is careful neither to be reductionistic nor dismissive. He does not deny there might be some value in the concerns expressed by this notion. He simply argues that it is not central to Paul's writings. More central, argues Yoder, is the concern for social reconciliation between various conflictual groups, especially Jews and Gentiles. Thus, once again, even this dimension of Paul's thought is seen to serve the overall thrust of Yoder's book: the reconciling, nonviolent, politics of Jesus is reinterpreted by Paul within a new context. Yoder was "astute" and even "prescient" at this point, as Hays ob-

---

39. Yoder, *The Politics of Jesus*, 210, emphasis his.
40. Hays, *The Moral Vision of the New Testament*, 245.

served, for, though the field of Pauline studies is quite complicated, the view Yoder articulated is now probably dominant within the New Testament guild. This was not the case in 1972.[41]

As Yoder noted in 1994, looking back on the 1972 edition of the book, the last chapter is different from the others. It contains no references to scholarly literature. Yoder does draw from the book of Revelation at several points, but he is grounding his closing reflections more broadly in biblical apocalyptic thought. Again he is seeking to demonstrate that biblical apocalyptic thought can be seen as but another way more fully to articulate and understand the basic message of the Jesus portrayed in the Gospels. Yoder closed this chapter in 1994 as follows:

> When read carefully, none of the biblical apocalypses, from Ezekiel through Daniel to Mark 13 and John of Patmos, is about either pie in the sky or the Russians in Mesopotamia. They are about how the crucified Jesus is a more adequate key to understanding what God is about in the real world of empires and armies and markets than is the ruler in Rome, with all his supporting military, commercial, and sacerdotal networks.
>
> Then to follow Jesus does not mean renouncing effectiveness. It does not mean sacrificing concern for liberation within the social process in favor of delayed gratification in heaven, or abandoning efficacy in favor of purity. It means that in Jesus we have a clue to which kinds of causation, which kinds of community-building, which kinds of conflict management, go with the grain of the cosmos, of which we know, as Caesar does not, that Jesus is both the Word (the inner logic of things) and the Lord ("sitting at the right hand"). It is not that we begin with a mechanistic universe and then look for cracks and chinks where a little creative freedom might sneak in (for which we would then give God credit): it is that

41. The literature on this subject is vast. See the bibliography in James D. G. Dunn, *The Theology of Paul the Apostle* (Edinburgh: T&T Clark, 1998), 334-35. (See Dunn's discussion, pp. 334-89.) Also see James D. G. Dunn and Alan M. Suggate, *The Justice of God* (Grand Rapids: Eerdmans, 1993), 1-42; N. T. Wright, *What Saint Paul Really Said* (Oxford: Lion Publishing, 1997); and James D. G. Dunn, "A New Perspective on Paul," in Dunn, *Jesus, Paul and the Law* (Louisville: Westminster/John Knox, 1990), 183-214.

we confess the deterministic world to be enclosed within, smaller than, the sovereignty of the God of the Resurrection and Ascension. "He's got the whole world in his hands" is a post-ascension testimony. The difference it makes for political behavior is more than merely poetic or motivational.[42]

While some of his exegetical forays are more successful than others, as a whole, Yoder, a self-described amateur in the biblical scholarship guild, did a brilliant job.[43] As Richard Hays puts it:

> Yoder's interpretation of these texts is informed by detailed and sophisticated interaction with historical-critical scholarship. . . . For instance, his attention to the social context and meaning of the texts, his placement of Jesus within the political matrix of first-century Palestine, his emphasis on the apocalyptic horizons of the "powers" language in the Pauline traditions, his interpretation of Galatians as an argument about the social form of the church (rather than the problem of individual guilt), his sympathetic understanding of the Torah as a vehicle of grace within Jewish tradition — all these elements of his presentation reflect careful harvesting of the best available insights of biblical scholarship in the early 1970s.[44]

Furthermore, I believe it would be possible to demonstrate, much more substantially than Yoder himself did in his 1994 "epilogues," that a considerable amount of recent biblical scholarship has strengthened

---

42. Yoder, *The Politics of Jesus*, 246-47.

43. I have referred here to Yoder as an amateur in the field of biblical studies. It was the way he referred to himself. And it is true in the sense that his doctoral thesis was in another field and most of his teaching was in other fields. However, it is also true that he took twenty-seven graduate level courses on the Bible, in addition to studying Greek and Hebrew.

44. Hays, *The Moral Vision of the New Testament*, 245. This is a much more accurate assessment of Yoder's use of the Bible than that of Philip LeMasters. See Philip LeMasters, *The Import of Eschatology in John Howard Yoder's Critique of Constantinianism* (San Francisco: Mellen Research University Press, 1992), 36-67. See also Mark Nation, review of *The Import of Eschatology in John Howard Yoder's Critique of Constantinianism,* by Philip LeMasters, *Encounter* 55 (1994): 218-19.

and deepened Yoder's overall readings of these biblical texts.[45] However, we sorely misunderstand Yoder's book and its intent if we conclude that because, for example, his reading of "the household codes" is less than persuasive for many, his overall purpose is defeated. Rather, in order to accomplish his purpose, Yoder only needed to establish that there is within the New Testament what might be termed a social ethic, an ethic that is centrally rooted in and defined by the cross of Jesus the Messiah.

Yoder was well aware that it is insufficient merely to provide readings of representative biblical texts. Even assuming he convincingly demonstrated the significance of these texts for social ethics, Yoder knew only half the task was accomplished. He wanted to make his case in "such a way that the ethicists across the way have had to notice it."[46] In order to do this within *The Politics of Jesus*, Yoder wrote two chapters discussing the various arguments for setting Jesus aside when it comes to social ethics.

Yoder begins the book not with a biblical study, but rather with a chapter in which he enumerates six reasons "mainstream" ethics has given (or assumed) for setting aside the normativity of Jesus for social ethics. Briefly, these are: (1) that Jesus taught an "interim" ethic, valid only for a short time; (2) Jesus was a simple, rural figure and, thus, taught a simple face-to-face ethic; (3) Jesus and his followers lived in a world over which they had no control; (4) Jesus' message was ahistorical by definition; (5) Jesus was a radical monotheist who pointed away from finite to infinite values; and, (6) the work of Jesus was the atonement, which means his life and death have no bearing on ethics.[47] In anticipa-

---

45. I would list here the books that affirm the basic thrust of Yoder's work, but the list would be too long. Authors that come to mind on the Gospels are Ched Myers, Frederick Dale Bruner, Richard Cassidy, Michael H. Crosby, David Rensberger, and Wes Howard-Brook. On Jesus generally Marcus Borg, N. T. Wright, R. David Kaylor, and Gerhard Lohfink. On the Pauline materials (including commentaries) see Walter Wink, N. T. Wright, James D. G. Dunn, Frank Matera, Richard Hays, Krister Stendahl, and Sam K. Williams. And on the apocalyptic material see Christopher Rowland, Elisabeth Schüssler Fiorenza, G. B. Caird, and Daniel Smith-Christopher.

46. Yoder, *The Politics of Jesus*, 2.

47. In the 1994 edition he names five more reasons for setting aside Jesus (Yoder, *The Politics of Jesus*, 15-19).

tion of later chapters, Yoder offers a brief discussion in this first chapter of the claim that even if Jesus might be perceived to be socially radical, such social radicalism is certainly changed by Paul.

About midway through the book, in chapter six, Yoder offers another similar discussion as a transition from the chapters focused on the Gospels to the chapters dealing with the rest of the New Testament. In chapter six he does two things. First, he provides a schematic overview of the rest of the book, stating that the social significance of the cross, already seen in Luke, is also present in Paul and throughout the rest of the New Testament: "Only at one point, only on one subject — but then consistently, universally — is Jesus our example: in his cross."[48] Second, Yoder names five more ways many within the Christian tradition have attempted to set aside the teachings that he is about to articulate in the rest of the book. This listing is a set of false choices: the choice between (1) the Jesus of history and the Christ of faith; (2) the prophet and the institution; (3) the catastrophic kingdom and the inner kingdom; (4) the political and the sectarian; (5) the individual and the social.[49]

Yoder is a brilliant polemicist. When in chapters one and six he names these numerous ways in which the normativity of Jesus for social ethics is set aside, he does not, point by point, rebut these claims. To do that adequately would require another, different sort of book. Rather, he challenges them in three ways. First, by naming the often unconscious and unstated reasons for setting Jesus aside, Yoder hopes that someone who is willing to be convinced can see, throughout the rest of the book, that the reasons for setting Jesus aside do not stand up next to the claims of the writings of the New Testament. The New Testament texts themselves serve to refute the claims. Second, the contrast between the refuted claims and the message of the New Testament helps illumine the social-political-ethical dimensions of the New Testament. And third, Yoder briefly but pointedly connects the implied claims of *The Politics of Jesus* with central Christian doctrines: revelation, the trinity, and the incarnation.[50] For instance, as he says in chap-

48. Yoder, *The Politics of Jesus*, 95.
49. Yoder, *The Politics of Jesus*, 103-9.
50. Yoder, *The Politics of Jesus*, 99.

ter one: "What becomes of the meaning of incarnation if Jesus is not normative man? If he is a man but not normative, is this not the ancient ebionitic heresy? If he be somehow authoritative but not in his humanness, is this not a new gnosticism?"[51] Thus to counter the claims of *The Politics of Jesus*, Yoder asserts, is to challenge orthodox teachings of the church.

Through the above combination of approaches Yoder was able to make a profound impact with *The Politics of Jesus*. He carefully harvested the best of biblical scholarship offered in the early 1970s. He responded to ways of setting aside claims contained in the texts of the New Testament by naming the typical reasons for setting Jesus aside in social ethics and then by debating these reasons subtly throughout the text and the footnotes. And finally, by arguing briefly but pointedly that the claims made in the New Testament and his book are rooted in central doctrines embedded in the Christian tradition, he made the powerful point that to set them aside is therefore to deny central doctrinal claims. It was through this combination of approaches that Yoder hoped he would be heard within the Christian ethics guild.

He has indeed been heard. In 1981 James Gustafson stated in his major work, *Theology and Ethics*, that "the radical Christian ethics of Yoder mark a substantive position for which there are sound defenses; to opt against it is to opt against some fundamental claims of traditional Christianity."[52] In 1982 Edward LeRoy Long, Jr., speaking of the world of academic Christian social ethics, stated that "*The Politics of Jesus* has become as frequently cited in discussions of social ethics as Paul Ramsey's *Deeds and Rules* in the discussion of norm and context."[53] Six years later, in 1988, Yoder, whose doctoral thesis was in historical theology, became president of the Society of Christian Ethics. In 1994 Philip Wogaman, in his book on the history of Christian ethics, named John Howard Yoder as one of seven "Formative Christian Moral Thinkers" in his section on "Christian Ethics in the Twentieth

51. Yoder, *The Politics of Jesus*, 10.

52. James M. Gustafson, *Ethics from a Theocentric Perspective*, Vol. 1, *Theology and Ethics* (Chicago: The University of Chicago Press, 1981), 76.

53. Edward LeRoy Long, Jr., *A Survey of Recent Christian Ethics*, 90.

Century."[54] And Richard Mouw, president of Fuller Theological Seminary, was hardly alone when, in 1994, he confessed, "My own wrestlings with [*The Politics of Jesus*] . . . have forever shaped the ways in which I think about questions of violence and the normativity of Jesus' redemptive ministry for the patterns of our social-political witness."[55]

Nevertheless, the temptation to dismiss the claims made by *The Politics of Jesus* is great. It is only those who have bothered to read the book closely and, even more, those who have gone on to read some of Yoder's other central writings, who can begin to understand why Stanley Hauerwas would say, "I am convinced that when Christians look back on this century of theology in America *The Politics of Jesus* will be seen as a new beginning."[56]

The Politics of John Howard Yoder

Why is it that someone might see *The Politics of Jesus* as a "new beginning" in theological ethics? The reasons are at once simple and profound. Hauerwas has named them in his essay where he refers to *The Politics of Jesus* as a classic. "Prior to Yoder," notes Hauerwas, "the subject of Christian ethics in America was always America."[57] Yoder makes two fundamental moves that offer an alternative. First he makes the life of the church vital for Christian ethics. According to Hauerwas, "Yoder's account of nonviolence requires theologians to acknowledge that their work makes no sense abstracted from the church."[58] Second, adds Hauerwas, "[i]n a manner that can only be described as catholic, Yoder returns Jesus to the center of Christian

54. J. Philip Wogaman, *Christian Ethics: A Historical Introduction* (Louisville: Westminster/John Knox, 1993), 233-35. The section is entitled "John Howard Yoder and the 'Politics of Jesus.'"

55. Richard J. Mouw, "Foreword," in Yoder, *The Royal Priesthood*, ed. Michael G. Cartwright (Grand Rapids: Eerdmans, 1994), vii.

56. Stanley Hauerwas, "When the Politics of Jesus Makes a Difference," *Christian Century*, October 13, 1993, 982.

57. Hauerwas, "When the Politics of Jesus Makes a Difference," 982.

58. Hauerwas, "When the Politics of Jesus Makes a Difference," 982.

ethics by freeing us from the political presuppositions sponsored by liberal social orders."[59]

To put it differently, one of the difficulties with the way in which Yoder is often read is that readers begin by acknowledging that Yoder is a pacifist. As a result, they read Yoder through the particular grid that the term "pacifist" conjures for them. This grid can lead to a serious misreading. As Hauerwas puts it, "to say one is pacifist gives the impression that pacifism is a position that is intelligible apart from the theological convictions that form it. But that is exactly what I wish to deny. Christians are non-violent not because certain implications may follow from their beliefs, but because the very shape of their beliefs form them to be non-violent."[60] For Yoder, as for Hauerwas, what is called "pacifism" is important not in itself but, rather, because it is integrally related to central Christian convictions. Yoder is not intending to call attention to some concept labeled "pacifism." Rather, he wants to enable us to hear dimensions of the gospel of Jesus that our pre-conceived notions prevent us from hearing.

One can see this in a brief essay describing his own pacifism as "the pacifism of the messianic community," where Yoder puts it this way:

> To say that this is the pacifism of the *messianic* community is to affirm its dependence upon the confession that Jesus is Christ and that Jesus Christ is Lord. To say that Jesus is the Messiah is to say that in him are fulfilled the expectations of God's people regarding the coming one in whom God's will would perfectly be done. Therefore, in the person and work of Jesus, in his teachings and his passion, this kind of pacifism finds its rootage, and in his resurrection it finds its enablement. . . .
>
> When we speak of the pacifism of the messianic *community*, we move the focus of ethical concern from the individual to the community experiencing in its shared life a foretaste of God's king-

---

59. Hauerwas, "When the Politics of Jesus Makes a Difference," 984.

60. Stanley Hauerwas, "Pacifism: Some Philosophical Considerations," *Faith and Philosophy* 2 (April 1985): 100.

dom. Persons may severally and separately ask themselves about right and wrong in their concern for their own integrity. That is fine as far as it goes. The messianic community's experience, however, is different in that it is a life for a society. It is communal in that it is lived by a covenanting group of men and women who instruct one another, forgive one another, bear one another's burdens, and reinforce one another's witness. . . . The existence of a human community dedicated in common to a new and publicly scandalous enemy-loving way of life is itself a new social datum. A heroic individual can crystallize a widespread awareness of need or widespread admiration. However, only a continuing community dedicated to a deviant value system can change the world.[61]

The above paragraphs offer a programmatic summary of what Yoder articulates in *The Politics of Jesus*. They were written originally at about the same time as *Politics*.[62] They name the two central theological concerns of Yoder's vast body of work: Jesus and the church.

Two things should be said about Yoder's approach to Christology. First, what he wrote constructively about Jesus the Christ is rooted in the biblical texts and connected with orthodox claims. There is nothing arcane, or peculiarly Mennonite, in his claims about Jesus. Indeed, Yoder claimed his view of Jesus in *Politics* was "more radically Nicene and Chalcedonian than other views."[63] Anyone who is interested in how Yoder would interact at greater depth with the biblical texts, classic creedal statements, and traditional systematic issues can examine his posthumously published *Preface to Theology: Christology and Theological Method*. This book was originally a set of lectures from a course he taught approximately twelve times between the early 1960s and the early 1980s.[64] But, more to the point, Yoder would have

61. John Howard Yoder, *Nevertheless: Varieties of Religious Pacifism*, revised and expanded edition (Scottdale, PA: Herald Press, 1992), 133-36, emphasis his.

62. See John Howard Yoder, *Nevertheless: Varieties of Religious Pacifism* (Scottdale, PA: Herald Press, 1971), 123-28.

63. John Howard Yoder, *The Priestly Kingdom: Social Ethics as Gospel* (Notre Dame: University of Notre Dame Press, 1984), 8-9.

64. John Howard Yoder, *Preface to Theology*, ed. Stanley Hauerwas and Alex Sider (Grand Rapids: Brazos Press, 2002). See also Alain Epp Weaver, "John Howard

been reasonably happy with the portraits of Jesus developed by a number of contemporary New Testament scholars.[65] Because, second, what needs to be understood is that few have argued that the portrayal of Jesus presented by Yoder was tendentious.[66] At the time he called more attention to the political dimensions of Jesus and the gospel than some others, but that that has become a relatively common trend in recent writings.[67] It is not, for the most part, the portrayal of Jesus given by Yoder that is the problem; rather, the normativity of Jesus for Christian social ethics is at issue.[68]

As with his views about Jesus, so Yoder's concept of the church is not arcane or unheard of either. In fact, again, it could easily be argued that his views are consonant with biblical teachings and with what would often be said about the church within orthodox doctrine.[69] However, Yoder has emphases that set his views apart from many others.[70]

Yoder and the Creeds: The Pattern of a Missionary Christology," *The Mennonite Quarterly Review* 74 (July 2000): 423-39; and Carter, *The Politics of the Cross*, 91-136.

65. Many of the recent studies of Jesus would serve to affirm and supplement the portraits of Jesus provided by Yoder. But I would think especially of the recent, extensive writings by N. T. Wright. See Wright, *The New Testament and the People of God*, and Wright, *Jesus and the Victory of God*.

66. N. T. Wright, in a 1996 book, wrote that *The Politics of Jesus* was "still a fascinating read more than twenty years later" (Wright, *The Original Jesus: The Life and Vision of a Revolutionary* [Oxford: Lion Publishing, 1996], 157).

67. This is true for many studies, including more "theological" works, such as the ones mentioned by N. T. Wright. An interesting, recent book is Scot McKnight, *A New Vision for Israel: The Teachings of Jesus in National Context* (Grand Rapids: Wm. B. Eerdmans, 1999). However, I do not know what McKnight means when, in his one footnote about Yoder, he writes, "At times J. H. Yoder strolls away from Jesus' nationalistic orientation toward too pietistic an outlook" (McKnight, *A New Vision*, 9, fn. 23).

68. This issue has already been touched upon in my discussion of *The Politics of Jesus*. However, it is dealt with more fully in Chapter Three, above, in discussing Yoder's essay, " 'But We Do See Jesus,' " from his book, *The Priestly Kingdom*.

69. Some studies that would offer views mostly complementary to Yoder's would include Gerhard Lohfink, *Jesus and Community* (Philadelphia: Fortress Press); Gerhard Lohfink, *Does God Need the Church?* (Collegeville, MN: The Liturgical Press, 1999); N. T. Wright, *The New Testament and the People of God*, 339-476; Robert Banks, *Paul's Idea of Community*, rev. ed. (Peabody, MA: Hendrickson Publishers, 1994); James Wm. McClendon, Jr., *Systematic Theology*, Vol. 2: *Doctrine* (Nashville: Abingdon Press, 1994), 325-452.

70. On Yoder's view of the church see Craig A. Carter, *The Politics of the Cross*,

Chief among these particular views is that Yoder held to a "believers' church" model.[71] The believers' church model holds that the church should be comprised of voluntary believers rather than be coterminous with general populations (as in parish systems). Contrary to some popular misconceptions, this view does not require perfection. In fact, it depends upon the recognized need for ongoing renewal or reformation. Still, believing does matter:

> [T]here is the ethical import of the insistence that church membership must be voluntary. This means that we cannot do ethics for everyone. The obedience of faith does not make sense apart from the context of faith. The substantial guidance, the experiential and social resources of conversion and membership are presupposed for it to be possible to speak of one's behavior as expressive of faith and obedience. Cross-bearing in the hope of resurrection, enemy-love as reflection of God's love, forgiving as one has been forgiven, behavior change describable as expressing regeneration or sanctification, do not make sense in the context of unbelief.[72]

A community of Christian believers provides, as Yoder said above, "a social datum," which is to say, they are a witness to the Christ who is their Lord. When functioning in a healthy way, a believers' church also provides a context for moral casuistry. Together its members discern what it means to live in the world in a way that is faithful to the God they worship and serve. Yoder put this provocatively in the introduction to his book, *The Priestly Kingdom*:

> The church precedes the world epistemologically. We know more fully from Jesus Christ and in the context of the confessed faith

---

esp. chapter four; and for a fuller discussion see Jeremy Thomson, "The Conflict-Resolving Church: Community and Authority in the Prophetic Ecclesiology of John Howard Yoder" (Ph.D. dissertation, King's College, University of London, 2000).

71. The book on this tradition that John Yoder referred to as a "classic" and around which he structured a course at the University of Notre Dame is Donald Durnbaugh, *The Believers' Church*, 2d ed. (Scottdale, PA: Herald Press, 1985).

72. Yoder, "Radical Reformation Ethics in Ecumenical Perspective," in *The Priestly Kingdom*, 110.

than we know in other ways. . . . The church precedes the world as well axiologically, in that the lordship of Christ is the center which must guide critical value choices, so that we may be called to subordinate or even to reject those values which contradict Jesus.[73]

Once these moves are made, it becomes meaningful to distinguish, as the New Testament does, between church and world. In many passages in the New Testament " 'the world,' " says Yoder, "is neither all nature nor all humanity nor all 'culture'; it is *structured unbelief*, rebellion taking with it a fragment of what should have been the Order of the Kingdom."[74] "Over against this 'world' the church is visible; identified by baptism, discipline, morality, and martyrdom."[75] Stanley Hauerwas agrees:

> It is from the church that Christian ethics draws its ethical substance and it is to the church that Christian ethical reflection is first addressed. Christian ethics is not written for everyone, but for those people who have been formed by the God of Abraham, Isaac, Jacob, and Jesus. . . . Therefore the first social task of the church — the people capable of remembering and telling the story of God we find in Jesus — is to be the church and thus help the world understand itself as world. That world, to be sure, is God's world. . . . For the church to be the church, therefore, is not anti-world, but rather an attempt to show what the world is meant to be as God's good creation.[76]

Again, it is important to emphasize that Yoder's central theological views are not particularly strange. Or, to put it differently, he was happy with various ways of approaching either Christology or ecclesiology. What he had little patience with were views and embodiments of views that rendered Jesus apolitical and irrelevant for our moral lives within

73. Yoder, "Introduction," in *The Priestly Kingdom*, 11.

74. Yoder, "The Otherness of the Church," in *The Royal Priesthood*, 62, emphasis his.

75. Yoder, "The Otherness of the Church," in *The Royal Priesthood*, 56.

76. Stanley Hauerwas, *The Peaceable Kingdom* (Notre Dame: University of Notre Dame Press, 1983), 97, 100.

the context of the church and the world God loves. One of Yoder's doctoral students, David Weiss, summarizes *The Politics of Jesus* this way:

> His thesis, simply put but thoroughly and eloquently argued, was that Christian ethics begins not by finding ways to set aside the radicalness of Jesus' ethic, but rather by finding ways in community to take those ethics seriously. In other words, the church is to bear the message of the gospel by *being* that message. If the gospel of God's reconciling love had political implications for the community of followers called into being by Jesus — if it decisively shaped the pattern of their life together — then it will continue to have such implications among those of us who link ourselves to that heritage and that calling.[77]

It has not been easy for many to hear Yoder's message. This is not because he did not communicate effectively, but rather because there has been in many traditions a strong bias against the message he sought to bring. Richard Mouw was quite candid about this in his foreword to Yoder's 1994 book, *The Royal Priesthood:*

> The views contained in this book are not detestable. That may seem like a strange way to invite readers into a serious engagement with a stimulating volume of essays, but it is for me an important concession to make. As a Dutch Calvinist, my earliest assessment of Anabaptist thought and practice was formed by the stern judgment of my sixteenth-century spiritual ancestors, as they expressed it in the Belgic Confession: "We detest the Anabaptists and other seditious people, and in general all those who reject the higher powers and magistrates and would subvert justice, introduce community of goods, and confound that decency and good order which God has established among men."
>
> I have come to realize that this verdict is seriously mistaken. And no one has influenced me more in coming to this realization than John Howard Yoder.[78]

---

77. David Weiss, "In Memory of John Yoder: Scholar, Professor, Friend," *The Observer* (student paper at the University of Notre Dame), January 27, 1998, 9.

78. Richard J. Mouw, "Foreword," in *The Royal Priesthood*, vii.

At least one of the reasons Richard Mouw changed his mind was because he and Yoder engaged in sustained debate.[79] Yoder was well aware that many in mainstream ethics could not give a serious hearing to his views because, even if they did not "detest" his views, they were given multiple reasons for dismissing them.

Thus he took it upon himself to engage in full frontal debate with several of the major alternative approaches to his views, especially when those approaches entailed the dismissal of the relevance of Jesus for social ethics and, thereby, the dismissal of pacifism. In 1953 Yoder wrote a critical essay in response to Reinhold Niebuhr's critique of pacifism.[80] In 1957, during his last few months in Basel, Yoder wrote a lengthy essay on Barth, which Barth read. That essay became a book on *Karl Barth and the Problem of War.*[81] (Larry Rasmussen adapted

79. In 1976 Mouw offered two critiques of Yoder's writings. Richard J. Mouw, *Politics and the Biblical Drama* (Grand Rapids: Eerdmans, 1976), 98-116, and Richard J. Mouw, "*The Politics of Jesus* and Political Theory," unpublished paper presented at the Mennonite Peace Theology Colloquium on *The Politics of Jesus*, Kansas City, MO, October 7-9, 1976, in possession of author. Yoder responded to all the papers at this colloquium. In 1979, at the American Academy of Religion annual meeting, Yoder read a paper on "Reformed vs. Anabaptist Strategies: The Limits of a Typology," excerpts of which were published in *TSF News and Reviews* (February 1980): 4-7. Five years later there was the following exchange: John Howard Yoder, "Reformed Versus Anabaptist Social Strategies: An Inadequate Typology," *Theological Students Fellowship Bulletin* 17 (May-June 1985): 2-7, and Richard J. Mouw, "Abandoning the Typology: A Reformed Assist," *Theological Students Fellowship Bulletin* 17 (May-June): 7-10. Then in 1989 they collaborated: John Howard Yoder and Richard J. Mouw, "Evangelical Ethics and the Anabaptist-Reformed Dialogue," *The Journal of Religious Ethics* 17 (Fall 1989): 121-37. In the early nineties Mouw added more pieces to the discussion: Mouw, "Jesus and Political Authority," in *Perspectives on Christology*, ed. Marguerite Shuster and Richard Muller (Grand Rapids: Zondervan, 1991), 253-67, and Mouw, "Creational Politics: Some Calvinist Amendments," *Christian Scholar's Review* 23, no. 2 (1993): 181-93. And, finally, Mouw, as indicated above, wrote a foreword to Yoder's 1994 *The Royal Priesthood.*

80. Published as John Howard Yoder, "Reinhold Niebuhr and Christian Pacifism," *The Mennonite Quarterly Review* 29 (April 1955): 101-17.

81. James Gustafson refers to the original essay as "a remarkable critical study of Barth on the point of pacifism." James M. Gustafson, *Christ and the Moral Life* (Chicago: University of Chicago Press, 1968), 208, fn. 38. Yoder's book on Barth is now included in John Howard Yoder, *Karl Barth and the Problem of War and Other Essays on Barth,* ed. Mark Thiessen Nation (Eugene, OR: Cascade Press, 2003).

Yoder's critique of Barth's use of the concept of *Grenzfall* to provide his own critique of Bonhoeffer's use of the same concept in his book, *Dietrich Bonhoeffer: Reality and Resistance*.)[82] In the summer of 1958 Yoder wrote a lecture responding to H. Richard Niebuhr's book, *Christ and Culture*. Almost forty years later, and after numerous expansions, this relatively well-known essay (for something distributed in photocopied form) had grown to a seventy-two-page critique. It was finally published as "How H. Richard Niebuhr Reasoned: A Critique of *Christ and Culture*."[83]

Yoder engaged in debates with Richard Mouw about the Reformed tradition in a way that overlaps with but is somewhat different from Yoder's critique of H. Richard Niebuhr. These debates all related to the positions of specific people, but Yoder knew that these positions were bigger than the people attached to them. Furthermore, he knew that there were other challenges that warranted responses. Thus he continued to write responses or counter-challenges.[84] Without going into the details of these critiques, I want to underscore a point: Yoder's substantial engagements with the major challenges and alternatives to his Christian pacifism are significant. They indicate he was quite conversant with these positions and therefore knew the alternatives to his own position and took them into account as he formulated his own views. Yoder's own mature views, therefore, represent a most serious engagement with alternative perspectives.

Because Yoder argued that the church is different from the world

---

82. Nashville: Abingdon Press, 1972.

83. John Howard Yoder, "How H. Richard Niebuhr Reasoned: A Critique of *Christ and Culture*," in Glen H. Stassen, D. M. Yeager, and John Howard Yoder, *Authentic Transformation: A New Vision of Christ and Culture* (Nashville: Abingdon Press, 1996), 31-89, 271-84.

84. For instance: John Howard Yoder, "What Would You Do If . . . ? An Exercise in Situation Ethics," *The Journal of Religious Ethics* 2 (Fall 1974): 81-105; John Howard Yoder, "Moral Theology Miscellany #21: Testing the Case for 'Nature' as Alternative, Corrective, or Complement to Grounding in the Particular," unpublished paper, 1994, in possession of author; and John Howard Yoder, " 'Patience' as Method in Moral Reasoning: Is an Ethic of Discipleship 'Absolute'?" in *The Wisdom of the Cross: Essays in Honor of John Howard Yoder*, ed. Stanley Hauerwas, Chris K. Huebner, Harry Huebner, and Mark Thiessen Nation (Grand Rapids: Eerdmans, 1999), 24-42.

and because he argued that Christian ethics are for Christians, he was often accused of encouraging disregard for and disengagement from the world. Nothing could be further from the truth. A careful reading of *The Politics of Jesus* shows that Yoder thought it inappropriate for the church to be separate from the world:

> There are thus about the community of disciples those sociological traits most characteristic of those who set about to change society: a visible structured fellowship . . . a clearly defined life-style distinct from that of the crowd. . . . The distinctness is not a cultic or ritual separation, but rather a nonconformed quality of ('secular') involvement in the life of the world.[85]

It is true that Yoder did not deal at any length with theoretical matters related to the discipline that is usually called social ethics within *The Politics of Jesus*. That is not what the book was intended to do.[86] However, he did reflect on these matters elsewhere.

Yoder's first published book, aside from his doctoral thesis, was *The Christian Witness to the State*.[87] In it he gave the outlines of a theological rationale for why Christians, including the Mennonite pacifists to whom the book was largely addressed at the time, should care about and engage the activities of the state in which they reside. Yoder's central theological warrant for concern for the world is that Christ is Lord over the world. God loves the whole world; thus we, as those covenanted to be faithful to the God revealed in Jesus, can do no less. The love of God embodied in Jesus Christ and exemplified through the cross of Christ is the central norm for behavior. Thus the church, as a body of people who have said yes to God's offer of salvation, realize that their first social ethical task is to embody the gospel,

---

85. Yoder, *The Politics of Jesus*, 39.

86. "[*The Politics of Jesus*] has quite rightly been found wanting by people who asked for a full contemporary social ethic; that was not intended." John Howard Yoder, "The Burden and Discipline of Evangelical Revisionism," in Hawkley and Juhnke, eds., *Nonviolent America*, ed. Louise (North Newton, KS: Bethel College, 1993), 34, fn. 43.

87. John Howard Yoder, *The Christian Witness to the State* (Newton, KS: Faith and Life Press, 1964). This book was reprinted, with slightly updated footnotes, in 1977. After again being out of print for a few years, it was published by Wipf & Stock, 1997.

to live lives of faithful discipleship, loving neighbors and enemies and serving the poor.

What about the world beyond the church? God has the same standard for all, a standard revealed in Christ. However, God in divine patience accepts the world's "no" to the offer of salvation. The church is to do likewise. Thus, God (and we) accept that the world will not live by the standards of discipleship. However, neither God nor we abandon the world because of its refusal of the offer of salvation. Rather, we still love and serve the world — even when the world persecutes us or becomes our enemy. And we, with means that are consistent with our identity as Christians and with the claims of the gospel, seek to speak to the powers that be in ways that move the world's actions closer to those that would be faithful to the gospel. We do not project a utopia toward which we expect the world to move. Rather, one issue at a time, we call upon the government or powerful agencies to be more just, less oppressive and violent. There are always particular injustices, particular wars, particular acts of abuse to which we can direct our critique and engage our energies.

In 1977 Yoder called such a stance in the world "Gospel Realism."[88] In all three of the synoptic Gospels Jesus is reported to have said, "The rulers of the nations lord it over them. Those who exercise authority let themselves be called benefactors." In both of these statements, says Yoder, there is wisdom that sheds light on the perennial political situation. Of course the abuses that accompany such rulership will vary from situation to situation, but rulers do "lord it over" their subjects. Furthermore, rulers from Belgrade to London to Washington "let themselves be called benefactors." They make claims about themselves and their beneficence — claims they fail to live up to. Thereby, the leaders and those who support them almost always provide us, contextually, with our language of critique.

In the 1950s, when Yoder wrote most of the material that came to be included in his small book *The Christian Witness to the State*, he was drawing from a variety of contemporary writers, including espe-

88. John Howard Yoder, "The Christian Case for Democracy," in *The Priestly Kingdom*, 155ff. (This essay was originally published in 1977.)

cially Herbert Butterfield, J. H. Oldham, and his teacher, Oscar Cullmann. He also made a reference to Karl Barth's use of analogy between the community of faith and the civil community.[89] In the last two decades of his life, Yoder would make much greater use of this aspect of Barth's approach, summarized by Barth as follows:

> There can be no doubt however . . . that the decisive contribution which the Christian community can make to the upbuilding and work and maintenance of the civil consists in the witness which it has to give to it and to all human societies in the form of the order of its own upbuilding and constitution. It cannot give in the world a direct portrayal of Jesus Christ, who is also the world's Lord and Saviour, or of the peace and freedom and joy of the kingdom of God. For it is itself only a human society moving like all others to His manifestation. But in the form in which it exists among them it can and must be to the world of men around it a reminder of the law of the kingdom of God already set up on earth in Jesus Christ, and a promise of its future manifestation. *De facto,* whether they realise it or not, it can and should show them that there is already on earth an order which is based on that great alteration of the human situation and directed towards its manifestation.[90]

Yoder uses Barth's concept of the Christian community as analogy for the civil community as a basis for his argument that "access to social ethics should consist in the exemplarity of the church as foretaste/model/herald of the kingdom."[91] This also fits well with Yoder's disavowal of what he refers to as "methodologism." Yoder refuses to marry his approach to social ethics to any one method or mode of ethics (deontological, utilitarian, virtue, etc.). He believes that a range of methods for dealing with ethics have their usefulness and limitations. What is paramount to him is that "the life of the community is prior to all possible methodological distillations."[92]

89. Yoder, *The Christian Witness to the State,* 18, fn. 2.
90. Karl Barth, *Church Dogmatics: The Doctrine of Reconciliation,* trans. G. W. Bromiley, IV/2 (Edinburgh: T&T Clark, 1958), 721.
91. Yoder, "Why Ecclesiology Is Social Ethics," in *The Royal Priesthood,* 106.
92. John Howard Yoder, "Walk and Word," in *Theology Without Foundations,*

I have not addressed Yoder's writings on current events and how his views applied to these. Although, as a theologian, he engaged the larger social world in various ways, including by addressing specific current issues, he addressed none as frequently as violence.[93] He wrote numerous essays, for instance, on the nuclear arms race.[94] And he wrote a number of articles, and half a book, against capital punishment.[95] These writings and those I have discussed in this section help us to understand the politics of John Howard Yoder.

Nevertheless

Yoder spent much of his time advocating his own type of pacifism. He did this especially through deflecting criticisms and by challenging the proposed alternatives. But he also spent considerable time seeking to help non-pacifists (as well as pacifists) appreciate the variety of religious (mostly Christian) pacifist approaches. The most obvious instance of Yoder's efforts on this front is found in his book *Nevertheless*. It was originally published in 1971 and was significantly expanded in 1992. In the expanded edition Yoder discusses twenty-nine different types of religious pacifism.

There are at least four ways to understand *Nevertheless*. On the

---

ed. Stanley Hauerwas, Nancey Murphy, and Mark Nation (Nashville: Abingdon Press, 1994), 82.

93. A perusal of my bibliographies of Yoder's writings will easily substantiate both of these claims.

94. See, for example, John Howard Yoder, "Nuclear Arms in Christian Pacifist Perspective," in *War No More? Options in Nuclear Ethics,* ed. James W. Walters (Philadelphia: Fortress Press, 1989), 17-31 and John Howard Yoder, "The Believers Church and the Arms Race," in John Howard Yoder, *For the Nations: Essays Public and Evangelical* (Grand Rapids: Eerdmans, 1997), 148-61 (originally presented as a lecture in 1978).

95. His first published article on this subject was 1959. He contributed articles to various Mennonite publications, to the Evangelical magazine *Christianity Today,* and to an often-reprinted anthology of essays on *The Death Penalty in America,* ed. Hugo Adam Bedau (New York: Oxford University Press, 1982, and other editions). His most substantial statement was John Howard Yoder, "Against the Death Penalty" and "Response," in H. Wayne House and John Howard Yoder, *Capital Punishment, Two Views* (Waco, TX: Word Books, 1991), 105-79, 197-208.

simplest level, it is a brief description of twenty-nine different types of pacifism. On another level, it provides a powerful argument for pacifism from twenty-nine different angles. Again Yoder displays his extraordinary talents as a polemicist. For although the book does describe twenty-nine different types of pacifism, it does much more than that. With twenty-one of the types, which includes his own type, Yoder first discusses the central axiom and strengths of the type and then points out its weaknesses. He concludes his discussion of each of these twenty-one types of pacifism by explaining how some more militant approach has similar weaknesses. But, in each case he points out that the type of pacifism under discussion is "nevertheless" superior to its more militant counterpart.

Eight other types of pacifism are discussed more briefly. They do not follow the pattern of the other twenty-one chapters. However, they display Yoder's careful attention to the multiple perspectives available.

Indirectly, the book provides a cumulative argument against violence. It carefully offers an argument for Yoder's own version of pacifism. It does this in two ways. First, and most obviously, Yoder's own position is stated as the one that "is closer than the others to the idiom of the Bible and to the core affirmations of the Christian faith."[96] But, more subtly and more powerfully, Yoder's position benefits from the fact that he, its adherent, can appreciate and affirm all that is best in the other twenty-eight types, even though he has named what he (and many of his readers) would see as the weaknesses of these alternative types.

Nevertheless was an ecumenical act on Yoder's part. He dedicated the book "[t]o the many friends, some still militant and some triumphant, whose different styles of pacifist commitment have judged and enriched my own."[97] He also wrote extensively, elsewhere, on how nonviolence could be effective as an instrument of social change.[98] He did it to display the relative practical effectiveness of

96. Yoder, *Nevertheless*, 137.

97. Yoder, *Nevertheless*, 5.

98. Aside from the relevant chapters in *Nevertheless*, see "Quakerism in Early America: 'The Holy Experiment,'" and "The Lessons of Nonviolent Experience," in *Christian Attitudes to War, Peace, and Revolution* (Goshen, IN: Co-op Bookstore, 1983),

nonviolent strategies. He did it as an apologetic strategy for those nonpacifists who were convinced that violence is always the more effective strategy. He also did it because his own view "includes the practical concern of the programmatic views . . . without placing its hope there."[99]

"As Close Kin": Yoder on Just War

John Yoder, as a pacifist, also engaged in respectful debate with those standing within the "just war" tradition. In the early 1960s Yoder first addressed himself to the issue of the just war tradition publicly. During the Vietnam War, during the American nuclear arms race with the Soviet Union, and during the 1991 Gulf War he published articles employing just war language to evaluate each of these actions.[100] For over twenty years he taught a course at a Mennonite seminary on the history of Christian attitudes toward war, peace, and revolution. This course included substantial material on the just war tradition. For more than a decade he taught a doctoral seminar on ethical method that focused on the just war tradition at the University of Notre Dame. And for a decade he coordinated a multi-disciplinary course on "The Legality and the Morality of War," primarily intended for military officers in training.[101]

But why would a pacifist have any interest in advocating a seri-

---

259-95, 487-507, and "The 'Power' of 'Nonviolence,'" a publication of the Joan B. Kroc Institute for International Peace Studies, University of Notre Dame, 1994. For the views of someone deeply influenced by Yoder see Glen H. Stassen, *Just Peacemaking: Transforming Initiatives for Justice and Peace* (Louisville: Westminster/John Knox Press, 1992).

99. Yoder, *Nevertheless*, 137.

100. John Howard Yoder, "Vietnam: A Just War?" *His* (April 1968): 1-3; "Can Modern Armed Conflict Be Conducted Justly?" unpublished paper presented as part of a Wilson Center panel discussion, October 5, 1979, in possession of author; "Just War Tradition: Is It Credible?" *The Christian Century*, March 13, 1991, 295-98.

101. See Yoder's comments on the latter in John Howard Yoder, "Military Realities and Teaching the Laws of War," in *Theology, Politics and Peace*, ed. Theodore Runyon (Maryknoll, NY: Orbis Books, 1989), 176-80.

ous use of the just war tradition? Yoder provides three reasons in his book on the just war tradition, *When War Is Unjust*.[102] The first reason is related to his general views about ecumenism. Since he has stated his own convictions clearly elsewhere, when he engages the just war tradition he does so respectfully. He is "on general ecumenical or dialogical grounds" and therefore accepts the integrity of his interlocutors. He accepts their claim that they intend to "limit the violence for which they will soberly accept responsibility to the minimum evil necessary to establish a just peace."[103] Second, he genuinely cares about violence, injustice, and the loss of life. As such, "it is still the case that every time just war proponents exercise effective discipline and limit the harm they do, fewer lives and other values will be destroyed than if they had not applied that restraint."[104]

And, third, he wants to challenge three popularly held but false notions about the just war tradition. One is that the just war tradition is the majority view. Yoder argues that normally something much less noble, something resulting in much less restraint, is the morally operative perspective when people (including church members) approach the war-making of their own nation. A second notion is that pacifism and the just war tradition are diametrically opposed. Yoder disagrees. Most of the time pacifists and just war adherents should reach similar, if not identical, conclusions about particular wars.[105] It is the other majority views that both of these positions should stand against. And, finally, Yoder challenged the notion that just war adherents can hold political offices, whereas pacifists cannot. If just war adherents do not realize the inherent difficulty in holding certain political offices it is only because they have not pondered seriously enough the potential implications of the just war tradition.[106]

---

102. John Howard Yoder, *When War Is Unjust: Being Honest in Just-War Thinking*, 2d ed. (Maryknoll, NY: Orbis Books, 1996), 5-7.

103. Yoder, *When War Is Unjust*, 5.

104. Yoder, *When War Is Unjust*, 5.

105. One testimony to Yoder's influence in this regard is a recent book of essays written by pacifists and non-pacifists: Glen Stassen, ed., *Just Peacemaking: Ten Practices for Abolishing War* (Cleveland: Pilgrim Press, 1998).

106. For one instance of a U.S. Senator who was influenced by Yoder who did

The above concerns fuel Yoder's engagement with the just war tradition. They lead him to explicate its history, distinguish it from other ways of approaching violence, name its shortcomings and more substantial uses, and generally provide a fuller accounting of the tradition so that when it is used in the future it might have more teeth.[107]

Has Yoder gotten a hearing within the just war camp? Drew Christiansen, a longtime Catholic colleague of Yoder's at the University of Notre Dame and a just war adherent, certainly thinks so: "[Yoder's] influence on my generation of Catholic moral theologians has been profound. His witness as a theologian in the peace-church tradition is highly esteemed, and the seriousness with which he has carried out his role as friendly critic of just war thinking has without doubt contributed to sharpening its formulation and application in the American Catholic setting."[108] Similarly, Charles Lutz, a Lutheran just war proponent, admits, "John Howard Yoder . . . speaks to us as close kin. He is not setting out to denigrate or demolish the just war ethic. Rather, he is calling us to integrity within the framework of our own claims. He asks us, for the sake of the world, to demonstrate the credibility of our ethic, to put it to the test, to be honest about where it leads us."[109]

Conclusion: For the Sake of the World

Yoder was undoubtedly pleased with the above tribute from Charles Lutz. He would have been pleased by the tribute from Jim Wallis, edi-

---

recognize the struggles, see Mark Hatfield, *Between a Rock and a Hard Place* (Waco, TX: Word Books, 1976).

107. I think Long overstates the similarities somewhat. Nonetheless, to see the overlap between the approaches of Paul Ramsey, one of the major just-war theorists of the twentieth century, and John Yoder see D. Stephen Long, "Ramseyian Just War and Yoderian Pacifism: Where Is the Disagreement?" *Studies in Christian Ethics* 4 (1991): 58-72.

108. Drew Christiansen, S.J., "A Roman Catholic Response," in John Howard Yoder, *When War Is Unjust: Being Honest in Just-War Thinking*, rev. ed. (Maryknoll, NY: Orbis Books, 1996), 102.

109. Charles P. Lutz, "Foreword to the First Edition," in *When War Is Unjust*, xix-xx. (Reprinted from the first edition of the book.)

tor of the influential *Sojourners* magazine, when he wrote, "John Yoder inspired a whole generation of Christians to follow the way of Jesus into social action and peacemaking."[110] An obituary of John Yoder in *The New York Times* on January 7, 1998, ends with an incident involving a friend of Yoder:

> Glen Stassen, a professor of ethics at Fuller Theological Seminary in Pasadena, Calif., recalled congratulating Mr. Yoder after scholarly papers presented at a session at the Society of Christian Ethics showed the deep imprint of Mr. Yoder's thought. "Your influence must really be spreading," Mr. Stassen recalled saying. "Not mine," Mr. Yoder replied. "Jesus's."[111]

Some who have read or heard this last comment see it as arrogant, as Yoder confusing his own influence with the influence of Jesus. Perhaps. But on one level Yoder saw all of his academic work as converging in a single task: to help us hear the voice of Jesus as he calls us to discipleship. As Yoder put it at the end of one of his few somewhat philosophical essays, "The real issue is not whether Jesus can make sense in a world far from Galilee, but whether — when he meets us in our world, as he does in fact — we want to follow him. We don't have to, as they didn't then."[112] Richard Hays summarizes the politics of John Howard Yoder well:

> Yoder's hermeneutic represents an impressive challenge to the church to remain faithful to its calling of discipleship, modeling its

---

110. Jim Wallis, "Lives of Peacemaking," *Sojourners* 27 (March-April 1998): 8. Ched Myers also said that *The Politics of Jesus* "influenced a whole generation of radical Christians in the U.S.A." (Ched Myers, *Binding the Strong Man*, 460).

These references are to Yoder's influence in the U.S. Yoder's influence extended to many other countries as well. For one testimony to his influence in South Africa see John de Gruchy, "Radical Peace-making: The Challenge of Some Anabaptists," in *Theology and Violence: The South African Debate*, ed. Charles Villa-Vicencio (Grand Rapids: Eerdmans, 1987), 173-85. For a testimony to Yoder's influence in Latin America see Ernest W. Ranley, C.P.P.S., "Christian Spirituality of Nonviolence as Reconciliation," in *The Wisdom of the Cross*, 115-27.

111. Peter Steinfels, "John H. Yoder, Theologian at Notre Dame, Is Dead at 70," *The New York Times*, January 7, 1998.

112. John Howard Yoder, "'But We Do See Jesus,'" in *The Priestly Kingdom*, 62.

life after the example of the Jesus whom it confesses as Lord. As Christian theologians increasingly are forced to come to grips with the demise of Christendom and to acknowledge their minority status in a pluralistic world, Yoder's vision offers a compelling account of how the New Testament might reshape the life of the church.[113]

113. Hays, *The Moral Vision of the New Testament*, 253.

Chapter 5   "Social Irresponsibility"
or the Offense of the Cross?
Yoder on Christian Responsibility

Christian responsibility, perhaps a surprising subject for an entire chapter, is a topic Yoder addressed a number of times, beginning early in his career. Examining and responding to recent criticisms of Yoder's early statements allows us to situate his statements within their historical contexts and within their fuller theological context in his writings. One cannot begin to understand Yoder's writings about topics like responsibility without realizing the ecumenical contexts within which he was writing, and without an awareness of the way in which he approached intellectual engagement with Christians from other traditions.

We will examine Yoder's views about Christian responsibility in several steps. First, we will look briefly at the current Mennonite situation as it relates to Yoder's legacy regarding peacemaking, noting how perceptions of his legacy may relate to assumptions about his views of responsibility and social engagement. Second, we will examine some of Yoder's most relevant writings from the early to mid-1950s that focus on the subject of responsibility within his ecumenical context in Europe. Third, we will look at Yoder's most direct writing on the subject of responsibility, namely, *The Christian Witness to the State,* an essay that has its roots in the 1950s, though it was not published until 1964.[1]

---

1. John Howard Yoder, *The Christian Witness to the State* (Newton, KS: Faith and Life Press, 1964). The third printing, 1977, includes updated footnotes to the 1964

Fourth, we will look briefly at the continuities, discontinuities and evolution of Yoder's thought beyond *The Christian Witness to the State*. And, finally, I will apply Yoder's thought to one of the most recent developments in Mennonite (and ecumenical) peace work, namely, the study of conflicts and how to transform them.

Mennonites on Peacemaking at the End of the Twentieth Century

The 1990s saw a spate of writings by Mennonites who were reflecting on their tradition of peacemaking.[2] This was not the first time such stock-taking had taken place. Although there was an unusual amount of such self-reflection within this decade, two trends within these writings are worth noting here. First, there was an emphasis on activism.

---

edition. This is the edition to which all references will be made. This latter edition has been reprinted by Herald Press in 2002.

2. These include: *The Mennonite Encyclopedia*, Vol. 5, ed. Cornelius J. Dyck and Dennis D. Martin (Scottdale, PA: Herald Press, 1990), s.v. "Church-State Relations," "Nonresistance," "Peace," "Peace Activism," "Reconciliation," and "Sociopolitical Activism"; Beulah Stauffer Hostetler, "Nonresistance and Social Responsibility: Mennonite and Mainline Peace Emphasis, ca. 1950 to 1985," *The Mennonite Quarterly Review* 64 (January 1990): 49-73; John Richard Burkholder and Barbara Nelson Gingerich, eds., *Mennonite Peace Theology: A Panorama of Types* (Akron, PA: Mennonite Central Committee Peace Office, 1991); John Richard Burkholder, "Mennonite Peace Theology: Reconnaissance and Exploration," *The Conrad Grebel Review* 10 (Fall 1992): 259-76; Leo Driedger, "The Peace Panorama: Struggle for the Mennonite Soul," *The Conrad Grebel Review* 10 (Fall 1992): 289-317; Duane Friesen, "Review of *Mennonite Peace Theology: A Panorama of Types*," *The Conrad Grebel Review* 10 (Fall 1992): 341-49; Howard John Loewen, "Mennonite Peace Theology: Continuing the Reconnaissance and Exploration," *The Conrad Grebel Review* 10 (Fall 1992): 277-87; Tom Yoder Neufeld, "Varieties of Contemporary Mennonite Peace Witness: From Passivism to Pacifism, From Nonresistance to Resistance," *The Conrad Grebel Review* 10 (Fall 1992): 243-57; Ervin R. Stutzman, "From Nonresistance to Peace and Justice: Mennonite Rhetoric, 1951-1991" (Ph.D. dissertation, Temple University, 1993); Leo Driedger and Donald B. Kraybill, *Mennonite Peacemaking: From Quietism to Activism* (Scottdale, PA: Herald Press, 1994); Keith Graber Miller, *Wise as Serpents, Innocent as Doves: American Mennonites Engage Washington* (Knoxville: The University of Tennessee Press, 1996); Perry Bush, *Two Kingdoms, Two Loyalties: Mennonite Pacifism in Modern America* (Baltimore: The Johns Hopkins University Press, 1998).

Peacemaking is to be a transformative activity, transformative especially in relation to the larger social world. Writers with an historical consciousness acknowledged that this emphasis signals a recent shift within Mennonite thinking and practice.

Second, somewhat surprisingly, John Howard Yoder did not play a particularly central role in these writings. I was surprised to discover this not only because Yoder is the author of *The Politics of Jesus,* one of the most influential books on Christian peacemaking in the second half of the twentieth century, but also because he has written more on peacemaking than any other Mennonite — ever.[3] I wonder if these two things I have named — an emphasis on activism and a minimal emphasis on the role of Yoder — are not related.

I was taken aback when I read the following in a 1993 essay by Mennonite scholar Rodney Sawatsky: "For one thing, particularly under the tutelage of John Howard Yoder, 'irresponsibility' became a virtue. In *Concern* No. 1 (1954) Yoder declared irresponsibility to be 'an implication of the Mennonite view of the church' of which Mennonites ought not to be ashamed."[4] This was a troubling discovery be-

---

3. John Howard Yoder, *The Politics of Jesus,* 2d ed. (Grand Rapids: Eerdmans, 1994). For a listing of Yoder's many other writings see Mark Thiessen Nation, *A Comprehensive Bibliography of the Writings of John Howard Yoder* (Goshen, IN: Mennonite Historical Society, 1997), and Mark Thiessen Nation, "Supplement to 'A Comprehensive Bibliography of the Writings of John Howard Yoder,'" in *The Wisdom of the Cross: Essays in Honor of John Howard Yoder,* ed. Stanley Hauerwas, Chris K. Huebner, Harry J. Huebner, and Mark Thiessen Nation (Grand Rapids: Eerdmans, 1999), 472-91.

4. Rodney J. Sawatsky, "J. Lawrence Burkholder: Sectarian Realist," in *The Limits of Perfection: A Conversation with J. Lawrence Burkholder,* 2d ed., ed. Rodney J. Sawatsky and Scott Holland (Waterloo, Ontario: Institute of Anabaptist and Mennonite Studies; Kitchener, Ontario: Pandora Press, 1996), 66. Sawatsky's reflections on Yoder echo J. Lawrence Burkholder's comments in the same book: "By contrast, for Mennonites 'social irresponsibility' was not unthinkable. Indeed, 'social irresponsibility' was declared in *Concern* No. 1 (1954) by John Howard Yoder as an implication of the Mennonite view of the church. . . . 'We should not be ashamed of our 'irresponsibility',' Yoder declared." J. Lawrence Burkholder, "The Limits of Perfection: Autobiographical Reflections," in *The Limits of Perfection,* 31. Given the polemical style of Sawatsky and Burkholder and the lifting of Yoder's quotes out of context, a reader might be excused for not realizing that the words "social irresponsibility" are intended as a scare quote in Yoder's original essay.

cause it was written as recently as 1993, and because the author referred to only one forty-six-year-old essay.[5]

Sawatsky's comments are unusual in their candor. However, I sometimes wonder if sentiments somewhat like Sawatsky's are not more common than the infrequency of such direct comments would suggest. I wonder if more than a few contemporary Mennonites imagine that John Yoder encouraged or encourages social irresponsibility.[6] Or, at least minimally, that he did not encourage active engagement of the larger social world. To determine whether or not that is the case will require more than a few quotes from only one of Yoder's earliest essays.

We need to focus specifically on Yoder's writings about responsibility as they relate to peacemaking for three reasons. First, the ways in which Yoder shaped his language about responsibility appreciably reflected his understandings of the ecumenical conversations as he entered them (especially in his writings of the 1950s). Therefore, today's readers should know that his comments about responsibility are addressed to these ecumenical conversations, albeit in terms that Yoder thought were faithful to an Anabaptist/Mennonite perspective. Second, some may not be aware of Yoder's many later writings that qualify or nuance his more polemical statements. For a full understanding, readers need to be familiar with Yoder's various ways of speaking about responsibility. And, third, some may not be aware of the larger theological framework within which Yoder's specific, direct comments are embedded. This is not to say that some would not dismiss Yoder

5. This was somewhat surprising because, just over ten years earlier, Sawatsky had published an essay that showed a broader awareness of Yoder's writings. See Rodney J. Sawatsky, "John Howard Yoder," in *Nonviolence Central to Christian Spirituality: Perspectives from Scripture to the Present,* ed. Joseph T. Culliton (Lewiston, NY: Edwin Mellen Press, 1982), 239-69.

6. Gordon Kaufman was already suggesting this in 1958 in an essay published in *Concern,* reprinted as Gordon D. Kaufman, "Nonresistance and Responsibility," in *Nonresistance and Responsibility, and Other Mennonite Essays* (Newton, KS: Faith and Life Press, 1979), 63-81. See also Scott Holland, "The Problems and Prospects of a 'Sectarian Ethic': A Critique of the Hauerwas Reading of the Jesus Story," *The Conrad Grebel Review* 10 (Spring 1992): 162; and Rodney J. Sawatsky, "The Quest for a Mennonite Hermeneutic," *The Conrad Grebel Review* 11 (Winter 1993): 16.

even if they were aware of this fuller presentation. But they should still know the whole story.

Before I begin an examination of some of the relevant writings of Yoder, it might be well to attend to two cautions, one from Yoder and the other from an interpreter of Yoder. The cautions are important at the outset of this discussion because many, including some Mennonites, continue to read Yoder through a sectarian grid that distorts the reading of Yoder.[7] First, Yoder cautions against a sloppy understanding of the words *responsibility* and *irresponsibility:*

> The strong emotional appeal of the word *responsibility* and the extreme pejorative ring of the epithet *irresponsible* have avoided the need for precise definition of the virtue in question. Rigorous analysis of the function the term discharges in the ethical argument of the Niebuhrian school would probably confirm that there is no more exact meaning than that *responsibility signifies a commitment to consider the survival, the interest, or the power of one's own nation, state, or class as taking priority over the survival, interest or power of other persons or groups, of all of humanity, of the "enemy," or of the church.* If it does *not* mean this, the concept of responsibility cannot prove what it is being used to prove in current debate. If it *does* mean this, it is clearly questionable at two points: (a) the priority of state over church; (b) the priority of oneself and one's own group over others or the "enemy," as the locus of value and decision. This basic egotism of the responsibility argument is clothed as a form of altruism.[8]

The other caution comes from a recent and incisive essay by Arne Rasmusson:

> In an odd way, twentieth-century Mennonite theology, through its newly recovered relationship with mainstream Protestant theology, let itself be forced into a distorted and unfruitful contrast between

---

7. For a very helpful discussion of how to move beyond the "sectarian" categorizing, see Philip D. Kenneson, *Beyond Sectarianism: Re-Imagining Church and World* (Harrisburg, PA: Trinity Press International, 1999).

8. Yoder, *The Christian Witness to the State*, 36, fn. 1, emphasis his.

faithfulness and responsibility that partly concealed some of its richest resources and put it into a no-win situation in relation to precisely this mainstream theology.[9]

According to Rasmusson, Mennonites have allowed mainstream Protestant theology (and thereby Ernst Troeltsch) to tell Mennonites both who they are and what social responsibility means. Thus, many Mennonites have allowed themselves to accept the dichotomy that says they can be faithful but inactive in the larger society or responsibly active and thereby participate not only in the ambiguities but even the sin of that social involvement — but they cannot be both faithful and responsible.[10]

These are the two cautions, warnings that should remind Mennonites (and others) that too often the language of responsibility is slippery and that the categories for thinking about social ethics are hardly neutral. In fact, they often force us into dichotomies that we can, and should, avoid. But how do we even begin to avoid the pitfalls of the typical social ethics categorization? Arne Rasmusson offers some important clues:

> To be able, at least to some extent, to think outside a given hegemonic cultural imagination you need an alternative community that tells another narrative, forms other practices, extols other virtues. Thinking is a bodily and social activity. . . . This shows the importance of ecclesiology, and an ecclesiology of a specific sort.
>
> In order to state such an ecclesiology convincingly, we have to overcome the individualistic and disembodied Protestant reading

9. Arne Rasmusson, "Historicizing the Historicist: Ernst Troeltsch and Recent Mennonite Theology," in *The Wisdom of the Cross*, 213.

10. Rasmusson uses Guy Hershberger and J. Lawrence Burkholder as his examples. Both accept the dichotomy, says Rasmusson; they simply take different positions in relation to the accepted dichotomy (Rasmusson, "Historicizing the Historicist," 213-20). For other construals of Guy Hershberger, J. Lawrence Burkholder, and the Mennonite social ethics context within which Yoder wrote, see John Richard Burkholder, *Mennonite Social Ethics: Continuity and Change* (Akron, PA: Mennonite Central Committee Peace Section, 1977); and Theron F. Schlabach, "Guy F. Hershberger Vis-à-Vis J. Lawrence Burkholder: Irreconcilable Approaches to Christian Ethics?" *The Mennonite Quarterly Review* 73 (January 1999): 9-34.

of Jesus, the church, and salvation that Troeltsch represents. . . . What is needed is a recovery of the bodily and social nature of human life and therefore of salvation.

One of the most powerful resources for doing this has been developed in precisely the same Mennonite context that created the theologies we have been considering. I am, of course, thinking of the remarkable work of John Howard Yoder. One way of reading him is an attempt constructively to liberate American Christian theology (and not just Mennonite theology) from the distorting categories of Troeltsch and the brothers Niebuhr.[11]

With these cautions and clues in mind we can proceed with the exposition of Yoder's thought on responsibility.

Yoder, Responsibility, and Ecumenism in the 1950s

Why is it that in an essay entitled "The Anabaptist Dissent," published in June 1954, John Yoder focused as much as he did on the topic of responsibility? There are at least two reasons, both of which are signaled in the first paragraph of the essay. Yoder says he is writing within "the context of current ecumenical discussions of the church's responsibility in society."[12] As discussed earlier in Chapter One, Yoder was involved in ecumenical discussions almost from the moment he arrived in Europe in 1949 until his departure in 1957. He was soon well aware that in Europe "the responsible society" was one of the key defining terms within ecumenical discussions of social ethics.[13] Yoder knew that if he was to address social ethics he had to respond to the dominant understandings of "the responsible society." Furthermore, about

11. Rasmusson, "Historicizing the Historicist," 235-36.

12. John Howard Yoder, "The Anabaptist Dissent: The Logic of the Place of the Disciple in Society," *Concern* 1 (June 1954): 45.

13. Ans van der Bent, a chronicler of WCC social thought, says, "The concept of the Responsible Society, proposed at the WCC's first assembly in Amsterdam in 1948, proved to be the key phrase in nearly two decades of ecumenical social thinking." Ans van der Bent, *Commitment to God's World: A Concise Survey of Ecumenical Social Thought* (Geneva: WCC Publications, 1995), 58.

the same time Yoder wrote this essay he published an essay on "Reinhold Niebuhr and Christian Pacifism."[14] Consequently, it is not surprising that he also says, in the first paragraph of "The Anabaptist Dissent," that he will address the issue of responsibility "with special reference to the problems involving the use of violence."[15] For what Mennonite, with a commitment to nonviolence and fresh from doing research on the writings of Reinhold Niebuhr, would not sense the need to respond to the claim of Niebuhr that "a responsible relationship to the political order . . . makes an unqualified disavowal of violence impossible"?[16]

Was the claim true that Mennonites, who, like Yoder, are committed to nonviolence, are irresponsible in relation to the political order? According to J. Lawrence Burkholder and Rodney Sawatsky the answer Yoder gave is "yes." They claim that Yoder's chief response, in 1954, was to encourage "the virtue of irresponsibility." Was that true of Yoder, even in 1954?[17]

The most straightforward refutation of such a view is found in Yoder's essay on Niebuhr. In the section on responsibility Yoder writes, "Of course, according to pacifist belief, there exists *a real Christian responsibility for the social order,* but that responsibility is a derivative of Christian love, not a contradictory and self-defining ethical norm."[18] If

14. John Howard Yoder, "Reinhold Niebuhr and Christian Pacifism," *Mennonite Quarterly Review* 29 (April 1955): 101-17. This essay was first read publicly in May of 1953 and first published as a pamphlet, in the Netherlands, in 1954.

15. Yoder, "The Anabaptist Dissent," 45.

16. Reinhold Niebuhr, *An Interpretation of Christian Ethics* (New York: Meridian Books, 1958 [originally published in 1935 by Harper & Bros.]), 170.

17. I will argue that it was not true. However, it should be noted that the tone and some of the language of Yoder's writings from this time were different from his later writings. As Yoder put it in 1993: "There was a time when I thought it was possible to accept the claim that when sociologists, or people who had learned from them, used the word 'sectarian,' it could be taken in the descriptive, Troeltschian sense, freed from the pejorative overtones left over from the age of establishment. I did so use it forty years ago. . . . Yet in the wider marketplace of ideas I doubt that the argument is worth it." John Howard Yoder, "The Burden and the Discipline of Evangelical Revisionism," in *Nonviolent America: History Through the Eyes of Peace,* ed. Louise Hawkley and James C. Juhnke (North Newton, KS: Bethel College, 1993), 21.

18. Yoder, "Reinhold Niebuhr and Christian Pacifism," 113, emphasis mine.

there exists, according to Yoder, "a real Christian responsibility for the social order," then why does he not simply affirm the notion of responsibility that is on offer in the early 1950s? Why does he proceed from his relative affirmation of responsibility to offering criticisms of the same term? It is because Yoder has entered a conversation that, he knows, is already in progress. The terms have largely been defined, including one of the dominant terms, "responsibility." Yoder believes that as the word "responsibility" is normally used, "this term is extremely dangerous, not because of what it says, but because of its begging the question and its ambiguity. The question that matters is not whether this Christian has a responsibility for the social order, it is what that responsibility is."[19] As Yoder puts it,

> the error here is not in affirming that there is a real Christian responsibility to and for the social order; it is rather in the (generally unexamined and unavowed) presuppositions that result in that responsibility's being defined from within the given order alone rather than from the gospel as it infringes upon the situation. Thus the sinful situation itself becomes the norm, and there can be no such thing as Christian ethics derived in the light of revelation.[20]

To use more recent vocabulary, Yoder recognizes the need to deconstruct dominant habits of thought before he can begin to reconstruct what would be an appropriate mode of Christian responsibility. Thus, Yoder's primary task is to re-define "the logic of the place of the disciple in society."[21] Then and only then will he be able, in an appropriately Christian manner, to say what it means to be responsible.

Two other things should be kept in mind from the first paragraph of "The Anabaptist Dissent." The first is that Yoder says he does not

---

19. John Howard Yoder, "Peace Without Eschatology?" in Yoder, *The Royal Priesthood: Essays Ecclesiological and Ecumenical,* ed. Michael G. Cartwright (Grand Rapids: Eerdmans, 1994), 162. (This essay was originally presented as a paper, read in May, 1954 in the Netherlands. On other details regarding the history of publication see p. 143.) For a similar comment on responsibility, see Yoder, "The Anabaptist Dissent," 49-50.

20. Yoder, "Peace Without Eschatology?" 162.

21. This is the subtitle of "The Anabaptist Dissent."

intend in this essay to specify particular courses of action "but rather to define principle consistently."[22] Thus we should not expect in this particular essay to find Yoder writing about specific actions related to responsibility. That is not his purpose here. Second, he intends "to elaborate a doctrine of social responsibility logically consistent with the concept of discipleship as understood and interpreted within the Anabaptist-Mennonite tradition."[23] *Concern,* the pamphlet series in which this essay appears, as Yoder knows, is a publication read mostly by Mennonites. So, in this particular essay he is mostly addressing his fellow Mennonites, but with concerns from the heart of contemporary ecumenical discussions. Thus in this essay Yoder is attempting to help Mennonites (and others convinced by an Anabaptist perspective) to be able to enter fully into ecumenical discussions, but in a way that is unapologetically "Anabaptist."

Following the introductory paragraph, Yoder continues "The Anabaptist Dissent" with two constructive comments. First he states that "the Christian life is defined most basically in ethical terms."[24] Second, he says that Christians can know what obedience means by looking at the ethical instruction in the New Testament. After these two comments, it must be said that, in this particular essay, Yoder is more interested in criticizing wrong assumptions than with constructing an alternative. Therefore, it would be understandable if someone accused Yoder of failing here to deliver on his promise to "elaborate a doctrine of social responsibility."[25]

Yoder had two fundamental concerns about the ways in which responsibility was often framed within the ecumenical contexts of the early 1950s.[26] The first relates to the way in which responsibility presumes a "Constantinian" arrangement. That is to say, there is an iden-

22. Yoder, "The Anabaptist Dissent," 45.

23. Yoder, "The Anabaptist Dissent," 45.

24. Yoder, "The Anabaptist Dissent," 45.

25. However, he would begin such an effort during this same period. We will look at that shortly.

26. Unless otherwise stated, the rest of this section of the chapter is borrowing from Yoder's essay, "The Anabaptist Dissent." Some of the points are stated more fully by Yoder in one or both of the contemporary essays, "Reinhold Niebuhr and Christian Pacifism" and "Peace Without Eschatology?"

tification of the church with the whole of society. On the one hand, the assumption is that the church will be the moral backbone or moral-giver of the whole of society. However, since the ethics formulated for the whole of society must be tailored for "everyone," such ethics must not be seriously Christian. Christians must not, for instance, presume that "everyone" will be interested in denying themselves and picking up their crosses. This costly form of living only makes sense, and is only possible, in light of the resurrection and the empowerment of the Holy Spirit, who is available to those who have experienced regeneration. On the other hand, because of the identification of the church with the whole of society, "responsibility" is defined a certain way. "Responsibility" cannot be defined according to the gospel, but instead is defined by certain ends, such as those fit for the values of that society (say, the preservation of the United States as the most powerful and wealthy nation in the world). In other words, if society as a whole (or really our particular country) is the primary locus of concern, "responsibility" is defined accordingly. If, with the Bible, however, we see that the primary meaning of history is to be carried by the people of God (Israel or the church), "responsibility" is defined differently.

Yoder's second fundamental concern is to articulate an adequate, biblical understanding of proper dichotomies in dealing with the call to love in relation to the presence of sin and evil in the world.[27] Yoder believes Niebuhr and others are right to wrestle with these difficult realities. He is, furthermore, not unwilling to use the language of dichotomies. However, he thinks they have the dichotomies wrong. According to Yoder, a proper understanding of responsibility is not possible apart from understanding where the dichotomies properly lie. Drawing from various New Testament texts, as well as the work of Oscar Cullmann, Yoder argues that the proper dichotomy is between church and world, orders of redemption and orders of conservation.[28] God has pro-

27. In "The Anabaptist Dissent" Yoder is quite willing to use clear contrast language like "dichotomies," and to appropriate them for his own use. In later writings he is less comfortable with this language, and softens it.

28. Cullmann was one of Yoder's teachers at the University of Basel. Yoder undoubtedly is drawing from a number of Cullmann's lectures and writings. The one he names is "The Kingship of Christ and the Church in the New Testament," in Oscar

nounced a "Yes" over the whole world, offering salvation to the created world. However, only the people of God have said "yes" in response to God's offer. Through divine patience God is willing not only to live with the "no" from the world but even to work with the world in two differing ways, one redemptive and one conserving. The church is to proclaim the good news of the coming of God's future reign, both through verbal proclamation and through visible embodiment of a new way of life made possible through the resurrection of Christ and the empowerment of the Holy Spirit. It is not as if those in the church do not sin — they do. However, the grace of God not only brings forgiveness for sin but also offers an empowerment that makes manifest the visible presence of the new reality, thereby witnessing to the coming Kingdom.

And what about those outside the church? The church calls them to follow Jesus; it evangelizes them. The church also influences them through its redemptive presence and by moral osmosis. For example, friends or children, even those who do not elect to become followers of Christ, are influenced by the redemptive lives of Christians. Furthermore, Christians trust that Christ reigns over the unredeemed world as well (Isa. 10; Rom. 13). God uses "good heathen" for God's ordering, conserving purposes, so that within a world that has mostly said "no" to God's offer of salvation there will be some sense of order rather than chaos. God uses the state (again Rom. 13) so that the good are protected, the evildoers are restrained, and the order of society preserves both from revolution and war.[29] Christians understand these "conserving" purposes better than non-Christians; therefore they should also witness to the state by offering critiques when these purposes are not being adequately served.

Yoder draws two "scandalous" conclusions regarding the Christian community's relationship to the world.[30] First, disciples should

---

Cullmann, *The Early Church* (London: SCM Press, 1956), 101-37. (This is an English translation of a lecture originally given in 1940.)

29. Yoder, "Peace Without Eschatology?" 159.

30. Actually these "conclusions" are stated in the introduction to "The Anabaptist Dissent." I think they make better sense as conclusions, as they appear in Yoder, "The Otherness of the Church," in *The Royal Priesthood*, 62-63. Here he refers to them as scandalous.

feel no embarrassment in being uninvolved in certain areas of society ("the world"). Such "conscientious involvement" (and, therefore, selective uninvolvement) is derived from their commitment to obedience and because of the stewardship of their time. Their primary vocation is, quite simply, to be Christian. Second, Christians do not expect Christian behavior from non-Christians.[31] These "scandalous" conclusions should make some sense in light of the foregoing discussion. They should also clarify what Yoder means when he says that Christians should refuse "to assume responsibility for the moral structure of non-Christian society."[32]

The discussions of "The Anabaptist Dissent" within this section of the book should make it clear that Yoder did not, in the early to mid-1950s, encourage social irresponsibility. However, to make that point even clearer, it is useful to point to Yoder's book, *The Christian Witness to the State*. This brief book was not published until 1964. However, Yoder admits that "most of the material" in it goes back to 1955.[33] There is actually little here that would not have been suggested in the essays we have discussed. However, because of its focus and greater length, the book both provides more detailed discussion and addresses issues the essays did not.

---

31. Throughout his life Yoder would maintain the distinction between church and world. He believed this distinction was biblical and theologically very important for a proper understanding of the Christian life. Nonetheless, language such as used here would later be modified somewhat. During this time, for instance, he would talk about the "distinctiveness" of Christian behavior. Later he would write about whether or not the behavior of Christians was specifiably Christian (that is, Christian behavior should be according to Christian norms). Whether it was "distinctive" or "different" was not decisive and would have to be tested contextually.

32. Yoder, "The Anabaptist Dissent," 46.

33. Yoder, *The Christian Witness to the State*, 4. An excerpt from a lecture given on the same subject in 1955 is published as John Howard Yoder, "The Theological Basis of the Christian Witness to the State," in *On Earth Peace: Discussions on War/Peace Issues Between Friends, Mennonites, Brethren and European Churches 1935-1975*, ed. Donald F. Durnbaugh (Elgin, IL: The Brethren Press, 1978), 136-43. It is interesting that among the group that advised Yoder in his re-working of the material that became *The Christian Witness to the State* there were two men, J. Lawrence Burkholder and Gordon D. Kaufman, with whom Yoder, then and later, would have significant differences regarding the subject matter at hand.

The Wiser Approach: Question the Definitions

As previously stated, one of the reasons many people, including some Mennonites, fail to understand Yoder is because they are trying to read him through a pre-established (Troeltschian/Niebuhrian) grid. However, Yoder has sought to re-shape the grid. Or to put it differently, Yoder has not primarily responded to the questions as asked; he has rewritten the questions. He summarizes his reasoning at the end of *The Christian Witness to the State* as follows: "It is normal for the newcomer to a debate which is already in process to accept the prevailing definitions of terms and choose one of the existing sides, whereas the wiser approach is to question the definitions."[34]

Near the beginning of *The Christian Witness to the State* Yoder writes, "Our purpose is to analyze whether it is truly the case that a Christian pacifist position rooted not in pragmatic or psychological but in Christological considerations is thereby irrelevant to the social order."[35] Yoder knows he must address those who are still captive to the dominant understandings.[36] There are those prototypical Mennonites who want to be reassured of the purity of their separatism along with the concomitant irrelevance of their position (and their lives) to the realities of the larger social order.[37] Conversely there are those

34. Yoder, *The Christian Witness to the State*, 90. One might ask how this approach relates to what I stated in the last section, namely that Yoder entered ecumenical conversations already in progress. I would say two things. First, Yoder always sought to be conscious of the various contexts into which he spoke and the languages that dominated the debates as he entered them. However, "being conscious of" does not equal allowing one's own language and normative positions to be captive to the dominant language. Second, Yoder evolved somewhat in this regard. One could argue that even his earliest essays in Europe "question the definitions." They do seek, in their own way, to redefine things. However, as he himself said, he was more willing in the 1950s than later to accept "sectarian" language as merely descriptive or helpful. As time passed he became less patient with the given categories. Thus one could also argue that he progressively deepened his questioning of the definitions.

35. Yoder, *The Christian Witness to the State*, 7.

36. In 1964, Yoder is still — certainly in the U.S. — addressing Mennonites more than any others. He is aware of this.

37. Yoder referred to this a number of times over the years. He wrote about it at length in John Howard Yoder, "Mennonite Political Conservativism: Paradox or Con-

(generally more educated and urbane) Mennonites who also embrace the separatist critique and who therefore accept the irrelevance of an Anabaptist ethic for the social order, but who are embarrassed by this sectarianism.[38] Yoder seeks to challenge the comfort of both groups. He does that by engaging in direct discussions of the pragmatic issues that matter to both, thus suggesting that, in their own terms, they are wrong. He also does that by simply refusing to fit his approach into preconceived categories.

In contrast to the common concerns posed in the previous paragraph, Yoder enters the world of social ethics with large theological claims. These theological claims are not decorative ornaments intended simply by their presence to somehow legitimate what could have been said just as easily without them; they are *defining* claims. Yoder believes Christian social ethics is shaped differently, is recast, when these theological claims are made central.

Yoder argues that if there is one overarching theological claim, it is the reign of Christ. In fact, he says on the very first page that the book is really simply an exposition of a couple of paragraphs from his essay, "Peace Without Eschatology?":

> The REIGN OF CHRIST means for the state the obligation to serve God by encouraging the good and restraining evil, i.e., to serve peace, to preserve the social cohesion in which the leaven of the Gospel can build the church, and also render the old aeon more tolerable.
>
> Thus the church's prophetic witness to the state rests on firmly fixed criteria; every act of the state may be tested according to them and God's estimation pronounced with all proper humility. The good are to be protected, the evildoers are to be restrained,

---

tradition," in *Mennonite Images*, ed. Harry Loewen (Winnipeg: Hyperion Press, 1980), 7-16.

38. See, for example, Gordon D. Kaufman, "Nonresistance and Responsibility," *Concern* 6 (November 1958): 5-29. (This was reprinted in Kaufman's 1979 book, *Nonresistance and Responsibility*.) See the critique of Kaufman's approach in Ted Koontz, "'Nonresistance and Responsibility': A Review and an Assessment," in *Mennonite Theology in Face of Modernity: Essays in Honor of Gordon D. Kaufman*, ed. Alain Epp Weaver (North Newton, KS: Bethel College, 1996), 156-76.

and the fabric of society is to be preserved, both from revolution and war. Thus, to be precise, the church can condemn methods of warfare which are indiscriminate in their victims and goals of warfare which go further than the localized readjustment of a tension. These things are wrong for the state, not only for the Christian. On the other hand, a police action within a society or under the United Nations cannot on the same basis be condemned on principle; the question is whether the safeguards are there to insure that it become nothing more. In practice, these principles would condemn all modern war, not on the basis of perfectionist discipleship ethics, but on the realistic basis of what the state is for.[39]

Clearly Yoder begins this book knowing he must respond to practical questions: does our theology relate practically to matters of the state? He knows that "by far the most current interpretation . . . is that the consistent Christian pacifist must accept the verdict of political irrelevance for his position."[40] Yoder wants to assure the readers at the very beginning that this interpretation is mistaken. Yoder both cared about such practical matters himself and did not want to lose his readers. Thus he begins as he does by naming a number of practical matters in these first two paragraphs.

But we err if we skip quickly over those first four words that he sets apart in capitals: "THE REIGN OF CHRIST." These words provide the center of this essay. Furthermore, we err if we forget that "reign of Christ" is, of course, a biblical concept, a theological term. It is a concept that is first of all at home in the life of the church. The church is the body of people who have said "yes" to the reign of Christ. They have committed themselves to a life of obedience, discipleship. According to the New Testament, it is the life of this church — not the existence of empires and nations — that bears the central meaning of history. Thus, we make a theological mistake if we fail to reformulate the question. We need to remember that the church, in biblical thought, is a *polis,* that is, a political entity.[41] Thus as Chris-

---

39. Yoder, *The Christian Witness to the State,* 5, emphasis, through capitals, his.

40. Yoder, *The Christian Witness to the State,* 7.

41. Yoder, *The Christian Witness to the State,* 18. Someone who was deeply influ-

tians who desire to be involved in politics it is important that we remember that the first *political* task for Christians is to be the church. This is because the church is a social entity that in its corporate life gives a social witness.

Because this is so often missed, we should not pass lightly over Yoder's claim that the church is, in itself, a political reality. This claim flies in the face of Reinhold Niebuhr's writings. Yoder claims that the church, through its embodiment of faithful discipleship, demonstrates what love looks like in social relationships. This witness to the gospel, however imperfect, is made possible through repentance, faith, and the empowerment of the Holy Spirit. Since the church bears the central meaning of history, there is no more important political purpose than to *be* the church — to follow Jesus the Christ faithfully — proclaiming through its life the coming reign of Christ.

Yoder continues: a part of what it means to be church is to witness to the surrounding world of the reign of Christ. Although the church witnesses in other ways than through its presence, it is worth reflecting on how the church provides a witness simply through its existence. First, the manner in which the church embodies discipleship will suggest, by analogy, the ways in which life in society at large can be altered. Second, the church witnesses through moral osmosis, as stated earlier. Christians will train their own children within the Christian faith. Then, even those who do not remain within the church will take what they have learned from the church with them. Moreover, the moral lives of members of the church will be observed by society. Those observations will have an indirect effect on the moral character of society. Third, the church will, out of its own vision, create projects — such as schools and hospitals — that will sometimes be seen by society as so useful that society at large will take them over, or at least use the idea to create something similar.

Again, because Yoder's thought runs against the stream, it is important to underline that it is the life of the church that defines the

---

enced by Yoder recently used this image for the title of a book; see Arne Rasmusson, *The Church as Polis: From Political Theology to Theological Politics as Exemplified by Jürgen Moltmann and Stanley Hauerwas* (Notre Dame: University of Notre Dame Press, 1995).

shape of the Christian witness to the state. The church not only shapes the lives of Christians; it also shapes their sensibilities as they go about their daily lives of "conscientious participation" in the world. For instance, the church helps Christians to know about the temptations of power and the persistence of sin.

Yoder continues by suggesting some of the other forms that a Christian witness to the state will take. First, he emphasizes that it is important to remember that the church is comprised of individuals, most of whom live out their daily lives in the midst of the "secular" world. Thus, because of the peculiar, Christian shape of their "conscientious participation" in that world, they will give witness to Christ within whatever job they have. This witness will always be to society, though not usually to the state as such. Second, Christians can and should evangelize non-Christian political leaders, calling upon them to follow Jesus in discipleship. Third, Christians can, with conscientiousness and with due consideration, vote for various candidates for political office (or, likewise, with conscientiousness and with due consideration, not vote).[42] Fourth, Christians can call upon the government to implement policies that pursue justice and minimize the use of violence.

This brings us back to the initial two paragraphs of Yoder's book. The church knows that they are called to be faithful to Jesus; that is, they know what faithful living means primarily by looking at the life of Jesus and responding to his call upon their lives. They confess that this same Jesus, the Christ, reigns over the world. The same one who calls them to deny themselves and follow him, to love their neighbors as themselves, and to love even their enemies, is the One who reigns over all of the "principalities and powers," including the state. Thus it is by looking at Jesus that Christians know not only what behavior Jesus desires for them, but also what he desires for the state. There is one norm for both. However, there is also a significant difference: The state is fallen. In God's divine patience, God allows states not only to continue in their fallenness, but God even uses them for di-

---

42. For an expansion of what *The Christian Witness to the State* says on this topic, see John Howard Yoder, "National Ritual: Biblical Realism and the Elections," *Sojourners*, October 1976, 29-30.

vine purposes. Thus as Yoder says at the beginning, "The REIGN OF CHRIST means for the state the obligation to serve God by encouraging the good and restraining evil, that is, to serve peace, to preserve the social cohesion in which the leaven of the Gospel can build the church, and also render the old aeon more tolerable."[43]

Yoder claims that the Lordship of Christ both motivates Christians and provides shape and content for their witness. Because of who Jesus is, the church will bear witness to the state especially by remembering the strangers, the marginalized, the enemies, and others who will normally be excluded from social and economic privileges. Because the world and the state are fallen, Christians will not project a utopia for earth, or for any particular state. This does not, however, mean Christians should be conservative or gradualists.[44] Sometimes behavior will be called for that requires something analogous to "faith" on the part of the state, which is to say, the state might take risks for the sake of principle. Normally, however, Christians will approach one issue at a time. The central defining norm for Christian witness is Jesus, though Christians will not often communicate that to the state, relying instead on terminology that will be intelligible to the state. Intelligibility does not require lowering the standard; rather, based upon knowledge of God's desires, revealed in Jesus, Christians address the state, calling it not to faithful discipleship, but rather to be the servant of God that the state can be. For it is always the case that there is room to call the state to be relatively more just and relatively less violent, thus moving in the direction of the norm revealed in Jesus.

Yoder offers three guidelines for the manner or spirit in which the church's pronouncements can be made to the state. (1) Only speak when there is clear conviction. (2) Only speak when what is said is consistent with your own behavior. And, (3) Only speak when you have something substantial to contribute. Christians should not feel that they have to cover the whole gamut of issues that the state confronts.

43. Yoder, *The Christian Witness to the State*, 5.

44. And although there is a certain way in which Yoder is "realistic," I am not sure his approach implies a conservative or even non-radical realism. However, see Mark Neufeld, "Responding to Realism: Assessing Anabaptist Alternatives," *The Conrad Grebel Review* 12 (Winter 1994): 43-62.

Perhaps Yoder best summarized his beliefs on social responsibility this way: "Of course, according to pacifist belief, there exists a real Christian responsibility for the social order, but that responsibility is a derivative of Christian love, not a contradictory and self-defining ethical norm."[45] Following from this, Yoder defines first things first. He names what for his approach is the defining norm for Christian love: the life, death, and resurrection of Christ. Second, Yoder makes it clear that God's central political purpose is expressed through the church. But having rooted Christian convictions and the shape of Christian involvement in Christ and in the life of the church, Yoder is then free to encourage active involvement in the world over which Christ, finally, reigns. In fact Yoder wants to encourage involvement

> by freeing us from feeling that we must always choose between faithful but irrelevant dualism and relevant but unfaithful compromise . . . by disassociating *involvement* from *moralism*. The incarnation is by definition *involvement*; Christ himself was in the middle of the socio-political maelstrom of military occupation and underground war, 'yet without sin.' To equate *involvement* with *compromise* and then *compromise* with *sin* so that sin is an *essential* dimension of the human situation is not only Christologically unorthodox and the death of fruitful thought; it sells out in advance to the same kind of legalism it intended to combat, for it defines *sin* as the breaking of absolute rules.[46]

Within *The Christian Witness to the State* Yoder devotes a chapter to reflecting on a variety of topics regarding national and international matters of peace and justice.[47] He believes Christians should care about the poor and work for justice and peace in the world, but such engagement does not end the critical questions Christians must ask — in fact, those who are actively engaged in issues related to the larger so-

---

45. Yoder, "Reinhold Niebuhr and Christian Pacifism," 113.

46. Yoder, *The Christian Witness to the State*, 57-58, emphases his. Clearly Yoder has framed these reflections to counter the thought of Reinhold Niebuhr.

47. Yoder, *The Christian Witness to the State*, 45-59. This is not to mention the many other writings where Yoder addressed himself to specific matters of peace and justice, some of which are discussed above in Chapter Four.

ciety may need such questions most. It is important to remember that faithful discipleship is always definitive for Christians.[48] They should ask careful questions about the stewardship of their time. Furthermore, Christians should ask critical questions about ends and means. They must not be fooled into believing that "responsibility" is self-defining; responsibility only has meaning in relation to some end — whether or not that end is specified. Even if some end is a (relatively) worthy objective, questions regarding means continue to have legitimacy. And for Christians these means are seen centrally in the light of Christ.

Yoder does not avoid difficult questions for his position, although he seeks to make it clear that such questions sometimes assume too large a role in such deliberations. For instance, *The Christian Witness to the State* mostly assumes that Christians as outsiders are "witnessing" to the state. But what about the issue of Christians holding positions of power within the state? Are such positions legitimate from Yoder's viewpoint? To begin with, Yoder wants to make it clear that very few are actually offered political power and are therefore put in a position of accepting it or rejecting it. He does contend that one has to pursue positions of power.[49] And one needs to be honest about the temptations connected with such positions. Furthermore, all Christians are called to be faithful (nonviolent) disciples. Also, all Christians should ask critical questions regarding the stewardship of their gifts and talents. But Yoder is not a legalist about these matters:

> [T]hose who think participation in the legislative and elective process to be major involvement in the wielding of the sword are probably mistaken and that it would be quite possible from the position of New Testament nonresistance to use selectively these means of communication without any compromise being implied. Not only the voter but, in fact, even the legislator, if he has no concern for his re-election or for developing a power bloc, could with-

---

48. Yoder specifically denies the classically Lutheran view wherein one's office or vocation can supersede Christ as the norm for our behavior. See John Howard Yoder, "The Two Kingdoms," *Christus Victor* 106 (September 1959): 3-7.

49. Yoder, *The Christian Witness to the State*, 57, fn. 9. One might add that the more power involved, the more actively and aggressively one has to pursue the position.

out compromise conceive of his office more as an occasion to speak to the authorities than as being an agent of the government. Whether such a nonresistant candidate would ever be elected and whether the investment of his efforts in such a context would be good stewardship of his vision and energy are questions on a quite different level, which might well lead to a decision against seeking or occupying legislative office. Perhaps a more fruitful investment of the same amount of concern and expertise would be achieved in the role of a journalist or lobbyist. That such a function would be conceivable without compromise is, however, a significant corrective to the current understanding that the Christian who eschews the sword is thereby implicitly condemned, if he would be consistent, to complete withdrawal from the political process.[50]

Without question Yoder's account of "the Christian witness to the state," more than most approaches, places Jesus and the church at the center of deliberations. However, one would be hard pressed to demonstrate that these theological commitments on Yoder's part caused him to encourage "withdrawal from the world." Quite the contrary. Yoder wrote *The Christian Witness to the State* precisely to provide a theological rationale that would encourage Christians (and especially Mennonites in 1964) to engage the larger social world. He did so at a time when such engagement could not be assumed.[51]

---

50. Yoder, *The Christian Witness to the State*, 27-28. Some would be surprised by this quotation from Yoder. Some would also be surprised to learn that later, Yoder significantly influenced U.S. Senator Mark Hatfield. Hatfield wrote to Yoder in 1983: "It means a great deal to me to have you keep in touch, John. I still count *The Politics of Jesus* as one of the 10 most influential books in my experience. Please let me know if you are going to be in the vicinity. I would enjoy some moments together" (Mark O. Hatfield, Washington D.C., letter to John H. Yoder, Elkhart, Indiana, July 11, 1983, transcript in the possession of author). For some of Hatfield's reflections that both affirm Yoder's concerns and indicate Yoder's influence on Hatfield, see Hatfield, *Between a Rock and a Hard Place* (Waco, TX: Word Books, 1976). For another, interesting account of how one pacifist U.S. Senator dealt with such powerful positions that, again, affirm Yoder's concerns, see Harold E. Hughes, *The Man from Ida Grove: A Senator's Personal Story* (Lincoln, VA: Chosen Books, 1979).

51. This was perhaps partly why Yoder, in 1958, in an essay on ecumenism, encouraged Mennonite participation in meetings of the Historic Peace Churches (with

Continuities and Discontinuities in Yoder's Thought

Thus far I have only traced Yoder's thought on social responsibility up through 1964 (and really mostly through the mid-1950s, when most of his thoughts on these topics were formed). There were no major shifts in Yoder's thought on these subjects after the early 1960s, but there was some development and some discontinuity in his use of language.

I have already mentioned that some of Yoder's language became less rigid over time. "Dualism," which was a term he used positively in 1954, had already shifted to "duality" by 1964 and would often give way to even less firmly oppositional language. Likewise, earlier Yoder referred to the "distinctiveness" of Christian ethics, but later he would refer rather to ethics being specifiably or identifiably Christian, with the distinctiveness varying depending on the context. Though Yoder never dropped the conviction that the church was the central bearer of the meaning of history, he did give less emphasis to the concept later, preferring rather to display the reality discursively. Finally, "middle axioms" language dropped from his usage after this period. "Middle axioms" was a term borrowed, again, from the world of ecumenism.[52] Yoder used it in an ad hoc fashion to relate identifiably Christian social concerns to a non-Christian world. He used other ad hoc means later.

It is much easier to see the further developments of what Yoder introduced in *The Christian Witness to the State* in later writings. Perhaps most obviously Yoder expanded some of the biblical reflections from this book — such as those on the principalities and powers and Romans 13 — into chapters of his book, *The Politics of Jesus*. Also, as early as 1964 he made reference to Karl Barth's use of analogy between the church and civil society.[53] In a number of writings in the

---

Brethren and Quakers) because "we might have something to learn in the way of social justice." John Howard Yoder, *The Ecumenical Movement and the Faithful Church* (Scottdale, PA: The Mennonite Publishing House, 1958), 41.

52. See W. A. Visser 't Hooft and J. H. Oldham, *The Church and Its Function in Society* (London: George Allen & Unwin Ltd., 1937), 209-10; and Michael Kinnamon and Brian E. Cope, eds., *The Ecumenical Movement: An Anthology of Key Texts and Voices* (Geneva: WCC Publications and Grand Rapids: Eerdmans, 1997), 277.

53. Yoder, *The Christian Witness to the State*, 18, fn. 2.

1980s and 1990s Yoder used this approach as an ad hoc replacement for earlier "middle axioms" language.[54] Yoder also went on to write substantial essays on a number of the subjects mentioned in *The Christian Witness to the State,* subjects pertaining to the world beyond the church.[55] Both through writing about various types of pacifism and through separate essays on the efficacy of nonviolence, Yoder sought to show some of the ways in which nonviolence could bring about significant changes in society. Finally, in various ways through many writings, Yoder sought to exhibit what he had said in 1967 was a component of "the Anabaptist Vision," namely that a "rejection of national, racial, and class selfishness and an active promo-

54. Most obviously see John Howard Yoder, "Why Ecclesiology Is Social Ethics: Gospel Ethics versus the Wider Wisdom," in *The Royal Priesthood,* 102-26, and "Firstfruits: The Paradigmatic Public Role of God's People," in John Howard Yoder, *For the Nations: Essays Public and Evangelical* (Grand Rapids: Eerdmans, 1997), 15-36. Also see Yoder, "The Christian Case for Democracy," in *The Priestly Kingdom: Social Ethics as Gospel* (Notre Dame: University of Notre Dame Press, 1984), 160-66; Yoder, "Sacrament as Social Process: Christ the Transformer of Culture," in *The Royal Priesthood,* 359-73; and Yoder, *Body Politics* (Nashville: Discipleship Resources, 1992).

55. See Chapter Four. It is also worth noting here some of Yoder's ongoing influence and perceived relevance. H. Jefferson Powell has utilized Yoder substantially in Powell, *The Moral Tradition of American Constitutionalism: A Theological Interpretation* (Durham, NC: Duke University Press, 1993). Another professor of law also showed Yoder's relevance for law and society in Thomas Shaffer, "The Jurisprudence of John Howard Yoder," *The Legal Studies Forum* 22/1, 2, 3 (1998): 473-86. Even more recently, Shaffer, by drawing on Yoder's extensive correspondence with him, showed Yoder's own reflections on contemporary culture in Thomas L. Shaffer, "John Howard Yoder: To a Hoosier Lawyer," unpublished manuscript in author's possession. A theologian has shown the relevance of Yoder's thought to tragedies such as that in Sarajevo in David Toole, *Waiting for Godot in Sarajevo: Theological Reflections on Nihilism, Tragedy, and Apocalypse* (Boulder, CO: Westview Press, 1998). I was recently informed of Yoder's significant contribution to the founding of a creative organization called "International Development Enterprises," "a nonprofit organization which works to improve the social, economic and environmental conditions of the world's poorest farmers by identifying and marketing low-cost, income-generating technologies." See "Introduction: International Development Enterprises," available from IDE, 10403 West Colfax, Suite 500, Lakewood, Colorado 80215. See John H. Yoder, "Memo to Whom It May Concern," regarding "The Paul Polak Project: A Brainstorm About Development Ethics," October 24, 1978, in possession of author. (His memo contributed to the formation of IDE.)

tion of international and interracial reconciliation is the obvious modern extension of the disciple's love."[56]

The present discussion, combined with the fuller comments in Chapter Four of this book, should make it clear that Yoder never — in 1954 or later — advocated irresponsibility in the face of the realities of power in the social world. In fact, from early in his writing life Yoder encouraged Mennonites in active engagement with the larger social world, thinking them too separate.[57] Nevertheless, he also was always concerned for the integrity of the Christian theology that informed such engagement.

Toward a Theology for Conflict Transformation

The field of conflict transformation studies has come into its own within the last three decades, becoming one of the academic (and professional) specializations connected to peacemaking.[58] This relatively new discipline utilizes the insights from other disciplines, especially in

56. "A Summary of the Anabaptist Vision," in *An Introduction to Mennonite History*, ed. Cornelius J. Dyck (Scottdale, PA: Herald Press, 1967), 106. (The author of each chapter is given in the preface. John Yoder wrote this chapter.)

57. This is hinted at in John Howard Yoder, *The Ecumenical Movement and the Faithful Church* (Scottdale, PA: Herald Press, 1958), 41. This concern is suggested in numerous places in John H. Yoder, "Anabaptist Vision and Mennonite Reality," in *Consultation on Anabaptist-Mennonite Theology*, ed. A. J. Klassen (Fresno, CA: Council of Mennonite Seminaries), 1-46.

58. One of the difficulties in writing about this subject is that the terminology is debated. For shorthand I will use the term "conflict transformation." I do this because as Carolyn Schrock-Shenk and John Paul Lederach define the terms, this term seems to have the closest affinity to John Yoder's theological concerns. See Carolyn Schrock-Shenk, "Introducing Conflict and Conflict Transformation," in *Making Peace With Conflict: Practical Skills for Conflict Transformation*, ed. Carolyn Schrock-Shenk and Lawrence Ressler (Scottdale, PA: Herald Press, 1999), 35 and John Paul Lederach, "'Revolutionaries' and 'Resolutionaries': In Pursuit of Dialogue," in *Mediation and Facilitation Training Manual: Foundations and Skills for Constructive Conflict Transformation*, 3rd ed., ed. Jim Stutzman and Carolyn Schrock-Shenk (Akron, PA: Mennonite Conciliation Service, 1996), 51-52. John Yoder used the term "conflict resolution" in the two lectures he gave directly on the subject, but that was over twenty years ago. The field has changed significantly since then.

the social sciences, to understand unhealthy and destructive conflicts and conflictual relationships. Theoreticians and practitioners in the field of conflict transformation seek to create strategies to transform conflicts through healthy and redemptive structures, processes, and relationships.[59] Since this is currently one of the cutting-edge disciplines in relation to peacemaking — one of John Howard Yoder's chief interests — and because it is seen as one of the ways to be "responsible" in relation to the larger social world today, it might be instructive to suggest, in outline form, the relevance of Yoder's theology for conflict transformation studies.

Yoder began his first lecture on theology and conflict transformation with an important caution.[60] It is often the case at Christian conferences, said Yoder, that someone is placed on the program to provide either biblical or theological input. And yet, far too often, perhaps especially in practical matters such as conflict transformation, the theological input is made to seem peripheral. There is no organic connection between what theologians say and what the sociologists, political philosophers, psychologists, and others in practice-related fields advocate — even if everyone involved would claim to be operating from within the same basic theological framework (say, they are all Mennonite). One of the ways this is reflected even in the theological writings is to create what Yoder refers to as "genitive theologies."[61] That is to say, theologians

59. The field of conflict transformation is quite complicated. For an entry into the discipline see Roger Fisher et al., *Getting to Yes*, 2d ed. (New York: Penguin Books, 1991); Robert A. Baruch Bush and Joseph P. Folger, *The Promise of Mediation* (San Francisco: Jossey-Bass Publishers, 1994); John Paul Lederach, *Building Peace: Sustainable Reconciliation in Divided Societies* (Washington, D.C.: United States Institute of Peace Press, 1997); John Paul Lederach, *Preparing for Peace: Conflict Transformation Across Cultures* (Syracuse, NY: Syracuse University Press, 1995); John Paul Lederach, *The Journey Toward Reconciliation* (Scottdale, PA: Herald Press, 1999); and Carolyn Schrock-Shenk and Lawrence Ressler, eds., *Making Peace With Conflict: Practical Skills for Conflict Transformation* (Scottdale, PA: Herald Press, 1999).

60. John Howard Yoder, "A Theological Point of Reference for an Approach to Conflict, Intervention, and Conciliation," unpublished lecture, Mennonite Central Committee Peace Theology Consultation, Kansas City, 6-8 April, 1978, 1-2. This consultation helped launch Mennonite Conciliation Services, which was a significant step forward in Mennonite involvement in the field of conflict transformation.

61. Yoder, "A Theological Point of Reference," 2.

write "theologies of" this or that. When this is done, too often the subject following the genitive becomes determinative of the content. Yoder intentionally avoids this error. He does not begin with the "givens" of some science called conflict transformation and then offer theological reflections. Rather, having read some of the relevant literature in the field, Yoder offers "a theological point of reference." This is intended to signal that for Yoder solid biblical or theological reflections should have a determinative place in deliberations about issues like conflict transformation.

The first thing to be said about Yoder's approach to conflict is brief, but quite important: Yoder would affirm theologically what those studying and working with conflict have also concluded, namely, that conflict is a part of reality and can serve quite redemptive purposes.

> Conflict is normal and natural. In the context of Christian ministry and witness there should be more rather than less of it, since truth telling, growth, change, and the demands of righteousness concur in bringing more of it to the surface. Rather than being denied or avoided, conflicts are to be processed, resolved, in the light of the message of forgiveness, which tells us that God himself has paid the cost of reconciling us and thereby made us ministers of the same reconciliation, and in the light of the promise of the Holy Spirit, who leads to truth by way of conversation. Conflict resolution is then a special Christian grace, but also a general Christian duty. Beyond that it is also a special gift or charisma of certain persons, who have been given the insight, the empathy, the moral authority to intervene to help others transcend their fear or anger and learn from their victims and opponents.[62]

One of the reasons the church, including the Mennonite Church, has often been unable to say anything redemptive to the world about violence is its inability to confront its own conflicts honestly and redemptively.[63] As Stanley Hauerwas has remarked, "in truth, we

---

62. John Howard Yoder, "Conflict Resolution," unpublished lecture, South Africa Christian Leadership Assembly, July 1979, 6-7. See also John Howard Yoder, *Body Politics* (Nashville: Discipleship Resources, 1992), 1-13.

63. Yoder repeatedly articulated basic theological guidelines for approaching dif-

must say that the church has too often failed the world by its failure to witness in our own life the kind of conflict necessary to be a community of peace."[64]

The second element of Yoder's approach to conflict is really the heart of the matter for Yoder: Jesus should be central for a Christian approach to conflict transformation. Yoder worked for many years to make credible the claim that "we know more fully from Jesus Christ and in the context of the confessed faith than we know in any other ways." Or stated differently: "the lordship of Christ is the center which must guide critical value choices, so that we may be called to subordinate or even reject those values which contradict Jesus."[65] This is not to say that other sources of wisdom need be renounced; rather, "The question is how to keep them subordinate to the centrality of the guidance of Jesus."[66] By the late 1970s Yoder was quite conscious that the particularity of this claim was offensive to many. What Yoder subsequently sought to demonstrate was that there is no alternative to particularity. Particularity is, finally, what we are stuck with. Some world may seem larger, better, less restrictive than our own. If so, perhaps we should become a part of that other, but still particular world. (Or perhaps we need to recognize how our learning from that other world can help us see our own particular world more clearly.) But we delude ourselves if we imagine that any of these worlds are other than particular. Into these various worlds we proclaim, and seek to live by, the message of Jesus:

> To ask, "Shall we talk in pluralist/relativist terms?" would be as silly as to ask in Greece, "Shall we talk Greek?" The question is what we shall say. We shall say, "Jesus is Messiah and Lord"; but

---

ferences and sin honestly and redemptively within the church. See John Howard Yoder, "Binding and Loosing," in *The Royal Priesthood*, 323-58 (originating as a 1967 essay); Yoder, "The Gift of Reconciliation," in *He Came Preaching Peace* (Herald Press, 1985), 116-22; and Yoder, "Binding and Loosing," in *Body Politics*, 1-13.

64. Stanley M. Hauerwas, "Peacemaking: The Virtue of the Church," in *Christian Existence Today: Essays on Church, World and Living in Between* (Durham, NC: Labyrinth Press, 1988; reprinted Grand Rapids: Baker Books, 1995), 95.

65. Yoder, "Introduction," in *The Priestly Kingdom*, 11.

66. Yoder, "Radical Reformation Ethics in Ecumenical Perspective," in *The Priestly Kingdom*, 120.

how do you say that in pluralistic/relativistic language? If that language forbids us to say that, do we respect the prohibition? Or do we find a way to say it anyway?[67]

"The real issue is not," says Yoder, "whether Jesus can make sense in a world far from Galilee, but whether — when he meets us in our world, as he does in fact — we want to follow him. We don't have to, as they didn't then. That we don't have to is the profoundest proof of his condescension, and thereby of his glory."[68]

We don't have to follow Jesus. And Christians who are involved in conflict transformation do not have to make Jesus determinative for their work. But this still begs a question: what would it mean to make Jesus determinative for Christians who are working in the field of conflict transformation? This is a complicated question and the responses can only be hinted at here. I believe one response would include something like the following.[69] Serious Scripture study and theological reflection would be a significant component. This involves much more than simply lifting out what appear to be immediately "relevant" texts for people involved in conflict transformation. And it involves more than simply using writers whose agenda is relatively close to that of those engaged in active peacebuilding.[70] This would include a commitment to avoid the temptation to make Jesus over into our own image,

---

67. Yoder, "'But We Do See Jesus': The Particularity of Incarnation and the Universality of Truth," in *The Priestly Kingdom*, 56.

68. Yoder, "'But We Do See Jesus,'" 62.

69. I am not necessarily suggesting that the following should primarily be done by those who deal with conflict transformation. For truly gifted and ambitious people, that may be possible. But it might be that the following suggestions would require serious, and perhaps ongoing, dialogue between those who teach/practice conflict transformation and theologians with various specialties. Minimally it would require serious, attentive involvement in the life and teachings of the church.

70. I think of the following writers who offer valuable insights but are inadequate as sole guides: Walter Wink, *Engaging the Powers* (Minneapolis: Fortress Press, 1992); Ched Myers, *Binding the Strong Man: A Political Reading of Mark's Story of Jesus* (Maryknoll, NY: Orbis Books, 1988); Ched Myers et al., *"Say to This Mountain": Mark's Story of Discipleship* (Maryknoll, NY: Orbis Books, 1996); and Robert R. Beck, *Nonviolent Story: Narrative Conflict Resolution in the Gospel of Mark* (Maryknoll, NY: Orbis Books, 1996).

or to make Jesus easily fit into a previously defined discipline. For instance, it might be tempting to adopt the Jesus created by A. N. Wilson as depicted by Charlotte Allen:

> Although Wilson's Jesus is supposed to be a first-century Jewish holy man, he is actually a nondenominational 20th-century therapy-group facilitator whose specialty is "enabling [people] to become themselves," and whose message is: "Suppress if you can the yang and exalt the yin! Keep down the urge to dominate, to score, to triumph, to fight, and exalt the urge to conciliate, to understand, to value."[71]

Of course, no one who writes of Jesus entirely avoids making Jesus into his or her own image. But Yoder is a good model here in the way he wrote *The Politics of Jesus*. He more or less dealt with the whole of the New Testament (and to a much lesser extent, the Old Testament). He drew on much of the best in contemporary biblical scholarship while remaining conscious of questions from the disciplines of ethics and systematic theology. In *The Politics of Jesus,* where he was seeking to show the social and political relevance of Jesus within his own context, Yoder dealt with such unlikely topics as apocalypse and justification by grace. By dealing with the whole of the New Testament he was fair to various strands of biblical thought and not just those immediately relevant to his case. He showed how even topics not normally seen to affirm his general case did in fact do so. The whole picture was enriched and made even more credible by the diversity of the texts and strands of thought drawn upon.[72]

71. Charlotte Allen, *The Human Christ: The Search for the Historical Jesus* (New York: The Free Press, 1998), 310. Allen's entertaining and informative book serves as a good reminder of "the perils of modernizing Jesus," to borrow a phrase from H. J. Cadbury.

72. Biblical studies are much more complicated now than when Yoder wrote the first edition of *The Politics of Jesus*. But among the books that should be included would be Walter Brueggemann, *Theology of the Old Testament* (Minneapolis: Fortress Press, 1997); N. T. Wright, *Jesus and the Victory of God* (Minneapolis: Fortress Press, 1996); Daniel Boyarin, *A Radical Jew* (Los Angeles: The University of California Press, 1994); Richard B. Hays, *The Moral Vision of the New Testament* (San Francisco: HarperSanFrancisco, 1996); Wayne A. Meeks, *The Origins of Christian Morality* (New

The third component of Yoder's theology for conflict transformation follows from his teaching concerning the centrality of Jesus: "We know more fully from Jesus Christ *and in the context of the confessed faith* than we know in other ways."[73] It is important that we know the Jesus of the canonical texts. It is also important that we understand something of the Jesus who has been confessed by the Church over the centuries.[74] Furthermore, it is important that we remember that the God we worship is the same God as the God revealed in Jesus, the Jesus whom we seek to follow faithfully. This worship, this following, has its roots in a gathered body of believers that we call church. It is the life together — as the body of Christ — that helps us discern what it means to follow Jesus faithfully today.[75] In fact this body helps to remind us, among other things, that "conflict resolution is not only a social science; it is also a set of skills,"[76] skills that are vital for our development as peacemakers. But, of course, it is also more than a set of skills. It is a way of life. As Stanley Hauerwas has observed:

> Peacemaking among Christians, therefore, is not simply one activity among others but rather is the very form of the church insofar as the church is the form of the one who "is our peace." Peacemaking is the form of our relations in the church as we seek to be in

---

Haven, CT: Yale University Press, 1993); and William C. Spohn, *Go and Do Likewise: Jesus and Ethics* (New York: Continuum, 1999).

73. Yoder, "Introduction," *The Priestly Kingdom,* 11, emphasis mine.

74. See John Howard Yoder, *Preface to Theology,* ed. Stanley Hauerwas and Alex Sider (Grand Rapids: Brazos Press, 2002). See also Alain Epp Weaver, "John Howard Yoder and the Creeds: The Pattern of a Missionary Christology," *The Mennonite Quarterly Review* 74 (July 2000): 423-39. For a reminder that this Jesus should not be far removed from either the canonical Jesus or the Jesus of Christian worship, see Luke Timothy Johnson, *Living Jesus: Learning the Heart of the Gospel* (San Francisco: HarperSanFrancisco, 1999).

75. Reflections on the significance of this for peacemaking are offered in Mark Thiessen Nation, "The First Word Christians Have to Say About Violence Is 'Church': On Bonhoeffer, Baptists, and Becoming a Peace Church," in *Faithfulness and Fortitude: In Conversation With the Theological Ethics of Stanley Hauerwas,* ed. Mark Thiessen Nation and Samuel Wells (Edinburgh: T&T Clark, 2000).

76. Yoder, "Conflict Resolution," 8.

unity with one another, which at least means that we begin to share a common history. Such unity is not that built on shallow optimism that we can get along if we respect one another's differences. Rather, it is a unity that profoundly acknowledges our differences because we have learned that those differences are not accidental to our being a truthful people — even when they require us to confront one another as those who have wronged us. . . .

. . . Peacemaking as a virtue is an act of imagination built on long habits of the resolution of differences. The great problem in the world is that our imagination has been stilled, since it has not made a practice of confronting wrongs so that violence might be avoided. In truth, we must say that the church has too often failed the world by its failure to witness in our own life the kind of conflict necessary to be a community of peace.[77]

Those practices that teach us what it means to live in unity and truth in the midst of our differences shape us to be true Christian peacemakers. Reflecting on these realities of life together in churches that wrestle honestly with their conflicts, Yoder offers the following observations:

To be human is to have differences; to be human wholesomely is to process those differences, not by building up conflicting power claims but by reconciling dialogue. Conflict is socially useful; it forces us to attend to new data from new perspectives. It is useful in interpersonal process; by processing conflict, one learns skills, awareness, trust, and hope. Conflict is useful in intra personal dynamics, protecting our concern about guilt and acceptance from being directed inwardly only to our own feelings. The therapy for guilt is forgiveness; the source of self-esteem is another person who takes seriously my restoration to community.[78]

Yoder lists a half-dozen personal qualities and community resources consonant with the Christian faith that are valuable for those who would intervene in conflicts:

77. Stanley M. Hauerwas, "Peacemaking: The Virtue of the Church," in *Christian Existence Today*, 95.
78. John Howard Yoder, *Body Politics*, 8.

a) Vulnerability, readiness to be shot at from both sides;

b) willingness not to get the credit;

c) the long-range holding power that comes from having one's psychic self-acceptance rooted in something other than immediate success;

d) Having behind oneself a network of understanding people with the same language and the same values to whom to turn for morale, for encouragement and also for acceptable criticism.

e) . . . the commitment of Christians to the dignity of the other party. In strict Biblical language we say this as "love your enemy."

[f]) One other element . . . is the pertinence for the concern of the doctrine of gifts. I shouldn't ask you to be like me, and I shouldn't feel bad when I'm not like you. It is a part of the nature of the richness of God working through the Holy Spirit that we have been given different things to do, and for that reason different capacities and different personalities.[79]

Of course, other skills could be mentioned, but what this listing chiefly reminds us of is that there are many skills, virtues, and character qualities that are derived from the life of the church that are invaluable for various peacemaking tasks, including intervening in conflicts. We dismiss a vital resource if we ignore the value of the church for shaping people to be people of peace.

In a new book of essays on conflict transformation, written mostly by Mennonites, a Jewish scholar, Marc Gopin, comments on the importance of the Mennonite community for shaping Mennonites to be effective peacemakers. "It must be remembered just how much the maintenance of community, Mennonite community, is key to the stories in our volume. . . . This is a vital component of who they are, and also something the field of conflict resolution in general may be able to learn from them."[80] It is significant that an outside observer makes this observation

79. Yoder, "A Theological Point of Reference," 6-7.

80. Marc Gopin, "The Religious Component of Mennonite Peacemaking and Its Global Implications," in *From the Ground Up: Mennonite Contributions to Interna-*

— one, I might add, that is repeated in various ways throughout the essay. As gratifying as such comments are, it is also important to remember, as Yoder would remind us, that the centrality of the church community is not justified pragmatically. Rather, the centrality of the church and the gospel of Christ it proclaims and embodies is a theological claim.

Gopin also notes that some Mennonites who are engaged in peacemaking and conflict transformation are sometimes "caught in a bind that is rarely articulated."[81] He is right to have named a bind. One of the substantial binds, inferred from Gopin's comments, is between mission and peacemaking. Gopin indicates that some who have contributed essays to the volume have problems with straightforward witnessing to the gospel of Jesus Christ; "They would see Jesus' principal endeavors as involving direct service, aid to and healing of those in need, and the teaching of non-resistance, not the construction of an empire of followers."[82] "The construction of an empire of followers," is, I assume, a far-from-neutral way of referring to creating churches and networks of churches (as "proselytizing" is a certain way to refer to witnessing to the gospel with the expectation that some listeners might convert to the Christian faith). And Gopin conjectures that the reason the Mennonite authors of this volume, to which he has contributed, have "rarely used words to describe what they loved about their faith, at least not in public," and their reticence to endorse proselytizing, is related to their embarrassment concerning mission work in the past, and their awareness of religious pluralism.[83] In other words, missionaries in the past were often arrogant, insensitive, ag-

---

tional Peacebuilding, ed. Cynthia Sampson and John Paul Lederach (New York: Oxford University Press, 2000), 241.

81. Gopin, "The Religious Component of Mennonite Peacemaking," 237.

82. Gopin, "The Religious Component of Mennonite Peacemaking," 236. The sentence quoted is followed by: "The latter they might see as a by-product of his work but not as its focus. This does not necessarily mean that they would be displeased by more Christians in the world. It is unclear, and that appears to be a sensitive issue" (236-37). The ambiguity of these two sentences is typical of Gopin's comments on this subject. I should also note that it is not of great importance, for the purposes of this chapter, who it is that Gopin has in mind. I believe his characterizations, in general terms, would accurately describe more than a few educated Mennonites at the beginning of the twenty-first century.

83. Gopin, "The Religious Component of Mennonite Peacemaking and Its Global Implications," 237.

gressive or even brutal; and people in other cultures also have their religions, they also know the truth; so, who are *we* to proselytize?

There are many, important, and complicated questions implied by the previous paragraph. We cannot hope to deal adequately with them in this chapter. However, I want to point up several things learned from John Yoder. If Mennonites who emigrated from Europe had not constructed "an empire of followers," there would not have been Mennonite authors contributing to a book on "Mennonite contributions to international peacebuilding." As Marc Gopin has noted, these Mennonite peacemakers have had their souls, their habits, their lives shaped by worshiping communities, by Mennonite churches:

> This method of engagement of radical humility, more than an ethical act or a strategy of intervention for Mennonites, appears to be a part of their being, a cultural characteristic that is at the heart of their religious experience of divine closeness and emulation. Every feeling of pain before the suffering of others is a living embrace of the life and person of Jesus. The community prayers, songs, and sermons often revolve around this theme.[84]

If in fact Mennonite peacemakers are shaped to be who they are by their church communities, then to denounce as illegitimate the building of such churches is, as John Yoder once put it, to run a cut-flower operation. Beautiful roses are very nice and they enhance our lives. But without the planting and nurturing of rose bushes we do not have such beautiful roses for long. Since it is precisely the community formed around Jesus that has nurtured us to be nonviolent, to care about justice, and to be humble, why would we not want to witness to this Jesus whom we proclaim Lord?[85]

---

84. Gopin, "The Religious Component of Mennonite Peacemaking," 243. I should say that these comments are a fine testimony to the Mennonites Gopin has known and the communities that have formed them.

85. Again, there is a danger here. Our witness to the gospel of Jesus Christ should not be *because* it motivates people to be good transformers of conflict. We are Christian because we trust in the God revealed in Jesus Christ. This entails a way of life for us and any others who would be so committed. This way of life involves many dimensions, including a commitment to being peacemakers in all that that involves.

None of this is to suggest that missions have not far too often been done poorly or even in an un-Christian manner. Without question they have. Many of us today cannot help but live with a painful awareness of these realities. In fact, this awareness joined to a heightened consciousness of the plurality of cultures, religions, and truth claims raises questions about the legitimacy of evangelization, of proselytizing.[86] These questions are only strengthened by our commitment to following Jesus, to embodying nonviolence. Yoder certainly identified with these basic questions. But then he wondered whether some of our responses in the light of these legitimate sensitivities did not replicate too much of the logic of the past, albeit in a new mode. Yoder offers a new possibility:

> Centuries ago it was self-evident to every Christian in Europe that Christian truth was universal truth. Other races and religions were known to exist, to the south and east; but they were no challenge to this confidence. When the technology was ready, this triumphal confidence circled the globe. Now, however, the other races and religions have found ways to talk back.
>
> There are *grosso modo* two ways Christians may respond. We can take as a norm the sense of consensus, the unchallenged confidence of that bygone age. In the search for a new consensus we can then jettison the particular, the local, the Jewish, the specific biblical content. Jesus then matters less and agreement more. Universality will be sought at the price of specificity. Dialogue will mean the uncovering of commonality. One will speak of common denominators, of anthropological constants, of several paths up the same mountain.
>
> But there is another way. It would be possible to say that the error in the age of triumphalism was not that it was tied to Jesus but

86. For reflections on some of these issues see John Howard Yoder, "On Not Being Ashamed of the Gospel: Particularity, Pluralism, and Validation," *Faith and Philosophy* 9 (July 1992): 285-300. Also see William C. Placher, *Unapologetic Theology* (Louisville: Westminster/John Knox Press, 1989); Lesslie Newbigin, *The Gospel in a Pluralist Society* (Grand Rapids: Eerdmans, 1989); Paul J. Griffiths, *An Apology for Apologetics* (Maryknoll, NY: Orbis Books, 1991); and Stanley Fish, *The Trouble with Principle* (Cambridge, MA: Harvard University Press, 1999), esp. the second half of the book.

that it denied him, precisely in its power and its disrespect for the neighbor. Then the corrective would be not to search for a new consensus but to critique the old. Its error was not that it propagated Christianity around the world but that what it propagated was not Christian enough. Then the adjustment to Christendom's loss of élan and credibility is not to talk less about Jesus and more about religion but the contrary.[87]

For Yoder, to talk less about "religion" does not mean to talk less about that organized, historical continuity of followers of Jesus called the church.[88] For to talk about Jesus is also to talk about the social reality of the church and to talk about a way of life that is centered on the worship of the God revealed centrally in Jesus the Messiah.

Ironically, some would say that it is precisely what they have learned from Jesus that leads them to minimize the centrality of Jesus and the community, the church, that gathers around him. This stems partly from an insufficient appreciation for the significance of the community in shaping us to be who we are. It also stems from an inadequate understanding of key components of the biblical portrayal of Jesus and what it means to follow him. We might begin with the reminder from Miroslav Volf: "[Jesus] was no prophet of 'inclusion' for whom the chief virtue was acceptance and the cardinal vice intolerance. Instead, he was the bringer of 'grace,' who not only scandalously included 'anyone' in the fellowship of 'open commensality,' but made the 'intolerant' demand of repentance and the 'condescending' offer of forgiveness."[89] Of course

---

87. Yoder, "The Disavowal of Constantine," in *The Royal Priesthood,* 257. For an example of the way in which Yoder's larger body of writings can be used to respond to the questions raised here see Gayle Gerber Koontz, "Evangelical Peace Theology and Religious Pluralism: Particularity in Perspective," *The Conrad Grebel Review* 14 (Winter 1996): 57-85. For some of Yoder's other comments see Yoder, "Radical Reformation Ethics," 119, and "Why Ecclesiology Is Social Ethics," 112-14.

88. I have an awareness of the tradition within which Yoder stood that led him to criticize "religion." Though I have mixed feelings about such critiques, I do have some appreciation of them. For Yoder's fuller development of his critique of "religion" see John Howard Yoder, "Civil Religion in America," in *The Priestly Kingdom,* 182-87. Also see John Howard Yoder, *The Fullness of Christ* (Elgin, IL: Brethren Press, 1987), 1-8, and what is implied by John Howard Yoder, *Body Politics.*

89. Miroslav Volf, *Exclusion and Embrace* (Nashville: Abingdon Press, 1996), 72-

those who would be followers of Jesus should be compassionate and kind. But a commitment to kindness need not entail a minimizing of specific religious convictions. As Paul Griffiths and Delmas Lewis argue,

> the non-judgmental inclusivist seems to believe that you can only be nice to people if you agree with them. This seems clearly false. It is both logically and practically possible for us, as Christians, to respect and revere worthy representatives of other traditions while still believing — on rational grounds — that some aspects of their world-view are simply mistaken.[90]

Without question our increased consciousness of the plurality of cultures and religions raises a number of complicated issues. I can only signal a place to begin our reflections on these challenges. Volf helps us begin such reflections: "Though sensitivity to plurality is essential, the *affirmation* of plurality is spurious. The only way to decide which among many options, all with their 'different visions' of 'the just,' ought to be affirmed, is by appealing to our own conception of justice. Instead of simply affirming plurality we must nurture an awareness of our own *fallibility*."[91] Christians should indeed nurture "an awareness of our own fallibility," a humility, that always informs how we live and relate to others. But just as this humility does not cause us to loosen our commitment to peace and justice, so likewise it should not prevent us from acknowledging that the center of our very existence is the God revealed through Jesus Christ.

There are varying conceptions of peace and justice, just as there are varying religious beliefs. This is because convictions, including convictions about matters like peace and justice, are formed within the context of particular cultures and traditions.[92] It necessarily follows

---

73. One of the challenges is to reflect more critically on current understandings of tolerance and intolerance. See, for example, Daniel Taylor, "Deconstructing the Gospel of Tolerance," *Christianity Today,* January 11, 1999, 43-52; and Paul Griffiths, "Proselytizing for Tolerance," *First Things,* November 2002, 30-34.

90. Paul Griffiths and Delmas Lewis, "On Grading Religions, Seeking Truth, and Being Nice to People — A Reply to Professor Hick," *Religious Studies* 19 (March 1983): 77.

91. Miroslav Volf, *Exclusion and Embrace,* 218, emphasis his.

92. For two instructive discussions of the way in which understandings of "jus-

that there is a plurality of beliefs. But an acknowledgement of plurality does not inevitably lead to an affirmation of "pluralism." As Gavin D'Costa has said, "there is no such thing as pluralism because all pluralists are committed to holding some form of truth criteria and by virtue of this, anything that falls foul of such criteria is excluded from counting as truth (in doctrine and in practice)." D'Costa continues, "by noticing this logical shape, our attention is drawn to the more interesting question as to what precisely are these criteria, how are they justified, and in what fashion do they work?"[93]

It would also be a mistake to imagine — as the minimizing of the importance of witnessing to the Jesus of the church would suggest — that one can simply dispose of the "religious" language of the church and get on with the important tasks of peacemaking. As William Spohn has noted, "Nonviolence understood as participating in the cross of Christ has a meaning different from Gandhian nonviolence. They are not the same moral practice outfitted in disposable rhetorical garments."[94] Neither Gandhian nonviolence nor a set of Harvard Negotiation Project's conflict transformation skills equals the life of the church.[95]

The fourth area of learning from John Yoder is one that distinctively sets his approach apart from many others, namely, retaining the distinction between church and world. This is very important for social ethics broadly and has implications for approaching conflict transformation. We are Christians. The shape that our peacemaking

---

tice" are always embedded within particular cultures, traditions, and communities, see: Alasdair MacIntyre, *Whose Justice? Which Rationality?* (Notre Dame: University of Notre Dame Press, 1988), and Michael Walzer, *Thick and Thin: Moral Argument at Home and Abroad* (Notre Dame: University of Notre Dame Press, 1994).

93. Gavin D'Costa, "The Impossibility of a Pluralist View of Religions," *Religious Studies* 32 (June 1996): 223-32, quoted on 225-26.

94. William C. Spohn, *Go and Do Likewise: Jesus and Ethics,* 15.

95. I mention the Harvard Negotiation Project simply because it is well known. (See, for example, Roger Fisher et al., *Getting to Yes.*) The point is that the language of peacemaking shaped by Christ and the church is never simply "a rhetorical garment" that can just as easily be transposed into the jargon of, say, any school of conflict transformation studies. The points of reference for Christians are always centrally derived from Christ and the life of the church, even if these same Christians are making connections between their own lives and, say, conflict transformation.

assumes, the approach we take to conflict transformation, is determinatively shaped by that community that worships and serves the God revealed in Jesus Christ. Our central identity and allegiance belong to this people rather than to any nation-state or particular culture. Stanley Hauerwas captures a part of what this means in his contribution to a symposium on whether the U.S. Government should intervene in Somalia:

> If Christians are going to think clearly about American intervention in Somalia, we first need to ask ourselves who we are. It is so easy to be quickly domesticated by the question, Do you not think we should intervene? The problem is in that "we." It makes all the difference who you think the "we" is.
>
> I suspect part of the problem in thinking about intervention in Somalia is that we assume the Christian "we" and the "we" of government are the same. When we do so we are robbed of what it means for Christians to think differently about these matters.[96]

"Our" thinking and "our" behavior as Christians should be identifiably Christian; they should be deeply shaped and nurtured by our commitment to follow Christ within the body of Christ. These *need* not be different on any given issue from the reflections and behavior of others, whether in government agencies or other organizations with whom peacemakers might work.[97] However, we should be prepared that they *may* be different in many ways, including our unwillingness to use violence. This because our first commitment is to the church.

Fifth, Yoder taught us to be careful in our choice and use of words. Truth and sin are big concepts about which much can be said, and though little will be said here, that little is not meant to indicate they are unimportant. There are truths for which we stand and sins that call for repentance. To make a "basically bad system a little more livable" is not the work of a true peacemaker.[98] If the whole system is

96. Stanley Hauerwas, "Who Is 'We'"? *Sojourners* 22 (April 1993): 15.

97. Earlier in his writing career Yoder referred to the distinctiveness of Christian behavior. Later he came to refer, rather, to behavior being specifiably or identifiably Christian. See Yoder, "A People in the World," in *The Royal Priesthood*, 81, fn. 19.

98. Yoder, "A Theological Point of Reference," 12.

wrong, it will hardly do to make a few adjustments to the system. It would hardly do, for instance, to help the various parties within a system of apartheid in South Africa to get along better while ignoring the basic injustices at the heart of the whole system itself.[99]

No, even when a peacemaker's task is to transform conflicts, she or he cannot forget that crucial questions of truth may be at stake in a given situation. We abandon the language of evil and sin at our own peril. If we have no language to describe evil, according to Andrew Delbanco, "we have no language for connecting our inner lives with the horrors that pass before our eyes in the outer world."[100] Likewise, as Christians, we act foolishly if we dispense with the language of sin, according to Thomas Long:

> Like other key theological terms, "sin" cannot be replaced with any other, more accessible, term. "Immorality" is too tame, too attached to the human will and social codes. "Estrangement and alienation," existentialist favorites, are too small, too focused upon the individual. "Evil" paints too broadly and lacks personal bite, while concepts like "co-dependent" and "psychopathic" are located on a single floor of the human mansion.
>
> No other word gathers up in a single stitch the intrapsychic, the interpersonal, the moral, the ecological, the social, the cosmological, and the theological character of the brokenness of human life and of all of creation. To be able to use the word "sin" is to be able to speak with honesty about who we are with and to each other. Because it places us on common ground, it is the soil of compassion, forgiveness, and hope. An anthropology that lacks a vigorous doctrine of sin is headed for constant disillusionment, chronic and bitter disappointment, and ever deepening spirals of

99. See Yoder, "Conflict Resolution," 6: "Resolving conflicts thus does not mean condoning injustice, as conflict avoidance may." As an outsider Yoder, probably rightly, did not deal much with the specifics of apartheid when he gave this lecture in South Africa in 1979. However, especially since I heard him report on his trip to South Africa in September of 1979, I believe the quote given in this footnote does include the injustices of apartheid.

100. Andrew Delbanco, *The Death of Satan: How Americans Have Lost the Sense of Evil* (New York: Farrar, Straus and Giroux, 1995), 3.

rage over the inability and unwillingness of human beings to act responsibly.[101]

Long is right; we make a serious mistake if we drop "sin" from our Christian vocabulary, including in language related to conflict transformation. Stanley Hauerwas exposes the temptation: "One can only think of Jesus' crucifixion as 'an unfortunate but avoidable failure in communication' if one believes that the remedy for sin is merely better training in the techniques of conflict resolution."[102] Though within the context of this particular article Hauerwas was primarily offering a critique of what he believed to be a faulty view of sin, nonetheless the second part of the sentence is a good reminder that sin is not something that can be eliminated through the use of the right techniques. Yoder would also want to remind us that, because of the reality of sin in the world, we should not project some future utopian world wherein violence is but a dim memory because all conflicts have been or are in the process of being transformed.[103]

One final area in which we can learn from John Yoder is integrally related to the five items already discussed, but bears being named as a separate concern: it relates to the thrust of conflict transformation. Conflict transformation, as a practical discipline, is geared toward results, toward pragmatism and effectiveness. Contrary to what some stereotypes would project, Yoder did not encourage ineffectiveness. He went to some effort to affirm an appropriate concern for effectiveness.[104] Nevertheless, being deeply rooted theologically,

101. Thomas G. Long, "God Be Merciful to Me, a Miscalculator," *Theology Today* 50 (July 1993): 166-67. See also Cornelius Plantinga, Jr., *Not the Way It's Supposed to Be: A Breviary of Sin* (Grand Rapids: Eerdmans, 1995).

102. Stanley Hauerwas, "'Salvation Even in Sin': Learning to Speak Truthfully About Ourselves," in *Sanctify Them in the Truth* (Edinburgh: T&T Clark, 1998), 67.

103. See John Howard Yoder, *The Christian Witness to the State*. This certainly would not mean, for Yoder, that we should not work to transform conflict redemptively; it simply means that we work with an honest evaluation of the sinful world in which we live.

104. See John Howard Yoder, *Nevertheless: Varieties of Religious Pacifism*, revised and expanded ed. (Scottdale, PA: Herald Press, 1992), esp. chapters four and five; Yoder, "The Lessons of Nonviolent Experience," in *Christian Attitudes to War, Peace, and Revolution: A Companion to Bainton* (Elkhart, IN: Co-op Bookstore, 1983), 487-507; Yoder, "The Kingdom as Social Ethic," in *The Priestly Kingdom*, 96-101; Yoder,

Yoder was relentless in arguing that any concerns for effectiveness should be constrained by central Christian teachings.

"Constrained by central Christian teachings" is one way to put it. Perhaps a better way to say it is that what we really need is to have our imaginations, our language, our thought patterns, and our lives determinatively shaped by the community called the church. Too often we forget that "effectiveness," "responsibility," "conflict transformation," and even words like "peace" and "justice" are not self-defining terms. As Stanley Hauerwas and William Willimon warn, "Big words like 'peace' and 'justice' . . . are words awaiting content. The church really does not know what these words mean apart from the life and death of Jesus of Nazareth."[105] Arne Rasmusson puts it this way:

> [W]hat is understood as "realism" depends on how the world is seen, which in its turn is related to one's communal practice. An alternative discourse-practice helps the moral imagination and vice-versa. It is this that makes ecclesiology so theologically important. Therefore, [John] Milbank can say that "theology has to reconceive itself as a kind of 'Christian sociology': that is to say, as the explication of a socio-linguistic practice, or as the constant re-narration of this practice as it has historically developed." Behind this assertion is his long argument in his book that "there can be no sociology in the sense of a universal 'rational' account of the 'social' character of all societies, and Christian sociology is distinctive simply because it explicates, and adopts the vantage point of, a distinct society, the Church." An alternative sociolinguistic practice provides possibilities to see the world from another perspective. . . . One of the many ways the church can be of service to the world is to nurture alternative ways of seeing the world that question what are thought to be necessities.[106]

"Christ, the Hope of the World," in *The Royal Priesthood*, 203ff.; and Yoder, *The Lamb's War,* ed. Glen Harold Stassen and Mark Thiessen Nation (forthcoming).

105. Stanley Hauerwas and William H. Willimon, *Resident Aliens* (Nashville: Abingdon Press, 1989), 38.

106. Arne Rasmusson, "Historicizing the Historicist," 234-35. The internal quotations are from John Milbank, *Theology and Social Theory: Beyond Secular Reason* (Oxford: Basil Blackwell, 1990), 380-81.

"To nurture alternative ways of seeing the world" is one way to understand the project of John Howard Yoder. And it is a relevant way to reflect on what he would say to practitioners of conflict transformation as they consider issues related to effectiveness. As he put it in the last paragraph of the revised edition of *The Politics of Jesus:*

> Then to follow Jesus does not mean renouncing effectiveness. It does not mean sacrificing concern for liberation within the social process in favor of delayed gratification in heaven, or abandoning efficacy in favor of purity. It means that in Jesus we have a clue to which kinds of causation, which kinds of community-building, which kinds of conflict management, go with the grain of the cosmos, of which we know, as Caesar does not, that Jesus is both the Word (the inner logic of things) and the Lord ("sitting at the right hand"). It is not that we begin with a mechanistic universe and then look for cracks and chinks where a little creative freedom might sneak in (for which we would then give God credit): it is that we confess the deterministic world to be enclosed within, smaller than, the sovereignty of the God of the Resurrection and Ascension. "He's got the whole world in his hands" is a post-ascension testimony. The difference it makes for political behavior is more than merely poetic or motivational.[107]

Conclusion: Cross-Shaped Responsibility

Yoder actively encouraged Christian responsibility throughout his adult life. For him such responsibility was always to be situated within the context of Christian theological concerns, centrally the confession of the Lordship of Christ within the life of the "binding and loosing" body called the church. This never meant, for Yoder, that Christians need to be disengaged from society. But such engagement — and the responsibility implied by the engagement — was always, for Yoder, defined in the light of the cross (and resurrection) of Christ. Thus, inasmuch as Yoder's way of encouraging responsibility is perceived to be irresponsibility, it is because of the offense of the cross.

107. Yoder, *The Politics of Jesus,* 246-47.

Conclusion   Yoder's Enduring Vocation

John Howard Yoder was a remarkably consistent thinker, both over a period of more than four decades and across several sub-disciplines within theology. Not only is there a remarkable consistency within his thought, his project demonstrates an inter-penetration of one category of thought with another. This complex integration creates difficulty for those who seek to interpret or summarize Yoder's contributions, because there is no particular center or privileged starting point within Yoder's thought.[1] It would be a mistake, for instance, to see catholicity (or ecumenism) as the center of this book, at least if by catholicity one means some term clearly defined before one reads Yoder. On the other hand, there is a remarkable consistency within Yoder's writings. Consequently, one could unfold Yoder's understanding of catholicity in such a way that much of the rest of his project would, at least, be implied. Or, one could begin with his view of Jesus and explore the rest — his view of the church, his commitment to ecumenism, his views on peacemaking and responsibility, and so forth — from this center. Herein lies the challenge for someone who would summarize his thought fairly. But this inter-penetration points to a richness, a bril-

1. One could argue that Jesus is central. In a sense this is true. Nonetheless divorcing this claim from, say, the importance of the church can easily skew one's understanding of Yoder's whole project.

liance that is quite remarkable. With these challenges in mind, I now summarize the five chapters of this book, offering concluding reflections on each chapter as I proceed.

Summaries and Reflections

The first chapter of this book provided an overview of Yoder's life, demonstrating the many ways in which John Yoder's life was given to ecumenical commitments. It would have been easy, perhaps too easy, to have focused merely on the many ecumenical involvements of John Yoder's adult life. That would have skewed the picture. For although Yoder was a committed ecumenist, he was profoundly shaped by his Mennonite heritage. At least the way Yoder saw it, his broad Christian commitments grew from the Mennonite soil that nurtured him. His father, great-grandfather, and his great-great-grandfather were each important leaders within the (Amish) Mennonite Church. Each was, in his own way, deeply Mennonite. This Mennonite tradition communicated to John Yoder the distinctive Mennonite convictions and practices that would always shape his life and thought. However, as John Yoder saw it, the immediate tradition to which he was heir was also progressive and outward looking. Thus, standing in the tradition of his own family and the Oak Grove Mennonite Church, young John Yoder was receptive to "the Anabaptist Vision" he was taught at Goshen College.

What we centrally need to learn from looking at this description of John Yoder is different at the beginning of the twenty-first century than what needed to be learned in 1949 when Yoder began his ecumenical involvements in Europe. Alasdair MacIntyre observes that we are all liberals now. Similarly, we are all ecumenists now. Both statements may be overstatements. But certainly most Mennonites, not to mention those in other denominations, who read Yoder in the twenty-first century would be ecumenical in ways somewhat unimaginable fifty years ago. What was remarkable about Yoder in the 1950s, and is vital for us today, is that he combined a commitment to the particularities of his own Mennonite church with a robust commitment to the universal church at many levels. Yoder did not feel a need to distance himself from his own denominational heritage in order to be involved ecumenically. Quite the opposite: he came to believe that his heritage compelled him to engage other Christians. Beginning in the 1950s, Yoder made vigorous arguments regarding why Mennonites should be involved with other Christians. Later he would make arguments for why all Christians ought to be ecumenical. While we still need to hear these arguments, today we may need to attend especially to Yoder's ability to be profoundly Mennonite while being committed to the church universal.

Chapter Two provided a description of Yoder's retrieval of his Anabaptist heritage, including some of the central learnings he derived from this heritage. We saw how Yoder interpreted this tradition both for his own denomination and for the broader Christian world. Yoder went to Goshen College at an ideal time, when Harold S. Bender and Guy F. Hershberger — both very important Mennonite leaders of their generation — were in top form. Bender communicated the excitement of "The Anabaptist Vision," while Hershberger reinforced the importance of peace as a part of what it meant to be Mennonite. Yoder was motivated to go to Europe to do service work for the Mennonite Central Committee, like his father before him. While in Europe, Yoder began a graduate program in theology, engaged in ecumenical discussions and debates about pacifism, joined in theological exchanges with other Mennonite graduate students, and began his own serious study of sixteenth-century Anabaptism. He emerged from all of this convinced that many Christians, including Mennonites, had much to learn from the Anabaptists. In the early 1950s he began to share some of what he was learning. He did this through face-to-face dialogue in Europe and through a periodical that was distributed in North America. He sought to bring renewal to the church, inviting more serious consideration of what it meant to follow Jesus. Yoder went on to write numerous essays wherein he sought to articulate what he had learned from Anabaptism (and the believers' church tradition more broadly) for an ecumenical audience. These are well represented in *The Priestly Kingdom.*

Yoder was a committed Mennonite until the day he died. His writings were the writings of a Mennonite. That said, Yoder showed the theological world that "Mennonite" need not mean narrow or sectarian. He spent a lifetime seeking to show both Mennonites and non-Mennonites that the central insights he gained from his study of sixteenth-century Anabaptism are relevant for all Christians; they are simply catholic convictions. Yoder repeatedly reminded us that the centrality of Jesus, the Christian community's vital importance for discerning and enabling faithfulness to Jesus, and the church's distinctiveness from those outside the church, are rooted in (catholic) Christian convictions. He articulated these convictions in numerous contexts. His perspectives received, and continue to receive, a significant hearing.

In Chapter Three we saw that the heart of Yoder's approach to ecumenism contained five important elements. First, Yoder stressed the biblical imperative for Christian unity. The duty of all Christians is to maintain familial relations with all others who confess the name of Christ. Second, Christian unity includes a call to faithfulness, not just in matters of doctrine and church order but also in matters of ethical behavior. When differences are serious enough to cause division, such differences should be confronted. If differences are only trivial they should be surrendered for the sake of unity. Yoder taught us to differentiate between appropriate diversity and a lazy form of pluralism. Third, inasmuch as it is up to us, we should not break fellowship with others. If a break in fellowship is to occur, it should not be initiated by us. When this view is applied beyond the Mennonite world, it offers a variation on the first point: Christian unity is an imperative. Fourth, it is vital that ecumenical conversation partners realize that the other interlocutors may be right and we may be wrong. Humility is essential. And, finally, we need to realize there are varying degrees of unity. The local fellowship should embody the highest level of unity. The largest and least frequent meetings will, quite appropriately, have the least unity. And there are varying degrees in between.

This relatively simple formulation of five elements expressed the combination of ingredients that not only compelled Yoder to remain ecumenically engaged throughout his adult life; they offer an agenda for the rest of us. Christian unity — a unity that includes the pursuit of faithfulness — continues to be an imperative.

In Chapter Four we focused on an important conviction that Yoder learned from his Mennonite upbringing, and that had been reinforced by his studies in sixteenth-century Anabaptism: pacifism is inherent in the gospel of Christ. He faithfully brought this conviction into ecumenical discussions. Yoder knew very well that both inside and outside of the Mennonite Church the "peace issue" was sometimes viewed as a hobby, a special interest of the peace churches. But he was convinced that there was no reason why the sort of theological and biblical arguments for pacifism used by the Anabaptists or Mennonites should be peculiar to them. He believed the sort of arguments he gave in *The Politics of Jesus* should be compelling to all Christians. He especially thought this case was compelling when accompanied by the arguments for the centrality of Jesus and for the vital importance of the life of the church in approaching these matters. However, he was committed to affirming (in a relative way) other Christians with other theologies who, despite theological differences, were nonetheless committed to nonviolence. He believed that a commitment to nonviolence was preferable to a willingness to kill. Furthermore, he thought a careful, disciplined approach to violence was preferable to an undisciplined approach. As a result, he also offered guidance (often solicited) regarding how to think carefully about how the use of violence could be selective and disciplined.

Yoder provided what I would argue is the most powerful articulation of a Christian theological rationale for pacifism that has ever been given. Several things are noteworthy about his writings on violence. First, in his most influential book, *The Politics of Jesus,* Yoder did not provide a "Mennonite" argument for his position. Instead, in *The Politics of Jesus,* he not only engaged current ecumenical and evangelical concerns, he also provided compelling readings of the Bible which many Christians from varying traditions would feel constrained to take seriously. Yoder showed how one could draw seriously from one's own tradition, even on a subject as contentious as pacifism, to make a broad, Christian argument that would be compelling to many. Second, Yoder supplemented the arguments of *The Politics of Jesus* in various essays, centrally in *The Priestly Kingdom,* so that interested persons could see how his views of the church, Jesus, and the relationship between church and world fit into a whole. Third, through the power and subtlety of his arguments in various writings, but especially in *The Politics of Jesus*, Yoder influenced many beyond those who embraced his whole project. That is to say, more than a few who were not convinced of Yoder's views as a whole were either convinced to be pacifist or had their pacifism strengthened through Yoder's pacifist writings. Others were strengthened in their resolve to use violence only in a disciplined fashion. I mention this latter phenomenon because it is important to remember that Yoder's writings on pacifism sometimes substantially influenced non-pacifists to be serious about their determination to avoid the use of violence in most cases. Fourth, of course, Yoder demonstrated that a pacifist could write intelligently about the just war tradition and about specific wars, thus demonstrating another way in which he exercised his Mennonite patience and communicated his convictions in a world of plural convictions.

Chapter Five differed somewhat from the previous chapters. In the first half of the chapter we dealt with one fairly discrete issue: the subject of responsibility as related to Yoder's writings. I sought to dispel some incorrect stereotypes of Yoder, stereotypes that suggest that he either discouraged, or at least failed to actively encourage, social responsibility. Yoder fully engaged the dominant ecumenical debates about responsibility that were current in the 1950s, though he did so by redefining the categories, refusing to allow others to pigeonhole his position and recognizing how the dominant categories tended to do so. Thus having redefined the terms of the discussion, Yoder encouraged Mennonites and other Christians to be actively involved in the world, to be socially responsible Christians. He continued to do this throughout the rest of his life in various writings and through various formulations. The second half of Chapter Five pointed to the ongoing relevance of Yoder's work by providing the outlines for Yoderian theological reflections on one of the fastest growing areas of interest for those involved in peacemaking, namely, the field of conflict transformation. Both halves of the chapter demonstrated the ongoing relevance of Yoder's writings concerning the matter of Christian responsibility in the midst of a world that is too often filled with violence.

Chapter Five concluded by addressing a common concern regarding the sort of pacifism advocated by Yoder: it is perceived as lacking concern for either responsibility or effectiveness. Yoder showed that such judgments are false, that pacifism is not antithetical to responsibility or unconcerned about effectiveness. Yoder helped those with similar positions to resist any categories that would suggest such dichotomies.

The five chapters of this book engaged and unfolded the teachings, involvements, convictions, and implications of Yoder's theological project. The particular angle used to examine and discuss his project was that of Mennonite patience, evangelical witness, and catholic convictions.

A Note about Yoder's Method

Yoder's project cannot be evaluated through the use of a single methodological framework. It is only after examining his life's work as a whole that one can understand why this is so. For this reason a brief summary concerning method is needed here in the concluding chapter.

Some students of Yoder's work have attempted to offer hints at Yoder's methodological framework. Joel Zimbelman, for instance, borrowed a method regarding the justification of moral discourse from David Little and Sumner Twiss to evaluate and compare the theological ethics and politics of Juan Luis Segundo and John Howard Yoder.[2] Craig Carter, in his conclusions, used labels to categorize (and evaluate) Yoder's thought: "Barthian, Anabaptist," "Postliberal," "Theologically Orthodox, Radical," "Non-Foundationalist, Non-Relativist," "Evangelical," "Jewish, Christian," "Christocentric, Trinitarian," and "Biblical, Ecumenical."[3] For this approach, I think Carter has done as well as can be done. He has used categories that, at

2. Joel Andrew Zimbelman, "Theological Ethics and Politics in the Thought of Juan Luis Segundo and John Howard Yoder" (Ph.D. dissertation, University of Virginia, 1986), 12-37.

3. Craig A. Carter, *The Politics of the Cross: The Theology and Social Ethics of John Howard Yoder* (Grand Rapids: Brazos Press, 2001), 225-34.

least in certain circumstances, Yoder himself would have been willing to use. And he has combined terms in such a way as to challenge stereotypes of Yoder's work.

Nevertheless, Yoder himself was wary of categorizing labels for his own work, and he avoided commitments to specific methods. This wariness was one of the reasons he gave for not writing "the big book," that is to say a book that definitively gave his views on Christian ethics. He finally articulated his aversion to method in an essay in 1994.[4] In this essay Yoder expressed his skepticism about either the search for first principles or "some prior definitional ('foundational,' methodological, 'meta-ethical') move to have avoided the pitfall of particular identity."[5] "Skepticism about methodological reductionism and respect for the 'thick' reading of any real history . . . ," says Yoder, "go naturally hand in hand."[6] As Yoder liked to remind us, he did not begin from scratch in the way he was Mennonite, the way he was an ecumenist, or the way he did ethics. He entered worlds and conversations already in progress.

I have avoided imposing some external methodological grid on Yoder's work precisely because I wanted to provide a "thick" reading of Yoder's particular identity as Mennonite, evangelical, and catholic — theologian and ethicist. As Yoder has said, "The fabric exists, and functions more or less well, before anyone asks for an accounting about why it works. The 'accounting' that we can do is therefore not 'validation' but *a posteriori* elucidation."[7] I have provided an *a posteriori* accounting. I trust my account has elucidated John Yoder's catholic vocation.

---

4. John H. Yoder, "Walk and Word: The Alternatives to Methodologism," in *Theology Without Foundations*, ed. Stanley Hauerwas, Nancey Murphy, and Mark Nation (Nashville: Abingdon Press, 1994), 77-90, 312-17.

5. Yoder, "Walk and Word," 77, 79.

6. Yoder, "Walk and Word," 88.

7. Yoder, "Walk and Word," 80. For a skepticism about method that is similar to Yoder's, as quoted here, see Rowan Williams, *On Christian Theology* (Oxford: Blackwell, 2000), xii-xiii.

Considered Criticisms

Anyone who would criticize John Howard Yoder's writings must be cautious. He was brilliant, relentlessly consistent, and incredibly prolific. He covered the various angles of most of the subjects he cared about. Because I believe he did such a thorough job in this regard, I offer no substantial criticisms. Nonetheless, I offer the following reflections, at least some of which may be perceived as criticisms. Most of them simply signal remaining research projects that would extend Yoder's ongoing influence.

The first set of reflections relates to the texture or feel of Yoder's writings. Upon reading Yoder's *Body Politics*, a well-known theologian in London said that it seemed to him that Yoder reduced the church to social ethics. Maybe this is similar to what David Wayne Layman had in mind when he observed that for Yoder (and James McClendon) the eucharist "seems to be nothing more than the symbolic expression of certain moral and ethical values. . . . it is really a tacit rationalism in which religion is the rational and volitional perpetuation of an ethical agenda."[8] I understand these concerns and believe there is some legitimacy to them. The flatness of some of Yoder's writings sometimes makes his theology seem reductionistic, especially, as in *Body Politics*, where he levels a polemic against "superstitious" or "magical" understandings of the eucharist. I say "seems" because I do not believe Yoder is really reductionistic. His frequent references to the Holy Spirit and apocalyptic, as well as his occasional but powerful references to the resurrection, would suggest that he was committed to richly textured accounts of the church and life in the presence of God. Still, this critique has resonance. Furthermore, especially since he taught for more than twenty years in a Roman Catholic university, Yoder's polemics against high-church views of the eucharist may have been in ecumenical bad taste, particularly since his particular views on the eucharist were not integral to any of his central positions.

8. David Wayne Layman, "The Inner Ground of Christian Theology: Church, Faith, and Sectarianism," *Journal of Ecumenical Studies* 27 (Summer 1990): 500. I will not here discuss whether Layman is right about McClendon; I am only discussing Yoder.

A second set of questions relates to ways in which Yoder made things a bit too easy for himself. First, I believe his discussion of and allusions to Constantinianism yield wonderful insights. Nonetheless, his characterizations were based centrally on Europe, especially medieval Europe. His brief discussions of newer and varied forms of Constantinianism were helpful, but he did not interact with recent sociological studies of American religion as these related to his understandings of Constantinianism. How would he have engaged such studies? It would have been helpful to know.

Second, Yoder's central essays were shaped primarily around the issue of violence. That is well and good; his writings contribute greatly to our understanding of violence. However, perhaps too often, Yoder would include a few throwaway lines to suggest that if he knew more he could also treat "this" or "that" issue. I would like to have seen him treat more issues in depth from his unique perspective, in order to know how he thought his perspective related to other issues. Other moral issues would have provided other challenges that would have forced Yoder to use other paradigms, other forms of logic. I believe that if Yoder had met some of these challenges, they would have elicited even more creativity.

A third set of comments relates to the additional research Yoder could have utilized during his lifetime. First, when *The Politics of Jesus* was first published in 1972, there were few recent books on the Bible and ethics. During the next twenty-five years, up to the time of Yoder's death, a spate of books tackled the relationship between the Bible and ethics. Many of these studies have greatly enriched our understanding of the Bible in relation to Christian moral behavior; some have even been significantly influenced by Yoder. We would be the beneficiaries had Yoder related his approach to many of those studies. For one reason or another, he chose not to interact significantly with most of these many writings. I would also like to have seen Yoder read more philosophy, especially political philosophy. As I indicated in Chapter Five, I believe Yoder's views on Christian engagement of the larger society contain much wisdom. Certainly there are not the "sectarian" problems with his approach that some have imagined. Nonetheless, his views, developed largely in the 1950s, could have been enriched by a deep reading in certain recent writings by political philosophers. His own perspective might have been updated in light of this reading. And, finally, Yoder did not see the need to say much about the details of how Christian communities shape Christians to be Christian in their moral behavior. Since he was aware of the focus on virtues, character, and narrative as important topics of study related to Christian ethics and discipleship, I wish he had given more attention to these things.

Because Yoder was an active theologian until the day he died, some of these criticisms, especially those in the last two paragraphs, may sound petty, as though I wanted him to be someone else. Rather, they are intended to reflect my profound admiration for Yoder. His arguments were logical and consistent, biblical and ecumenical, and deeply and creatively rooted in his own Anabaptist tradition. It is precisely because of my admiration for Yoder that I would like for him to have developed his thought further in the ways I have suggested. Thankfully, others have taken up some of these projects.

The Yoder Legacy Continues

One testimony to the fruitfulness of Yoder's ecumenical vocation is evident in the depth and breadth of his ongoing influence. Furthermore, most of the (minor) shortcomings in Yoder's work are more than made up for through the ongoing work of others who have been influenced by his work. Much of this has already been indicated, in the notes in this book. However, it is appropriate to indicate briefly something of the continuation of the Yoder legacy through the work of others.

Two major theologians — James McClendon, a Baptist, and Stanley Hauerwas, a Methodist — had their approach to theology and theological ethics transformed as a result of Yoder's influence.[9]

---

9. In the writings of James McClendon this is most obvious in his systematic theology. See James Wm. McClendon, Jr., *Systematic Theology*, Vol. 1: *Ethics* (Nashville: Abingdon Press, 1986; rev. ed., 2002); *Systematic Theology*, Vol. 2: *Doctrine* (Nashville: Abingdon Press, 1994); and *Systematic Theology*, Vol. 3: *Witness* (Nashville: Abingdon Press, 2000). Most of Hauerwas's many writings exhibit something of the influence of

While both theologians express deep indebtedness to Yoder, they nonetheless differ enough, from Yoder and each other, to enrich our understanding of how approaches influenced by Yoder can vary. McClendon has shown how, with Yoder's help, one can develop a systematic ordering of Christian convictions regarding ethics, doctrine, philosophy, and culture — all rooted in an Anabaptist tradition. Yoder himself was uninterested in undertaking this project; however, he praised the fruit of McClendon's efforts.[10] Also, both McClendon and Hauerwas have reflected on virtue, narrative, and community in ways that have deeply enriched our understanding and have supplemented Yoder's views on these matters.[11] Hauerwas has shown how someone who is profoundly influenced by Yoder can reflect on many different moral issues.[12] Hauerwas has also demonstrated that there is nothing in Yoder's approach that requires a low-church view of the eucharist.[13]

Several studies have related Yoder's work to social and political philosophy. One of the most significant is a book by Swedish theolo-

---

Yoder. One obvious example is Hauerwas, *The Peaceable Kingdom* (Notre Dame: University of Notre Dame Press, 1983).

10. Yoder provided endorsing blurbs for the two volumes that were published during his lifetime. I should also mention another systematic theology written with significant engagement with Yoder's thought is a recent one by Joe R. Jones, *A Grammar of Christian Faith: Systematic Explorations in Christian Life and Doctrine*, 2 vols., (Lanham, MD: Rowman & Littlefield Publishers, Inc., 2002).

11. See McClendon, *Ethics*. Among Hauerwas's many relevant writings, see Stanley Hauerwas and Charles Pinches, *Christians Among the Virtues: Theological Conversations with Ancient and Modern Ethics* (Notre Dame: University of Notre Dame Press, 1997), and Hauerwas, *The Hauerwas Reader*, ed. John Berkman and Michael Cartwright (Durham, NC: Duke University Press, 2001). See my "Review of *The Politics of the Cross* by Craig A. Carter and *The Hauerwas Reader* by Stanley Hauerwas," *The Mennonite Quarterly Review* 76 (October 2002): 485-88.

12. As a small sampling of the many issues Hauerwas has addressed, see Stanley Hauerwas, *The Hauerwas Reader*.

13. See Stanley Hauerwas, "A Homage to Mary and the University Called Notre Dame," in *In Good Company: The Church as Polis* (Notre Dame: University of Notre Dame Press, 1995), 81-90. Even more, see William T. Cavanaugh, *Torture and Eucharist: Theology, Politics, and the Body of Christ* (Oxford: Blackwell, 1998). This book is by a former doctoral student of Hauerwas. Writings by many of Hauerwas's former students indirectly or directly show the influence of John Yoder.

gian Arne Rasmusson concerning the church as polis.[14] Theologian David Toole relates Yoder's thought to contemporary violent tragedies.[15] Political scientist Thomas Heilke sometimes uses Yoder in his work on political philosophy.[16]

These studies and writings suggest that inasmuch as Yoder's project was incomplete at the time of his death, his legacy continues through the many that have been influenced by his writings.[17] These current writings testify to the fact that John Howard Yoder's contributions to theological ethics were quite outstanding. Yoder issued a call to commitment to the church universal and demonstrated a commitment to active peaceful engagement of our social world. He helped us to see how such engagement can continually be shaped by Jesus when

14. Arne Rasmusson, *The Church as Polis: From Political Theology to Theological Politics as Exemplified by Jürgen Moltmann and Stanley Hauerwas* (Notre Dame: University of Notre Dame Press, 1995). Even though the second half of this book is about Hauerwas, references to Yoder abound, and Rasmusson is quite consciously aware of its relationship to Yoder's writings as well.

15. David Toole, *Waiting for Godot in Sarajevo* (Boulder, CO: Westview Press, 1998), esp. chapters seven and eight.

16. Thomas Heilke, "On Being Ethical Without Moral Sadism: Two Readings of Augustine and the Beginnings of the Anabaptist Revolution," *Political Theory* 24 (August 1996): 493-517, and Thomas W. Heilke, *Eric Voegelin: In Quest of Reality,* 20th Century Political Thinkers (New York: Rowman & Littlefield, 1999), esp. chapter five. Heilke is, as of this writing, working on a larger project related to Yoder's writings.

17. It is impossible here adequately to represent the many scholars who reflect a deep influence by Yoder. Mention should be made of a few obvious indications of such influence. First, I would mention the *Festschrift* that was published to honor Yoder: Stanley Hauerwas, Chris K. Huebner, Harry J. Huebner, and Mark Thiessen Nation, eds., *The Wisdom of the Cross: Essays in Honor of John Howard Yoder* (Grand Rapids: Eerdmans, 1999). As one of the editors I was well aware that we could have easily had many more than the twenty contributors we included. See also John D. Roth, ed., *Engaging Anabaptism: Conversations with a Radical Tradition* (Scottdale, PA: Herald Press, 2001). Almost all of these thirteen non-Mennonites testify to the influence of John Yoder on their thinking and lives. And third, a conference on Yoder's work was held at The University of Notre Dame in the spring of 2002. Some of the more than forty papers presented were published in the July 2003 issue of *The Mennonite Quarterly Review*. Many of the others are published in Ben C. Ollenburger and Gayle Gerber Koontz, eds., *A Mind Patient and Untamed: Assessing John Howard Yoder's Contributions to Theology, Ethics, and Peacemaking* (Telford, PA: Cascadia Publishing and Scottdale, PA: Herald Press, 2004).

evangelical witness is firmly rooted in the life of the church and when the church encourages, challenges, and holds us accountable to the faithfulness of the call to follow Jesus. John Howard Yoder was a patient Mennonite who provided an evangelical witness and who was firmly committed to catholic convictions, convictions to be embodied in the universal — the catholic — church.

Index

138,-142, 152, 162-63, 171, 176, 184, 186, 193-94, 198, 201

virtue, virtues, 69-70, 72, 119, 137, 149-50, 152, 172, 176-77, 181, 199-200

Volf, Miroslav, 181-82

voluntary church membership. *See* church membership

Waldensians, 63

Wallis, Jim, 26-27, 142-43

Walters, James W., 138

Walton, Robert C., 35-37

Wayne Country, Ohio, 3-4

Weaver, Alain Epp, 128, 159, 175

Weaver, J. Denny, 11

Wegner, W., 103

Weiss, David, 25, 132

Wells, Samuel, 175

Wenger, J. C., 21, 32

Williams, Rowan, 196

Williams, Sam K., 123

Willimon, William, 187

Wilson, A. N., 174

Wink, Walter, xviii, 27, 109, 115, 123, 173

Winona Lake, Indiana, 54

Witherington, Ben, III, 118-19

witness, xi, xviii, 7, 27, 71-72, 74, 87, 95, 105-6, 109-10, 117, 126, 128, 130, 135-37, 145-46, 156-59, 161-72, 176, 178-79, 183, 185, 202

Wogaman, J. Philip, xvii, xviii, 125-26

Wooster, Ohio, 13, 16, 28

word care, xii, 184

Wright, N. T., 113, 121, 123, 129, 174

Yale Divinity School, 54

Yeager, D. M., 134

Yoder, bibliography of works of, x, 19, 23, 38, 52-54, 147

Yoder, Christian Z. (C.Z.), 4-6, 28

Yoder, editorial work of, 13, 24-25, 35-36, 39-40

Yoder, Ethel G., 6-7, 28

Yoder, Howard C., 6, 28

Yoder, John K., 3-4

Yoder, John S., 6

Yoder, lectures and speaking engagements of, 16, 18-19, 23-24, 98, 128, 169

Yoder, Paton, 3

Yoder, polemics of, xi, 48, 102, 124, 139, 147-48, 197

Yoder, professional organizations, 24

Yoder, published and unpublished works of, x-xi, xxi, 2, 19, 21, 23, 26-27, 34-36, 39-40, 43-44, 51-55, 74, 78, 88, 91, 96, 98, 100, 103, 110-11, 128, 134-35, 138, 140, 145, 151-53, 157, 198, 200

Yoder, teaching roles of, xxi, 4, 23-24, 53, 128, 140, 197

Zimbelman, Joel, 195

Zürich Council, 33

Zwingli, Ulrich, 32-33, 35-38, 63, 84